A Practical Guide to

Information Architecture

by Donna Spencer

A Practical Guide to Information Architecture
by Donna Spencer

Published in 2010 by Five Simple Steps
Studio Two, The Coach House
Stanwell Road
Penarth
CF64 3EU
United Kingdom

On the web: *www.fivesimplesteps.com*
Please send errors to *errata@fivesimplesteps.com*

Publisher: Five Simple Steps
Editor: Bill Harper
Production Editor: Emma Boulton
Art Director: Mark Boulton
Designer: Nick Boulton
Printed in the UK by Paramount Print

ISBN: 978-0-9561740-6-2

A catalogue record of this book is available from the British Library.

Acknowledgements

This book didn't come from nowhere – it came from teaching information architecture in workshop form for many years – at loads of conferences and in-house for clients.

So the first thank you goes to everyone who has been in one of those workshops and asked good questions and shared good stories. I don't figure things out until I have to do them or answer questions about them, so a lot of my thoughts are a direct result of questions people ask me.

Thanks to all my clients who have let me play with their content, and paid me to do it. How cool is it to be paid to do something so fun!

I sent a really rubbish draft out to a pile of smart people to see what they thought. Thanks to the following folks for reading the draft and sending me comments – they really did help make this book better. In first name order (yes, I am an IA): Arun Martin, Brian Hoffman, Christopher Frost, Daniel Souza, Gary Barber, Kirsten Hall, Kushal Pisavadia, Margaret Hanley, Marianne Colwell, Mike Pauley, Nathan Wall, Rachel Peters, Rowan Peter, Ruth Ellison, Patrick Foster and Steph Beath. And thanks to everyone who shared stories that helped to emphasise points in various chapters.

My editor Bill Harper was amazing. I looked at the first chapters he sent back and thought he hadn't done anything – I couldn't see any differences. But he had done tons of work – he'd managed to improve my writing out of sight and still keep it sounding just like me. Bill, I hope you can edit for me for every other book I write (and I'm glad you're my friend).

To my lovely kid who has just spent months watching TV and reading books while I work evenings and weekends – thanks for putting up with me as your mum. I promise to spend more time with you until the book bug bites again.

And to Steve who has only known me in writing mode – thanks for saying "I understand" and meaning it.

Foreword

Derek Featherstone

Long before I was a web developer or an accessibility specialist, I was a high school teacher. One of the things I miss the most about that time was ongoing discussion about education, teaching and learning with my peers. We tried to do as much as we could to understand what our students were saying, doing, and thinking – it was the only way to truly assess their progress. We were trying to get inside their head, so to speak, to uncover their existing knowledge about a subject and how that framed what we were currently learning in class. Why? So that we could teach, and they could learn, more effectively.

In teaching, we used many of the types of exercises we use in user research: card sorts, think aloud activities, probing for existing knowledge and more. It was all about understanding people.

I learned those techniques from some of the best teachers I could have hoped for. Many of the discussions we had about education left a lasting impression. My time learning to teach was the first time that I truly understood the meaning of the ancient Chinese proverb:

> *"Give a man a fish and you feed him for a day. Teach a man to fish and you feed him for a lifetime."*

This proverb doesn't mention one critical aspect of success: the balance between fish and fishing. Yes, I need to be able to fish for myself, but in the short term, if you don't feed me some fish, I'm going to starve.

When I was learning to teach, I had support from friends, peers and my professors both in terms of helping me learn to fish, AND feeding me some fish so that I didn't starve while I was still learning.

I left teaching in 1999, and started my own company. That change of context left me with nobody to help me learn to fish, and, suddenly, I had no fish to eat. Oh, I struggled through, making things up, learning along the way, picking up every bit of knowledge I could from books, articles, and anything else I could find. Sure that information helped me learn the things I needed to build web sites and applications and to understand people. But what they lacked, at least for me, was the relationship to the whole. I needed something to connect those nitty-gritty tactics I was learning to the big picture strategy.

Having read through Donna's book, it just feels like the right balance between fish and fishing. She gives you some fish – techniques you can use right away to 1) understand the mindset and motivations of people using your sites, 2) implement and test a draft of your work and 3) iterate to a more complete solution. At the same time, she beautifully connects those techniques to the big picture of user experience and Information Architecture.

As you read this book, you'll find it will work for you in different ways, at different times in your careers. If you're just getting started out as an IA, or are a web designer/developer team of one that is responsible for IA as part of your job, this book gives you the fish you so desperately need when you're hungry. And you'll feel like Donna is right there guiding and supporting you with insight from her years working in the field. She'll tell you not to expect perfection in your work (that's why we iterate, after all!). She'll tell you to just get on with it and try something. And she'll always tie it back to the big picture to give you enough context to make sense of your work. She'll feed you some fish, but teach you how to fish for yourself along the way.

I'm not just saying this because Donna and I have grown to be good friends over the course of our careers. I'm saying this because I really mean it: this is the book that I needed 10 years ago.

Contents

PART 1

About information architecture 1

WHAT IS INFORMATION ARCHITECTURE? 3

IA IN A PROJECT 9

WHO DOES IA? 19

IA FOR NON WEB 31

BEFORE YOU START 37

PART 2

Understanding people 51

LEARNING ABOUT YOUR USERS 53

ANALYSING USER RESEARCH 75

COMMUNICATING ABOUT USERS 85

HOW PEOPLE LOOK FOR INFO 97

HOW PEOPLE THINK ABOUT CATEGORIES 113

Part 3

Understanding content 121

CONTENT YOU HAVE 123
CONTENT YOU NEED 133
COMMUNICATING ABOUT CONTENT 137
CONTENT PLANNING 143
CLASSIFICATION SCHEMES 155

Part 4

Designing an information architecture 177

IA PATTERNS 179
LABELS AND LANGUAGE 209
HOW TO CREATE IA 217
TESTING IA 229
COMMUNICATING IA 245

Part 5

Designing navigation 255

NAVIGATION CORE 257
NAVIGATION EXTRAS 271
DESIGNING NAVIGATION 283
TESTING NAVIGATION 289
COMMUNICATING NAVIGATION 295

Introduction

I'll tell you a secret. One that my friends and family mostly know about, and many people who meet me eventually figure out. But it is one of those slightly embarrassing secrets – one that I don't usually just tell people when I meet them for the first time. But you're going to be my friend for the next 300 pages, so you may as well know this.

I **really** like organising stuff. Like, really. There are few things I enjoy more than having a day off and tidying the pantry, re-organising all my yarn (I'm a weaver and have crates and crates of yarn) or pulling all my wine off my wine rack and putting it back in a different order. Well, that would be if I actually had time to do any of those things. But when I do, I get into the zone and organise and tidy. It's bliss.

So knowing that, can you imagine how I feel when someone calls me up and says "Our intranet/website is in a total mess. No-one can find anything and there's stuff hidden in there that has been out of date for years. We need help!" Yep, you know where I'm going with this – I love it. And I love that people pay me to do it.

But there is actually one thing I like even better than organising things. I love teaching other people how to do it. I've been teaching information architecture workshops at conferences and in-house for about 8 years now. It's been cool to watch how things have changed, and how people's general awareness of IA has increased over that time. It's been cool to spend a day with people and hear them say "Wow, I actually knew a whole lot of that, I just didn't know I knew it" and go away feeling more confident about their messy projects.

Now I've written down some of what I know about IA. Now you too can read this book and say "Wow, I actually knew a whole lot of that" (I do hope you learn some new things too of course) and can go away feeling more confident about your messy projects.

At least that's the plan – I hope it works out for you.

Happy organising!

Part 1

About information architecture

What is information architecture?

IA in a project

Who does IA?

IA for non web

Before you start

1

What is information architecture

Imagine your local supermarket/grocery store has just been renovated. The owners have expanded it to include more items, and improved the layout so you can move around more easily. And you're seeing it all for the first time.

You walk in craving chocolate, head to where it's usually kept and realise that, wow, everything has been moved. Yikes! How can you quickly make sense of it and find the chocolate? After all, you don't want to check every item on every shelf. You look at the signs, but they all point to where stuff used to be. No help there. You start looking up the aisles. No, this aisle is all canned food... this one is soft drink... this one is bread...

Aha! Here's one that looks like it's full of sweet things (the bright colours and everything at children's eye level gives it away). You decide to give this one a go. And lo and behold, there's the chocolate.

Why was this relatively easy, even though they'd moved everything around? It's because they put similar things together into groups. And they put those groups into bigger groups, and those groups into even bigger groups. So they put all the chocolate – dark, light, white, bars and pieces – together. Then they put it near other sweet things, which are also arranged into groups of similar items. And so, when we glance down the aisle, we can quickly figure out what the whole aisle is about.

Now let's extend that idea to our websites, intranets and other information systems. We could just list everything we have on the home page, but we usually don't. Instead we put our content into groups, break those groups into sub-groups, and so on. This is much easier to use than showing all our content in one long list.

However, it isn't just grouping items that make supermarkets and websites work well. It's about creating groups that **make sense to the people who use them**. After all, supermarkets could group by colour, or even where things were made. They could put the chocolate with the gravy and other things that are brown. They could put the Swiss chocolate with the Swiss cheese, and the Belgian chocolate with the Belgian beer. But as tempting as that may sound, most times it won't help anyone find the chocolate in their newly-renovated supermarket.

Even when we create categories that make sense to people, we need to describe them well. So no *seacláid* signs in a supermarket full of non-Irish speakers, or aisles called *Sweeties Treaties*.

We also need to help people find their way to the thing they want. In the supermarket this can be done with layout, signage and visual guides; on websites we use navigation bars, buttons and links.

And that's what information architecture is all about:

1. Organising content or objects
2. Describing them clearly
3. Providing ways for people to get to them.[1]

Where we find information architecture

While most information architecture work these days is used for websites and intranets, you can find it wherever you need to organise things (information and/or objects) that other people need to use.

So it's just as useful for figuring out how to organise your music and movies, your file system at work, and even physical things such as your paper files at home or groceries on a supermarket shelf.

[1] The Information Architecture Institute define information architecture as:

- The structural design of shared information environments.
- The art and science of organizing and labeling web sites, intranets, online communities, and software to support findability and usability.
- An emerging community of practice focused on bringing principles of design and architecture to the digital landscape.

> *"I file everything one way, my husband files it a completely different way. We nearly ended up coming to blows over the filing until we sat down together one day and went through a complete IA process on our own goals and content. We slowly worked out terminology and structures that worked for both of us and having documented it he went ahead and re-sorted our files accordingly. Now it works well and we both know where to find and file things - and what's even better is he now understands what it is I do at work each day :-)"*
>
> Steph Beath, Information Architect/Interaction Designer

Throughout this book I talk about information architecture primarily in terms of content-heavy websites and intranets, and use a lot of examples from websites. I use the word 'site' as a convenient way to avoid saying 'website, intranet, document management system, filing system, user manual or web application'.

Oh, and from the next chapter I'll be calling it 'IA' instead of 'Information Architecture'. Not only is it shorter, it's also a bit cooler, don't you think?

Why information architecture is important

Information architecture has always been important. Whenever we create groups and describe things other people need to use, the information architecture (how things are grouped and labelled) directly affects how easy things are to use.

As the amount of information available to us keeps growing, information architecture becomes even more important. The more information there is, the harder it can be to sift through and find what you need. Good information architecture can help people find their way through the information, and ignore what isn't relevant.

But good information architecture can do more than just help people find objects and information. It can empower people by making it easier for them to learn and make better decisions.

So what's a good information architecture? It's one that is both easy for people to understand and works well for whatever is being grouped. A bad one is just the opposite – it's hard for people to use, and the content doesn't easily fit. For example, an online supermarket with a good information architecture may put all the chocolate together and group it with other snack foods. One with a bad information architecture may group all grocery items by manufacturer, making people check every manufacturer to see who produces chocolate.

This isn't easy. For any set of things:

- There will always be more than one way of organising them. Unfortunately it isn't always clear which way is the best way.
- People have different needs.
- People often have different ideas about what goes together and what doesn't.
- Some people may know a lot about a topic, while others may know nothing at all.

As you can see, three of these reasons relate to people. If you're organising things that will be used by other people, you'll need to do it in a way that makes sense to them – that fits with their idea of what goes together, and is described in a way that makes sense to them.

This can be easy if they think the same way as you, but that's rare – I've only worked on a couple of projects for people just like me. It's far more likely that whoever's using your information will think differently to you – sometimes very differently.

What you need to create a good information architecture

You need to understand three very important things before you can design an IA that works really well:

- **People**: What they need do to, how they think and what they already know
- **Content**: What you have, what you should have and what you need
- **Context**: The business or personal goals for the site, who else will be involved and what your constraints are.

Figure 1 – 1. IA is all about meeting the needs of people, content and context

Without a good understanding of these three things, you simply can't create a good IA.

- If you **don't know enough about people** you won't be able to group content in ways that make sense to them, or provide ways for them to find it easily.
- Without a good **understanding of your content**, you won't be able to create an information architecture that works well for current and future content.
- And if you **don't know all about the context**, you won't be able to create something that works for people and the business, and you'll have endless trouble in the project.

Don't worry. I'll be talking about all these things in this book. Part 2 is all about the people who will use your site. Part 3 is about the content itself. And parts 4 & 5 are about actually designing an information architecture (the groups and labels) and navigation (ways for people to get to it). Context is covered in chapter 5 (Before you start).

Chapter summary

- Information architecture is all about organising content or things, describing them clearly and providing ways for people to get to them.
- A lot of information architecture work relates to websites and intranets, but is just as relevant for music and movies, a computer file system, your paper files at home or even groceries on supermarket shelves.
- Good information architecture helps people to find information they need. It can also help them learn and make better decisions.
- You need to understand three things to create a good information architecture: People, content and context.
- The term is often abbreviated to 'IA' (just as I'll be doing from now on).

2

Information architecture in a project

In the previous chapter I described IA in general terms, and how it can help organise and group any type of content or object.

However, most of you reading this book will probably be working on something like a website or intranet – either designing a new one or redesigning an existing one. So let's look at how IA fits with that type of project.

Imagine you've just been asked to be responsible for the IA of a new website or intranet. What might that mean?

An information architecture project

I've worked on many IA projects – for small sites and large, for new sites and redesigns. Although they differ in the details, they all follow the same basic approach.

Figure 2 – 1. The basic parts of an IA project. Don't worry if yours don't look like this - every project is different

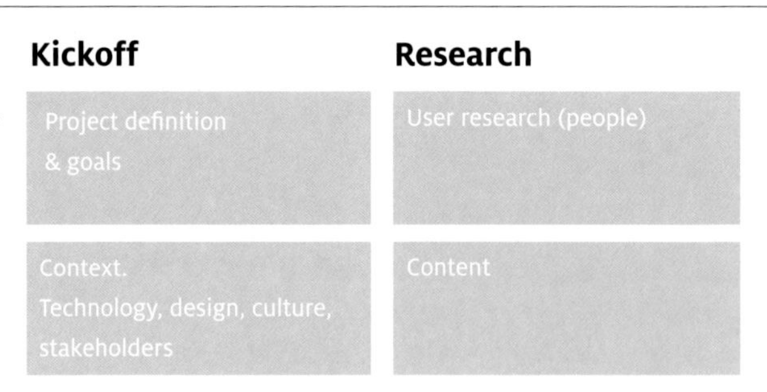

The first part of a project is always to figure out exactly what is involved – to define what the project is about, identify the goals and anything else that will affect it (the context) such as:

- the technologies you may have to use
- any design constraints
- the culture of the organisation (how things get done in that organisation)
- who should be involved (the stakeholders)

(These are all covered in detail in chapter 5: Before you start)

The second part of a project is research – gathering good information and analysing it to help you make a wide range of decisions during the project. As I mentioned in the previous chapter, you'll need to learn all about people (what they need, what they know, etc.) and about your content (current and future). Part 2 of this book covers people in depth, and part 3 covers content.

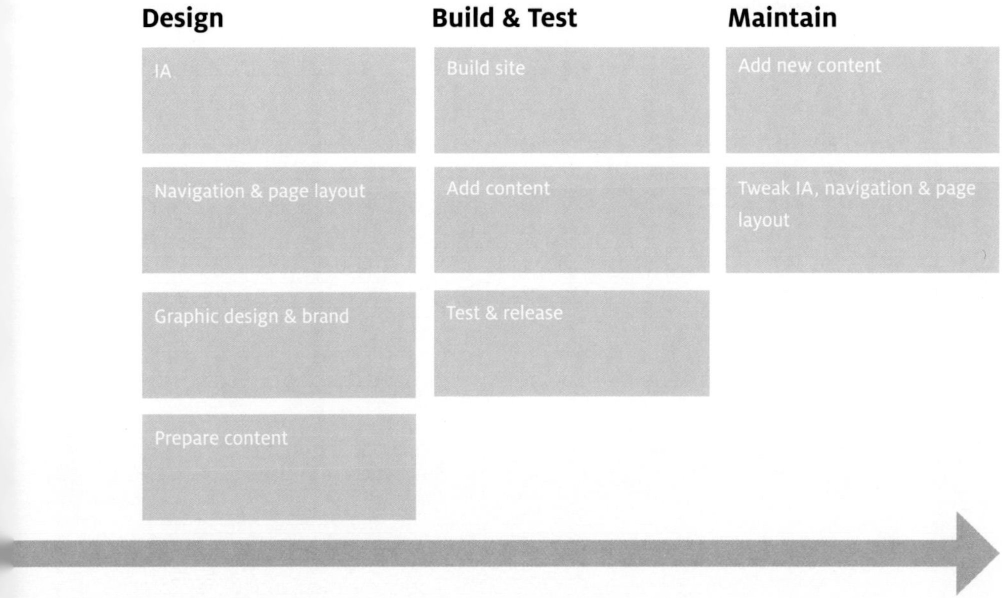

Design

IA

Navigation & page layout

Graphic design & brand

Prepare content

Build & Test

Build site

Add content

Test & release

Maintain

Add new content

Tweak IA, navigation & page layout

The middle part of the project is where you design a solution. Here I use “design” in its broadest sense – not just how things look, but also creating solutions to defined problems. You’ll come up with a new IA and navigation for the site, and then test both to make sure they work before starting to build the site. If new content needs to be prepared, this is the time to get it started. Part 4 of this book covers how to create the IA and part 5 covers navigation.

When all that’s sorted out and you know the details about what the site will do and how it should work, you can start to the technical work – building the site, adding content, and testing it before release.

As you can see from the diagram, you need to do a lot of work upfront before you can start building. It’s *very* important that you do this work. Sometimes managers or clients will tell you not to bother with all that stuff, and to just get on with doing the IA and building the site. That’s not only silly, as you would have no idea what you need to do, but there’s no way you’ll create anything useful to either the business or the users. Just like in the physical world of architecture you have to think about what you need, plan it in detail, and write it down before you go digging foundations and putting up walls.

Information architecture deliverables

There are two core IA deliverables in the diagram and description overleaf:

An information architecture

The IA will describe:

- The overall structure (or shape) of the site: In the broadest sense, how the main parts of the site relate to one another.
- Groups and sub-groups: The main groups and sub-groups that will eventually be used in navigation. This will describe what will be included in each and what they will be called (labelling).
- Metadata: For some sites (particularly product sites), this is what you'll use to describe each product and the descriptive terms for each

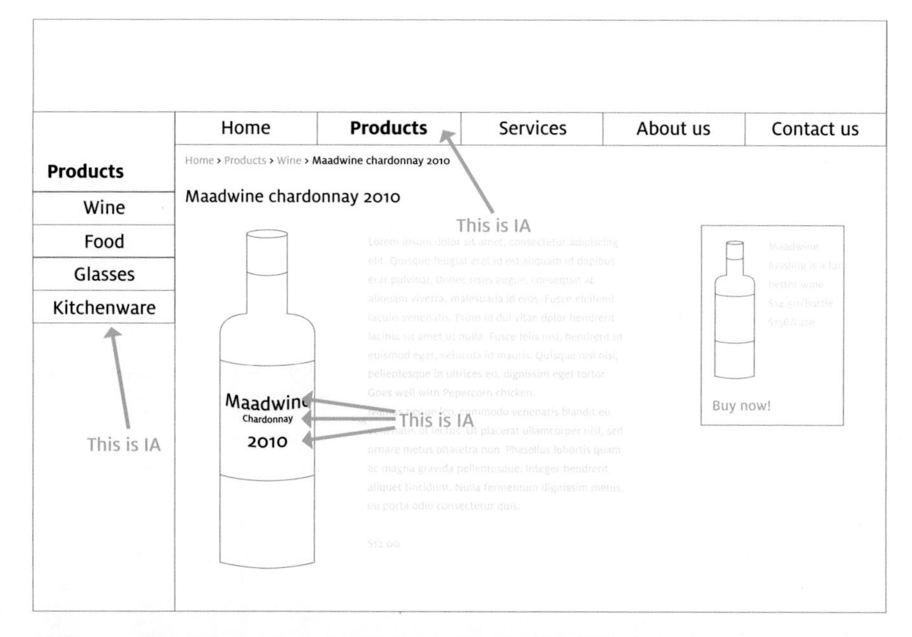

Figure 2 – 2. IA describes the groups and subgroups, plus metadata for content

Navigation

Navigation is the way people will get around the site. It is absolutely dependent on the IA, but in a project it's done after the IA is drafted. It will include things like:

- navigation bars
- related links
- in-page navigation elements (such as hyperlinks)
- helpers like A-Z indexes and site maps

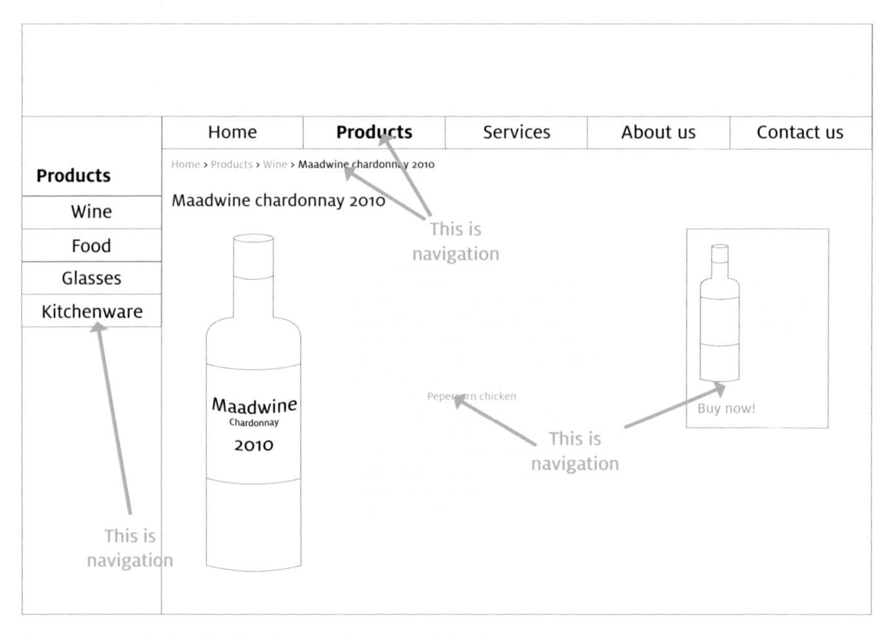

Figure 2 – 3. Navigation describes how people get around the site

How long this takes

People often ask me how long the IA part of the project takes. You already know my answer to that – it depends.

It will vary depending on:

- How much you already know about your audience and content: If you don't know much, it will take longer to learn about them than if you already know a lot.
- The amount of content you are working with: Large sites take more work than small sites.
- How experienced you are with IA work: The more experience you have with IA, the faster you'll be able to come up with solutions that work.
- How much communication work will be needed: If you're working with a small client, this will be easier than working with a large organisation with distributed authors.

For very small projects such as a new website for a small business with simple content, this can be a pretty quick process. You can find out what people need, brainstorm a content list, draft an IA and sketch some navigation in less than a day.

At the other end of the spectrum you have something like a large corporate website that has been growing uncontrollably for a few years. It could take you a month just to figure out what content is already available. It could take you many more months to talk to all the content authors and figure out what needs to be kept and what can be deleted. And when you have drafted a new IA, you may need to go back to all those authors and talk to them about it, where their content will be and what they'll need to do to maintain it.

In both types of project, actually drafting the IA and navigation is pretty quick. It is the research and communication that takes the most time. Of course, you can't eliminate these – they are crucial parts of the project.

Without good research into people and content, you won't be able to make good decisions. It will be hard to draft the IA in the first place. Then when you start talking to the stakeholders about it, they'll have all sorts of objections and questions you won't be able to answer. If you start to design IA, navigation and the graphic design without good research, you'll have to make significant changes – not a good thing if you've already shown people what the site will look like.

If you don't leave time for communication, you'll have trouble during the project – people will hear about it and want to know what's happening. And afterward it may be very hard for people to maintain the site if you haven't explained important ideas throughout.

But if you get the upfront research right, and communicate well throughout, you'll have a much easier run. You'll make better decisions from the start, and people will understand where you are heading.

Agile IA

Anders Ramsay

> *"A common question when discussing how IA manifests itself in an Agile project is "What changes?" How is the work different to a traditional project?*
>
> *The underlying principles of how information should be structured, organized and presented are just as applicable in an Agile project as in a traditional project. The difference is in the journey travelled – primarily communication amongst team members."*

Lean Communication

In a traditional practice, documents are generally the primary method for communicating project information, with other forms of communication playing a supporting role.

In an Agile team, this is turned on its head. Communication is conversation-centered – direct conversation is the primary means of communication, with documents playing a supporting role. Agile documents contain barely sufficient detail and are intentionally created to convey the instability of the information they are communicating. For example, a site map that may traditionally be created using drawing software might instead use sticky notes on a whiteboard with hand-drawn connectors.

In a traditional project, a site map may have been created by an individual team member, possibly following a team session in which the site map perhaps was sketched out. In an Agile project, the document created by the team is the primary artifact – project artifacts are created less by individuals and more by the team during working sessions.

Unless there is a specific requirement or direct business value, documents are never seen as an end in their own right, but rather as a means to an end, which is to create a high quality software product. A document is not expected to remain up-to-date or be comprehensive. It is only expected to be enough to move the project work forward, to be a placeholder for conversation among team members.

Iterative IA

A key difference between an Agile project and a traditional project is when the team actually starts to build working software. Commonly, this will be anything from two weeks to two months after the project starts. From that point forward, the software product is built in iterations, with working software being released in recurring cycles.

In other words, far less IA is defined up front, and is instead defined throughout the project, leveraging what has been built so far to inform later iterations.

Rather than defining the entire IA before development begins, the focus is on big-picture IA plus detail for the part of the site currently being developed. For example, if your team was building an auto parts site, the initial round of IA may focus on the ability to place an order for an auto part. While the auto parts ordering feature is being built, you may work on a parts detail page, which will be created in the next iteration.

Distributed IA

Another key difference is how the team work together and ownership of knowledge.

Having an individual team member as the primary keeper of specialized knowledge such as a site's IA makes the team too dependent on the work of a single person and risks creating a bottle-neck in the workflow. Instead, the entire team is actively engaged in creating the IA, such as by creating IA artifacts during team sessions or pairing with other team members in doing IA work, which creates a shared sense of ownership and reduces overall project risk.

More rewarding

Overall, a lean, iterative, and distributed approach to IA tends to make for a more rewarding practice – with fewer hours toiling away in isolation on detailed design documents, and more time interacting directly with end users and team members. There is less noise in the communication channel, less time spent on creating great-looking documents and more time spent on creating great-working software.

Chapter summary

An IA is often made up of the following parts:

- defining what the project is about and its goals
- researching people and content
- designing the IA, navigation, visual approach and content
- building and testing
- maintaining

The main IA deliverables in a project include:

- the information architecture
- navigation
- metadata

The length of each individual project varies, from as little as a day, to as long as a year, depending on how much you know up front, the size of the project, your experience and how many people are involved.

3

Who does information architecture?

One of the most common questions I'm asked is who should be responsible for the IA for a website or intranet.

Although there is a specific 'information architect' job role, you don't need to hire a specialist for anything but the largest, most complex sites. A lot of people are naturals for IA work.

Roles

All sorts of people can be involved in IA, including business analysts, usability specialists, graphic designers, writers, web developers and even information architects!

Business analysts

Business analysts usually identify business needs for a system, prepare requirements and other project documentation (and so much more). They can be particularly good at IA due to their experience collecting information, analysing existing systems, focusing on detail and synthesising solutions.

If you're a business analyst who hasn't worked on an IA project before, you may need to do more user research than you ordinarily would, focusing on how people use information, what they need to do with it and their terminology (a lot of traditional BA work involves collecting requirements, which are different). If you haven't designed an IA or navigational approach, the most useful chapters for you are those on IA and navigation design.

Usability specialists

Usability specialists are often involved in the design of the IA as part of their project role. They are very attuned to user needs, and usually have a basic understanding of the content from activities such as usability testing.

I've never worked with a usability specialist who had a lot of experience with content analysis – if you're the same, pay particular attention to this. If you haven't worked on many IA projects, or are working on a larger project than usual, the most useful chapters are those on IA and navigation design.

Writers

Writers are a natural fit for IA work. Good writers will be naturally focused on the user, and are accustomed to organising large amounts of content. Writers may need to brush up on navigation design concepts.

Graphic designers

IA often falls to the graphic designer on a project, as part of their role in designing navigation and page layouts. The most important thing for graphic designers to remember is that the IA should be designed before the navigation so the navigation suits the IA, not the other way around. Now I'm not saying you all do this, but I've worked on enough projects where I've been told, "We're using horizontal navigation and have space for five categories", with no consideration for what is really needed.

If you're a graphic designer and have been asked to design navigation without being given an IA, please push back. Ask for it to be done (or even if you can do it) first.

Web developers

Just like graphic designers, the job of designing the IA is often left to the front-end web developer.

I've worked with some web developers who have a natural empathy with users and are good at figuring out how to organise information. They've been a quite natural fit for IA work.

The important thing to remember as a web developer is to take on the IA design as a mini-project. Collect information (as I outline later in the book), design the IA, design the navigation, test it with users, and then implement it. Don't start the IA and navigation design as you are developing the front end – you simply can't do both at once. I know this sounds silly, but I've seen it happen more than once.

Project managers

Some projects don't have anyone with the skills or time to do the IA, and it may fall to the project manager. A project manager usually has the big picture view of the project, and has been involved in requirements gathering and maybe even some customer research. This can put them in the best place to draft the IA, as they may know more about all the pieces than anyone else.

Whoever!

Really, it doesn't matter who designs the IA. I honestly don't care what your title is on your business card. The most important thing is that you have the right set of skills for the work.

Skills

The skills that help most with IA work include:

Empathy with people

One of the most important aspects of a good IA is that it works well for the people who need to use it. Sometimes it can be hard to come up with something that works well for the business and content, and also helps people find what they are looking for. The person creating the IA must genuinely care about understanding the people who will use the site, and be willing to represent their needs (and go in to bat for them when the pressure is on).

If the person doing the IA is also heavily involved in the content (e.g. as a subject matter expert or content writer), they need to be able to look at the information objectively, and from the perspective of those who will use it. This can be harder than you imagine – it takes a lot of effort to see your own content from someone else's perspective.

Language

The person doing the IA must have excellent skills in the language you are working in. So much of this work involves grouping content into concepts and describing it, so great language skills are a must.

Synthesis, strategy & detail

As I've mentioned already, a good IA works well for both the users and the content, and also meets the goals of the business. As the person creating the IA, your job is to come up with something that synthesises information from different areas, such as user research activities (which we talk about in chapter 2.1). You need a deep understanding of the content and a detailed understanding of the business. Chances are you'll have competing needs from each of these areas, so you need to be able to pull things together into a solution.

You also need to be able to think about overall strategies (what's the site for?) and nitty-gritty details (what will this hyperlink be called?) at the same time.

You'll need great attention to detail to make sure your ideas will work in the real world.

If you work best going step-by-step, and like to see how each step of a process leads to the next one, you may not be the best person to create the IA. It's not a linear process – you definitely need creative leaps and insights.

If you're a great strategist but don't much like detail, you'll need to work with someone who can make sure your strategies support the actual content.

Communication

The person creating the IA is often one of a few people on a project who understands all the ins and outs (because they understand the strategy, people and content). This means they'll often be asked to explain how the information architecture should work, as well as all sorts of other details about the project.

Communication skills are vital. The person creating the IA should be able to talk with a wide range of people, including users, managers, content experts and developers. They should be able to have one-on-one discussions with people, and present to groups.

They should also be able to communicate in more than one style – verbally, in writing, and visually (representing things either by sketching or diagramming) – and not rely on a standard approach to communicating.

In most of my projects, the most feedback, comments and questions come when people see something for the first time – either a draft IA or draft navigation and page layouts. At this point, the person doing the IA must be able to:

- listen to the feedback and questions
- understand the underlying issues that come up
- be prepared to **make changes** based on feedback

What you don't want is someone who creates a draft then defends it to the end. They must be able to listen to other people, figure out the underlying message and decide what to do about it.

What's an information architect?

So what about an information architect? What do they do? A person with a title of IA will usually do a range of things. Of course, they will be primarily responsible for designing:

- The IA: The overall structure of the site, groups, sub-groups and labels
- Navigation: Navigation bars, links and other ways of getting people to information (e.g. A-Z indexes, search)
- Documentation: Writing it all down (or communicating it in another way) so it can be built

They may also be involved in:

- User research: Understanding what information people need, how they may approach it, and how they think about groups and concepts
- Usability testing: Making sure the IA, navigation and other aspects of the project actually work for people
- Other interface and interaction design, such as the interfaces for web-based applications
- Creating prototypes for communication and testing.

And depending on the project, they may be involved in:

- identifying site strategy and goals
- content writing
- search engine optimisation (SEO) (This is coming up in more and more job descriptions as people realise IA can have a big impact on SEO)

How I got into IA

I asked a range of people about how their skills in a previous role helped them in IA. Here's what they told me.

Patrick Kennedy

User researcher and experience strategist, gurtle.com

"As lead web developer for an interactive agency, I worked in a team consisting of three groups: tech, creative and 'suits'. The respective concerns of each discipline were well handled; visual design by creative, dev build by the techies, and business/marketing requirements by the suits. But often things fell between the cracks. How did it all fit together? How would it be received by the users? What did users want?

I saw this as an opportunity to take a more holistic view of a project, plugging the cracks, introducing those arcane arts 'usability' and 'information architecture'.

I did the usual things – read books, went to seminars and conferences – but above all I just started doing it. Some of those initial 'discussions' with my colleagues were painful (after all why wouldn't you put the main navigation at the bottom of the page?). It took a lot of negotiation and relationship management.

I also made myself the 'go-to man' for usability and IA. Call it shameless self-promotion, or just being eager, but within an organisation that had no knowledge of, let alone expertise in, the field of IA, it was important to make it visible, tangible and valuable (that is, demonstrating value).

Coming from the technical perspective had obvious benefits – such as knowing how feasible it was to build a certain design – but also some that were not so obvious. For example, my colleagues respected my opinion and were accustomed to coming to me for advice and insight on technical matters. This was an excellent platform from which to start to introduce IA philosophy; a luxury I probably wouldn't have had if I had been this new 'IA guy' that they didn't know."

Benjamin Bykowski

Internet strategist

"My career on the Web began while I was studying Computer Science & Engineering. I was classically trained in data structures and algorithms and my first Web projects focused on interfaces based more on databases than users.

In computer science, the skills that we are taught involve taking a system and building in a sense of structure and order. Classes are designed for inheritance and refactored for improved performance, methods are diagrammed, integrated circuits are mapped.

Yet taken out of context I might as well have described the work I do as an Information Architect. Having successfully made the transition into IA, I've the found that the skills I learned as a computer science engineer were invaluable to creating IA, designing navigation, and building interfaces.

As an Internet Strategist I discovered the power of communicating design as means of articulating a vision for online destinations. The lessons I've learned, of starting with the user, being active in my community, and communicating information design, are valuable not just professionally but in all aspects of my life."

Leslie Dann

Lead interaction designer (LBi) and Video producer (Cruz Dann Productions)

"I studied graphic design at the University of Cincinnati and soon found I was more interested in the initial phase of projects – understanding the content, information and communication strategy – rather than the visual design phase.

I got into IA in 1994 when I was hired as a graphic designer at a Silicon Alley multimedia firm. My first task was to do the storyboard for a CDRom and I enjoyed it so much that I stayed on that side of projects, not getting into the graphic interface work. This eventually led into creating wireframes for screens and flow charts. At the time we were known as 'Navigation designers'.

I realised that a large part of what IAs do uses graphic design skills:

- Understanding the importance of a creative brief, how to collaborate in developing one and how to apply it to a project.
- Visual problem-solving: A lot of our work is 'a puzzle'. We have to figure out how to make complex information and visuals as simple as possible, but no simpler than the target audience and creative brief require.
- Understanding the importance of creating a design system and applying it consistently but with flexibility, knowing when you should break the rules (consistency without boredom).
- Good information design skills are key to creating the deliverables themselves: To create balanced page compositions, clear/ consistent visual hierarchies and flow of information in our wireframes and site maps.
- Knowing the language of design and design critique skills to be able to communicate and collaborate closely with the creative team. The more we know about what they do and their challenges, and vice versa, the more we respect each other's work, resulting in strong teamwork.

I also produce short documentary and fiction films, as an extension of wanting to communicate stories and topics I've learned about through another immersive media. I'm glad to see that video is becoming more and more part of online user experiences and would like to keep working in both my IA and video careers."

Renata Phillippi

Freelance Interaction Designer

"Design and business have been a common theme in my life as far back as high school – I even worked in a design job straight out of high school while I studied for my Bachelors degree.

In 2002 I started working in change management and worked my way up to a business analyst. In this role I really enjoyed bringing design thinking to business. My first project as a BA was to help redesign the intranet for two of the internal teams for the client. The second project built an online application to track hospital spending.

Later when I went on to become an IA I realized a lot of the work I did as a BA helped prepare me for the job:

- Being able to understand and translate business requirements to prototypes, functional specs, and communicate with developers
- Taking content audits to contribute to laying out information based on the users needs and desires
- Collaborating across various job functions to ensure we meet the needs of the end user
- Communicating to business how solutions would drive results

While this is just the BA side, I know that having also been a visual designer has helped me to visualize the business needs into appropriate solutions for the end user."

Avi Soudack

Information Architect and User Experience Consultant, brightroom.ca

"After working as a researcher, first on educational media and later in communication and marketing, I began to do usability testing. It was a natural development for someone with training in observational research methods and an interest in information and communication technologies. But there was now an Internet, a web, that needed examination.

After a few years or so I'd amassed quite a few hours watching people use software and the net. Along the way, I worked as an instructional designer, developing e-learning programmes for adult learners at home and in the workplace, and as a writer and editor of technical material.

Increasingly the 'usability' consulting I was doing involved suggesting interaction design and content strategies. Then the balance began to shift and i was doing less user testing and more straight-ahead content, navigation and interaction design – information architecture. It was a comfortable move: I was able to put together a user-centred approach founded on my research training and tons of time with 'users', with hands-on experience in developing content, organizing information and designing online interactions."

Chapter summary

People suitable for designing the IA for a site could include:

- business analysts
- usability specialists
- writers
- graphic designers
- web developers
- project managers

Their skills should include:

- empathy with people
- language
- ability to synthesise different types of information
- attention to detail
- great communication skills

4

Information Architecture for Things Other Than Websites

When I teach workshops, people often leave wondering how IA is relevant for their non-website project. Yes, IA is most applicable for things such as websites and intranets. But you can use it for other things as well.

Let's look at some non-website examples, and see how IA fits in.

Menus

Many applications, both on and off the web, use menus to provide access to functions and tools. Menus are a perfect example of IA – each grouping together similar functions.

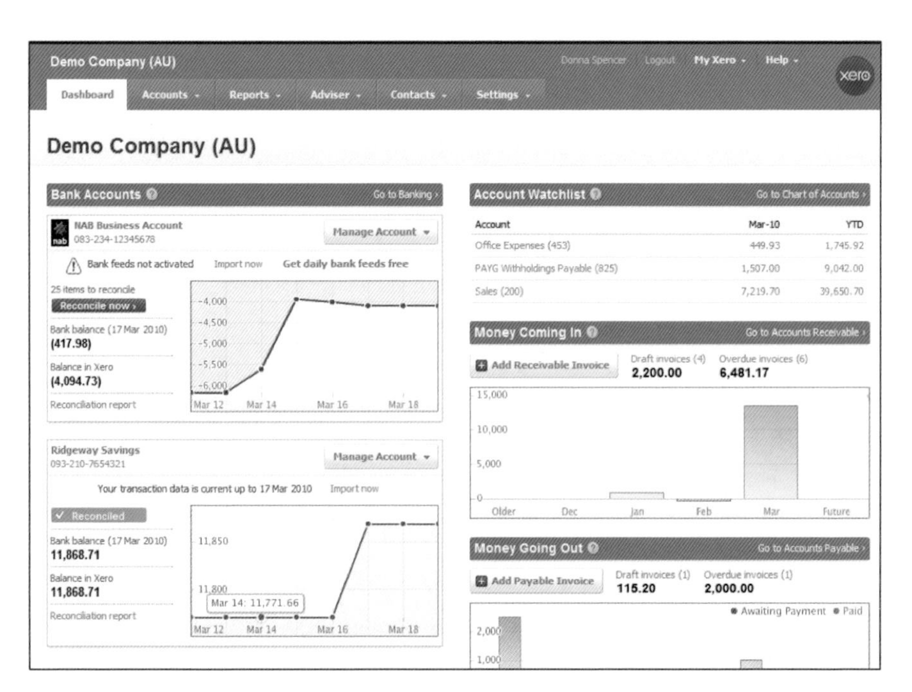

Fig 4 – 1. Xero is an online accounting application. The menu at the top groups similar functions together (xero.com)

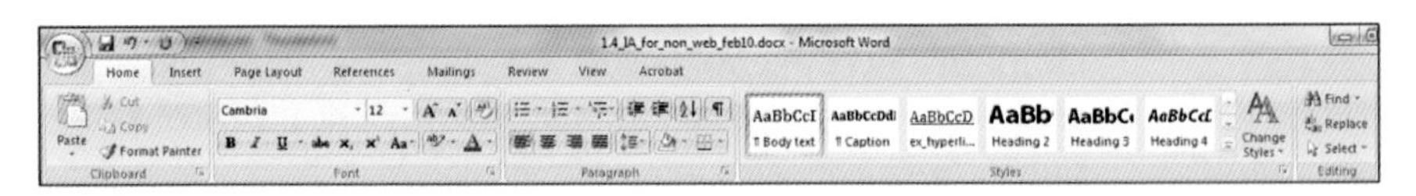

Fig 4 – 2. Love it or hate it, Microsoft Word's ribbon and menus are examples of IA for a software application

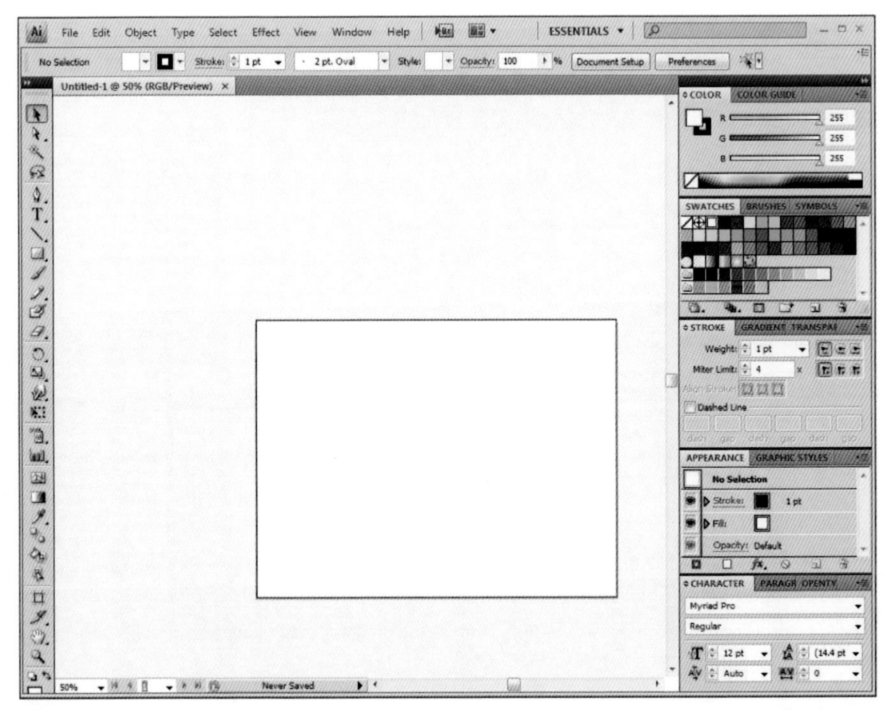

Fig 4 – 3. If you've ever used a drawing tool, you'll know how hard it is to find the right tool or setting in all the menus and palettes

Data-heavy applications

I work on a lot of internal business applications. While a large part of my work is figuring out how they should work, it's also making sure the data fields are grouped in sensible ways so people know what each set of fields is about and what to do with them.

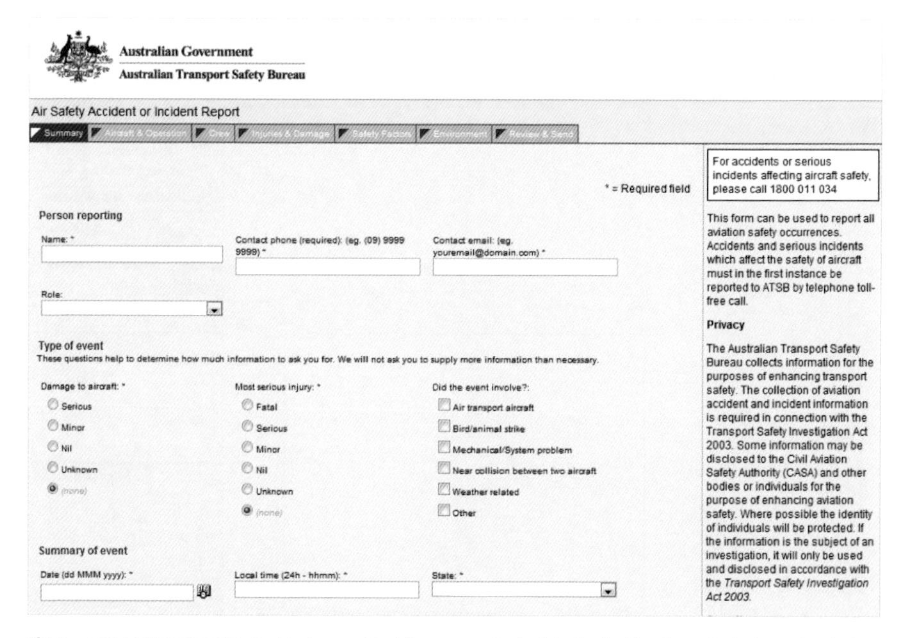

Australian Government
Australian Transport Safety Bureau

Air Safety Accident or Incident Report

Summary | Aircraft & Operation | Crew | Injuries & Damage | Safety Factors | Environment | Review & Send

* = Required field

Person reporting

Name: *

Contact phone (required): (eg. (09) 9999 9999) *

Contact email: (eg. youremail@domain.com) *

Role:

Type of event

These questions help to determine how much information to ask you for. We will not ask you to supply more information than necessary.

Damage to aircraft: *
- Serious
- Minor
- Nil
- Unknown
- (none)

Most serious injury: *
- Fatal
- Serious
- Minor
- Nil
- Unknown
- (none)

Did the event involve?:
- Air transport aircraft
- Bird/animal strike
- Mechanical/System problem
- Near collision between two aircraft
- Weather related
- Other

Summary of event

Date (dd MMM yyyy): *

Local time (24h - hhmm): *

State: *

For accidents or serious incidents affecting aircraft safety, please call 1800 011 034

This form can be used to report all aviation safety occurrences. Accidents and serious incidents which affect the safety of aircraft must in the first instance be reported to ATSB by telephone toll-free call.

Privacy

The Australian Transport Safety Bureau collects information for the purposes of enhancing transport safety. The collection of aviation accident and incident information is required in connection with the Transport Safety Investigation Act 2003. Some information may be disclosed to the Civil Aviation Safety Authority (CASA) and other bodies or individuals for the purpose of enhancing aviation safety. Where possible the identity of individuals will be protected. If the information is the subject of an investigation, it will only be used and disclosed in accordance with the *Transport Safety Investigation Act 2003.*

Fig 4 – 4. The online air safety incident or accident form can collect a lot of data. Figuring out what goes in what tab, and how it is grouped on the page takes IA skills too

Classifying

Many applications are about classifying data so people can find and use it. For example, a document management system usually needs you to classify each document according to a number of criteria.

I've worked on projects where two organisations wanted to merge or share data. The biggest barrier (and the biggest part of the project) was that their data was classified in different ways. Even a small difference in defining something like a geographical boundary makes it hard to compare and combine data.

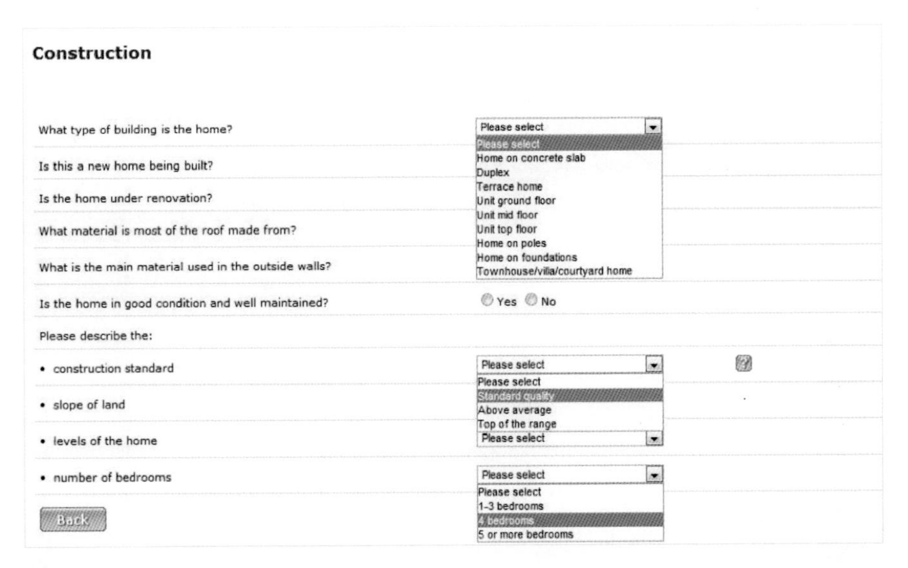

Construction

What type of building is the home? — Please select: Please select / Home on concrete slab / Duplex / Terrace home / Unit ground floor / Unit mid floor / Unit top floor / Home on poles / Home on foundations / Townhouse/villa/courtyard home

Is this a new home being built?

Is the home under renovation?

What material is most of the roof made from?

What is the main material used in the outside walls?

Is the home in good condition and well maintained? — Yes / No

Please describe the:

- construction standard — Please select: Please select / Standard quality / Above average / Top of the range
- slope of land
- levels of the home — Please select
- number of bedrooms — Please select: Please select / 1-3 bedrooms / 4 bedrooms / 5 or more bedrooms

Back

Fig 4 – 5. Insurance forms are full of classifications, and your answers affect how much you pay.

Mobile

If you are designing a mobile app, you'll need to do some IA work. A lot of mobile apps work as a hierarchy, with menus providing access to different parts of the application. This IA is just the same as it is for everything else.

Everything in this book (except navigation design) is just as relevant for these examples as it is for websites and intranets.

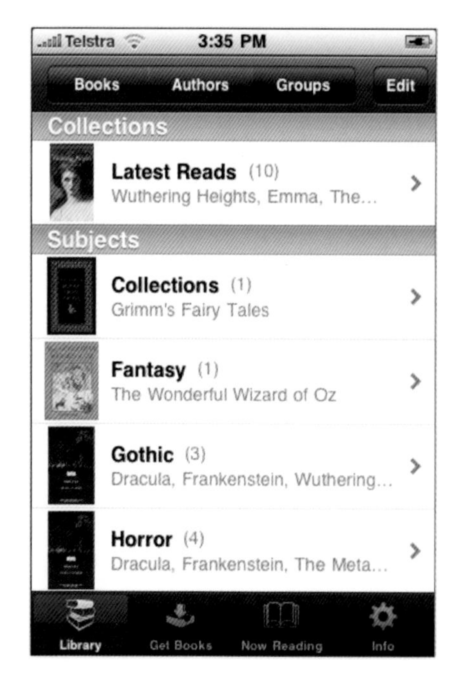

Figure 4 – 6. Stanza allows access to books by authors and groups

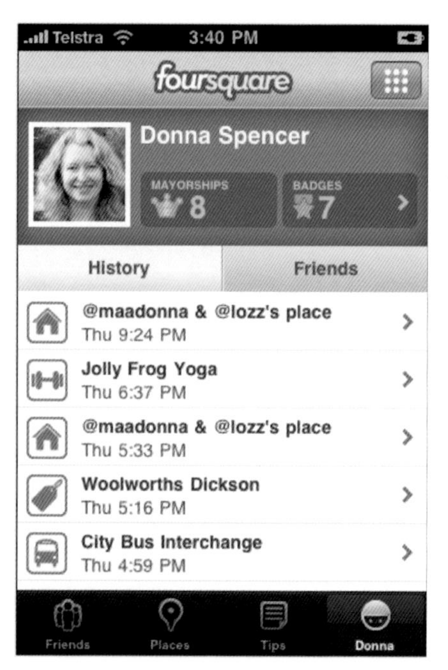

Figure 4 – 7. Foursquare arranges functions into four groups (at the bottom) then some into further groups

Chapter summary

IA is not just for websites and intranets, and is relevant to:

- Anything with a menu: Software, web applications and mobile applications
- Applications that collect or process a lot of data
- Any system that involves classification of information
- Mobile applications

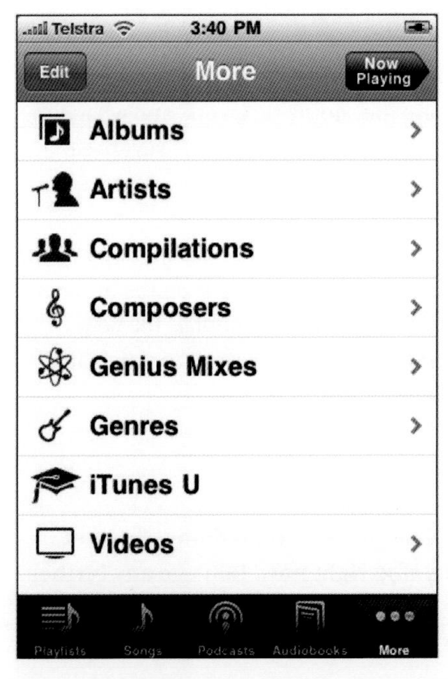

Figure 4 – 8. The iPod groups your music

5

Before you start: *Context*

So far we've talked a lot about what IA is. In this chapter we start the actual work by looking at what you'll need to know right from the start if you want your project to go smoothly – the project's context.

As we discussed in chapter 2, you'll want to know about:

- **Goals**: What are the aims or goals of doing this work?
- **Technology**: What are the technology opportunities and constraints?
- **Design**: Are there design constraints you need to consider?
- **Culture**: What sort of culture are you working within, and how will that affect your project?
- **Stakeholders**: Who is, and who should be, involved in the project?

Project goals

When I start a piece of work with a client, I want to know two things straight away: why are they doing this work, and what do they want to achieve when it's finished. You may be surprised (though I'm not any more) to hear that in most cases no-one actually knows.

In my experience, people often know there's something wrong – "Our website sucks", "No-one can find anything on the intranet", "We wrote the online help but everyone still phones the help desk". However, it can be much harder to get them to articulate what the end result should be.

I'm going to be very blunt about this.

If you can't clearly articulate the reason for doing the work, and the desired outcome, stop right now. Don't go any further until this is clear.

Case Study

UX *Australia*

Let me introduce you to a project I'll be using as an example and case study throughout this book.

When I'm not doing IA work, teaching and writing books, I run a conference called UX Australia that focuses on user experience topics. It's a small, community-focused conference and is great fun to be involved with. At the time I'm writing this book we're in the early stages of planning the second conference, which will be held in Melbourne, Australia.

Naturally, the conference has an associated website that has information about the upcoming conference (including the program), resources from the previous conference, and online registration.

It's a good example for the book as it has some complexity – a combination of structured and unstructured content (which we'll talk about later) – while being a familiar enough topic for you to understand.

In each chapter, I'll use this example (and others, of course) to illustrate key points.

If you'd like to see what it's all about, visit uxaustralia.com.au.

Case study: UX Australia website goals

Our goals for the website for UX Australia were:

- Allow attendees to find out a range of information about the conference – from broad ideas like what it's about, to detail like how to get a cheap room at the conference hotel. (This reduces our administration costs as we don't have to answer questions, and increases sales as people can find out enough to decide they will attend.)
- Make sure people can see how they'll benefit from the conference.
- Help people convince their boss to let them attend.
- Ensure potential speakers know exactly what is expected before submitting a proposal (reducing the amount of chasing up we have to do).
- Be a place people would visit for user experience articles and information (increasing awareness and potential future attendance).

If you don't know where you're heading, you can't possibly get there. My worst projects – where I feel like we've been spinning around in circles, redoing work and not getting anywhere – have all been problems because the project goals weren't clear.

Project goals help define what you are doing. A good set of project goals describe what the project is all about, why it is being done and what the end result will be.

They are useful to help you:

- Set directions and priorities
- Make sure you are on track
- Assess requirements and requests: When someone asks for a new feature (like the organisation's mission statement on the home page), you can find out whether it will contribute to the project goals.
- Make decisions: Will this new design feature support the goal? Is one approach better than another?

They will also directly affect the IA. As you draft an IA, you'll be trying to make it work as best as possible for people, fit the content and achieve the goals of the project. This can be tricky sometimes, especially when the business wants to achieve one thing (sell more music) and the people want to achieve something else (download music for free). With a solid understanding of the goals of the project, you'll be able to create an IA that works for both the business and for people.

You'll also be able to communicate and sell the draft IA more easily. When you can show how it will achieve the goals of the business, stakeholders will accept it more easily.

Learning about goals

If you're lucky, your client or team may already know the goals of the project. They may have had to figure out what they wanted from the project to get the funding, or they may just be very organised and disciplined.

Yeah, right.

In a lot of cases, you'll probably have to work it out yourself. If that's the case, try to learn these pieces of information.

What is the overall goal of this project?

This is the key question, and can be one of the hardest to articulate. After all, it's such an abstract question. But it does need to be answered, or you'll get to the 'end' of the project and find out that you've done a lot of work for no outcome.

Sometimes the answers are fairly obvious. But it is still worthwhile to check that everyone is on the same page and wants to achieve the same thing.

Goals usually fall into three different types – making more money, reducing costs or helping people make better decisions. Example goals include:

- Increase sales by 10%
- Increase customer retention by 5%
- Allow customers to find information about our services (which may lead to increased sales and reduced sales costs)
- Make it easier for existing customers to place orders (increased sales)
- Reduce follow-up calls to customers (decreased costs)
- Improve the quality of data from customers (reducing processing times and costs)
- Raise awareness of an issue (encouraging people to make different decisions as a result)
- Build a community around a product (increasing loyalty and increasing sales)

How do we know that we have 'finished' it?

It can often be hard to figure out if a project is 'finished' or ready to launch. How do you know that it's good enough to go? Sometimes it will be that you've used up your time or budget, but that shouldn't be the deciding factor in whether or not you've finished.

Before you even start a project, think about when you'll know it's ready enough for you to launch. You may decide you need only a couple of pages of content ready and it can grow from there, or you may want to make sure everything is 'perfect' before you launch. Of course, that begs the question of what 'perfect' is and how you will measure it.

How will we measure the impact of any changes?
At the end of a project you may need to show that the site has actually improved (particularly for redesigns). This may help you decide whether you are ready to launch, but more often it will be to show that the money spent on a project was worthwhile. (I know of lots of projects that spent a lot of money and could show no outcome.)

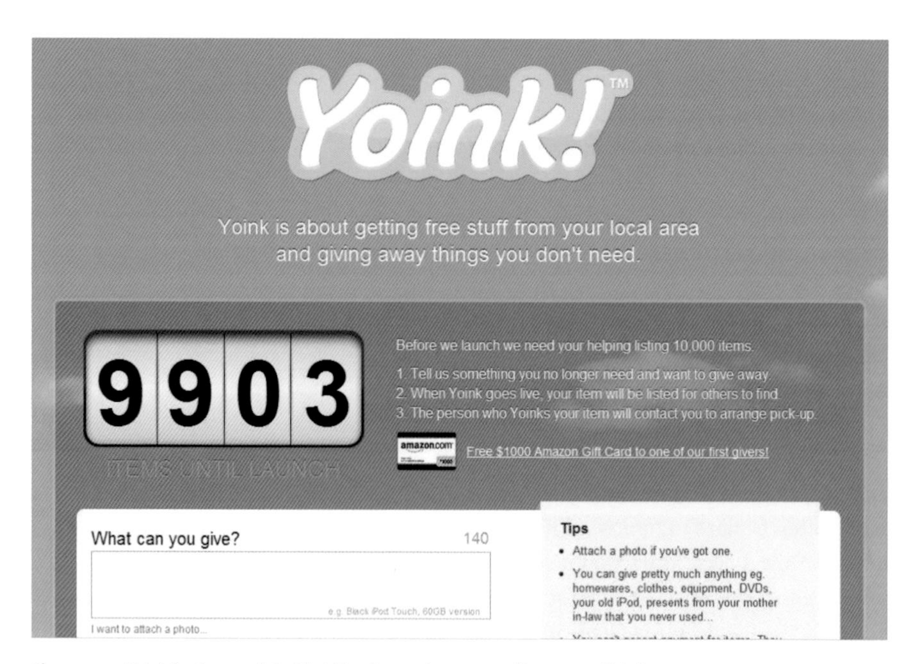

Figure 5 – 1. Yoink (`yoink.com`) decided 'done' was when 10,000 items were listed

To measure change, you'll need to know how you are doing at the beginning, and again at the end. Depending on your project, you may want to measure things like:

- overall visits to the site
- product purchases (how many people visit a product and buy it)
- shopping cart abandonment (what proportion of people add items to their cart but don't follow through with the purchase)
- time to complete a task
- quality of incoming data
- number of calls to the call centre or help desk

Of course, the fact you need these details at the beginning of the project as well as the end means your first step may be getting systems in place to measure them.

Ways to collect goals

The way you create project goals will depend on your project and your role in it. If your project is part of a larger corporate initiative, start by finding out what the goals of that project may be. Also review any business strategies to see where the project fits in terms of achieving broader organisational goals.

For some projects, you may be able to get a set of goals from a brief conversation with your client or a senior manager.

For something bigger you may need to run a workshop with a range of stakeholders. How you do this will depend on the organisation. I've worked with some clients who are very strategic. They're aware of how they work and what they need, and can usually articulate their goals fairly easily. But many just don't have the experience to do it easily.

Here are three methods I find useful for working out goals.

1. Scenario planning

Scenario planning takes a story-telling approach to identify goals. By telling stories, people can better visualise and describe an outcome, and you get great information on what the goals really mean.

Ask your client or stakeholders to describe an ideal outcome, in story form. They may say something like:

- "Someone visits the website, easily narrows down to just a set of products that interest them, finds one (after comparing a couple) and pays for it in one simple step."
- "When someone is thinking about a job with us, they find out what sort of company we are, the types of jobs that are available and can either contact us for more information or apply for a job straight away."
- "The next complaint form I open will have enough detail for me to start investigating the issue without having to contact the customer for more information."
- "People stop phoning me with the same simple questions over and over, but call when their situation is different to normal, or when they need to clarify a point of detail."

For each basic story you could dig deeper – describe what happens before the story, explore the middle further, and identify what happens after it finishes. Although the stories may initially sound just like tasks, by paying attention and asking questions, you can tease out goals. For example:

- The first example above (narrowing down to find products and pay in a single step) is all about helping customers to be more efficient which, ultimately, may increase sales.
- The second (looking for a job) is all about attracting the right candidates, which should get better staff and reduce administration for unsuitable applicants.

You can also do scenario planning in reverse – ask stakeholders to describe what a failure looks like (again, in story form). Use this as a starting point to figure out how to address the likely points of failure. With the right organisation this can be very fun and much more productive than tackling the goals head on.

2. Pain points

One place to start is to identify current points of pain. Find out what is going wrong, and see if you can get to the bottom of why it is happening.

Pain points are a good starting point for a discussion, as they give everyone something concrete to discuss. (The hardest thing about setting goals is thinking abstractly about the future, so anything concrete is good.) As you discuss the pain points, you can start to identify consistent patterns, discuss the underlying issue and turn it into a goal.

For example, if over-the-phone purchases are increasing, and sales staff's workload is increasing, discuss why. It might be that pricing information isn't clear, product details are missing or just that your audience are not comfortable completing full transactions online. Your goal may not be to reduce phone sales (which you could do by making the phone number harder to find as one client of mine did), but to remove the barriers that customers are facing when buying online and gradually convert phone sales to online sales.

3. Backcasting

Backcasting[1] is like forecasting in reverse. You start with an end and work backwards to identify what you need to do to get there.

The end positions are described in scenario form, and may describe a few different outcomes you are trying to reach. I usually create a scenario for an ideal future, an acceptable outcome and something in between. By looking at what would be needed to reach each end point, you can tease out a lot of issues. You can also identify intermediate goals that are more achievable than one big end-goal.

Technology opportunities and constraints

Another thing to understand before you really get started is the technology you may be using. I've rarely created an IA before the technology was chosen. It's much more common to have something in place – be it a content management system, existing system that runs the intranet or document management system.

If there's a system you need to use, or if the project team has ideas about the type of system they want to choose, learn a little about how it works before you get into the IA. For example some content management systems are very good for hierarchical information, but don't do so well with structured content (we'll discuss structured content in chapter 16) and vice-versa. Some let you easily display related content, and some don't. Some may do what you need, but in a clumsy way that's hard to maintain. Some offer a series of navigation templates you'll need to work with. Some are easy to customise to do what you want, and some can be harder or more expensive.

If you're not a technical person, talk with folks who are. Ask them to explain the basics of how the system stores the content and how pieces of content are displayed on a page.

Every system is different, so it's hard for me to tell you exactly what to look out for and learn. But when you know the basics, keep checking whether the ideas you have for the information architecture can work within the system you are using.

And if you have no technology constraints to work with, congratulations!

[1] See `http://www.slideshare.net/mmilan/backcasting-101-final-public` for a thorough explanation of the process, tailored to IA work

Design constraints

You may also face constraints in some aspects of design. You may have to use an existing approach to the site navigation, a standard approach to page layout, branding requirements that affect navigation design (such as big banners that take up a lot of screen space), preferred terminology, or the need to have the CEOs photo on every page (I'm joking!).

If you're working with government sites (and increasingly for corporate), you'll probably have to meet accessibility guidelines. You may also need to meet policy and/or legal requirements.

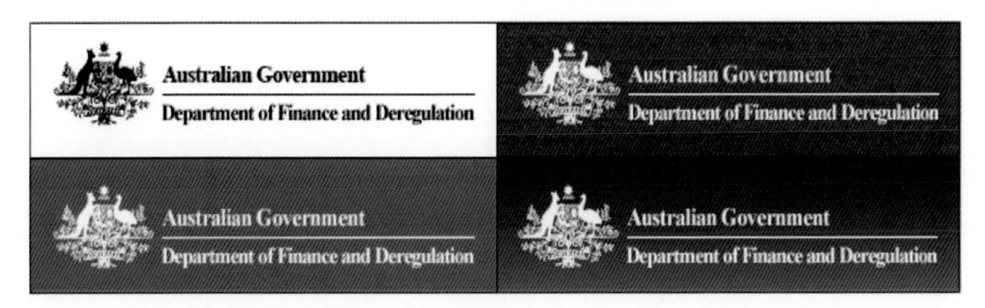

Figure 5 – 2. All Australian Government websites must adhere to standard branding requirements (`http://webpublishing.agimo.gov.au`)

Whatever these are, it's good to know them up front so you can work with them as you come up with the IA. Few things are more annoying than working right through a design only to be told the navigation has to be in a particular part of the page to fit with the organisation's overall approach (which of course you haven't done).

Culture

You may need to know a little about the organisation's culture before you start a project. Sometimes it doesn't matter very much, but sometimes it does.

Organisational culture is all about the way an organisation works. (The best description I've heard is "The way we do things 'round here".)

The main thing a culture affects is how communications are conducted. Will you be able to talk to whoever you want whenever you want, or will all meetings have carefully constructed invitation lists and be scheduled well in advance? Will you be able to present a rough draft of an idea for feedback, or only present detailed final deliverables?

Stakeholders

When planning a project, consider who is (and who should be) involved. Understand their role in the organisation and where their influence lies.

The things you most want to avoid are:

- People popping out of the woodwork well into the project with an entirely different perspective on what the goals of the project are.
- The person you think is making the decisions not actually being the decision-maker.

On many projects I discover people being excluded who really should have something to contribute. Sometimes it's because other people don't understand what they do. Sometimes there's an internal political agenda.

One of your roles in a project may be to introduce stakeholders to fundamental ideas behind what you are working on. A lot of my projects will involve some simple education about 'the web', how it works and how people use it.

Doing this early can make it much easier to present ideas later – you won't be interrupted with quite so many comments about everything needing to be on the home page, that people don't scroll, and other fallacies about the web.

Other constraints

Lastly, don't forget to check whether you have time and budget constraints. These will exist for most projects and you'll never have enough of them. But you need to know and work within them.

Chapter summary

Before starting a project, you'll need to find out all about the context of the project, including:

- What the project goals are. These may already be defined, or you may need to help figure them out.
- The technology you will be using, what it does well and what it does poorly.
- Any existing design constraints and requirements you have to work within.
- The culture of the organisation, and how will you be allowed to communicate with people.
- Who is, and who should be, involved in the project.

Further reading

See the list of articles at `http://delicious.com/practicalIA/goals/`

Case Study

How goal setting helped our project

Ruth Henry, Space-time research, spacetimeresearch.com

When we went to redesign our website, we started with what we called a Competitor Comparison Workshop to compare and discuss our current website. All the relevant stakeholders were present including the CEO, Product Manager, and Marketing Communications Manager. We discussed the following:

- What is the underlying structure of our website and competitor websites?
- Which websites have information below the fold?
- What elements are common to all websites?
- What is the accessibility of the website?
- What is your first impression of the website? In a five seconds viewing what do you first see and can you work out what the company does?

From this research the objectives were defined and documented in the *Website Re-creation Brief*. This document was used to brief the designer and scope the required project work.

With the objectives clearly defined, it was easy to allocate the project work into phases so we could quickly go live with the new website.

- **Phase I**: Gaining Control – This included integrating the templates, populating the existing content, and building features such as integration between forms and salesforce.com.
- **Go Live**: After Phase I we turned the website on.
- **Phase II**: Building a Community – Integrated the Forum, FAQ, MediaWIKI, Twitter feed, Blog feed, and Blog.

Using the *Website Re-creation Brief* it was clear what was in and out of scope, which kept our project on track. Any ideas for improvements were captured in a Phase III document to be discussed at a later date. The supporting information in the brief was re-used in the contract with the website company and in the Project Charter document.

An extract of the *Website Re-creation Brief*:
The external website's purpose is to inform and excite readers to find out more about Space-Time Research's solutions, products, and to contact Space-Time Research.

From analysis of our competitors' websites we have identified that the website must have the content separate from design. The structure and design must be separate from the marketing branding.

Therefore the website construction is defined in layers:

- features
- content
- structure
- design
- branding

The objectives of the website re-creation are:

- Create a website structure and design that will allow marketing and supporting content to be added or modified with ease.
- Create 'calls to action' that are part of the sales funnel.
- Create a website front page that can allow new content to be showcased.
- Create content that is focused to different kinds of readers based on the website's audience. For example statistics, executives, government employees.
- Create a community.
- Demonstrate that we are 'thought leaders' in the area of self-service business intelligence.
- Use structural elements common to competitors' websites. This will allow readers to be instantly familiar with the website as the structure is similar to other websites.
- Use design elements common to competitors' websites. This will allow readers to be instantly familiar with the design elements as they have used them on other websites.

Part 2

Understanding People

Learning about your users

Analysing user research

Communicating about users

How people look for info

How people think about categories

6

Learning about your users

Have you ever been asked to help a colleague with something on their computer and been surprised about how they've set it up or what they're trying to do? Have you ever helped a customer over the phone, and had to step them through some basics before you could even begin to answer their question?

It's weird isn't it? I'm still surprised when someone double-clicks a hyperlink, types a URL into Google's search box, or wonders whether a page has finished loading. I'm even more surprised when people phone me with questions I'm sure I've answered on my website, or give me good suggestions for things I've already done. And I've lost count of how many times I've had to help people shut off their iPhone just as the aircraft is taking off.

But they help me remember two important things:

- Not everyone knows as much as I do about computers and the internet.
- Even when I think I've made something completely obvious, it might not be.

That's why I do some type of **user research** for all my projects. If I don't take active steps to learn about people, I'll assume all sorts of things that just aren't true. And I might miss out on some very important things that could provide real insights for the project.

What you can learn about people

User research is an important part of any project. For IA work you can learn all about the types of information people need, how they use it, where they use it and how they think about it. This helps you to select content they need, make sure it is useful and easy to understand, and is organised in a way that makes sense.

What do people need?

One of the main things you'll learn from user research is what information people need or are looking for.

You can learn this by asking people directly what they use and/or look for. You can also do it by looking at their existing behaviour, such as what pages are already popular. For example, when I'm working on a corporate intranet, I look at the most popular pages and also ask staff "What's the one piece of information on the intranet you couldn't live without?" or "What would cause you a lot of trouble if we took it away?" Funnily enough, it's usually something I don't expect – the weather page, or maybe the canteen menu. It's rarely the corporate news or whatever management thinks is most important.

Understanding people's needs helps you:

- assess existing information to make sure it meets key needs
- identify information gaps
- make key information easy to find
- prioritise content activities – release or rewrite the most important pages before the least important

What do people do with information?

Beyond knowing what information people need, I like to find out what they do with it. People rarely want to just 'find' information – they usually want to do something with it as well.

They may want to grab a fact, or dive in deep and learn everything about a topic. They may want to filter a big set of products and then compare items. They may need to send it to other people, save it for later, or copy a part of it into a report. They may even want to print it![1]

People may also read your information before taking another step in a process. For example, they may need to check system requirements before downloading software, read the product description before adding it to their shopping cart or looking at similar products. You need to know what their next step is so you can help them take it easily. (And remember, there may be more than one "next step".)

[1] Chapter 9 is all about the different tasks that people may need to do and what you'll need to do to design for them

Where do they use it?
Sometimes knowing where people use information may be important. Will they be in an office with a large monitor, good lighting and plenty of time to read? Or will they be using a mobile device with a small screen in bright light? Knowing this could really change the amount and type of information you provide. You may even decide to provide the same content in different ways for people to use in different locations.

What do they already know about the topic?
Everyone starts with some level of knowledge about a topic.

Your audience may know very little about the topic you're presenting. If so, you'll want to know how much they do know and create ways to get them up to speed quickly.

Or they may know a lot about the topic – maybe even more than you if it's legal, scientific or something technical. You'll need to work out how to give them what they need without basic information getting in their way.

Most likely you'll find that some people know nothing about what you're working on, while others will know a lot. This is common. It sounds tricky to design for, but if you get to know both groups well, you'll see opportunities to meet everyone's needs in an elegant way.

How they think about the information – their current opinion or feeling about it – may also be important. For example, people may be more interested in getting a refund than paying a bill, and will be willing to spend more time learning how to do it.

What do they already know about the technology?

If you think you'll be doing something new (or newish) with technology, or if you know some people may not be comfortable with new technology, you'll want to learn how much experience they have.

I remember teaching a workshop where I flippantly said, "Don't worry about long pages, everyone knows how to scroll these days".

One of the participants politely pointed out some research she'd just finished with her internal staff that showed most of them had no idea there was content out of their immediate view.

I was stunned, and asked more about their background. It turns out they'd been using a mainframe system for years, and most didn't use computers at home (another surprise and reminder to me). The idea of something being out of view just wasn't in their paradigm of how computers worked. It didn't stop them implementing an intranet with content below the fold, but it reminded them about doing some extra training to help people know it was there.

How do they describe things

One of the most important things you'll learn from user research, and one you can't get any other way, is the terminology people use and the way they think about concepts.

This is so important to know that you'll use it over and over again as you work.

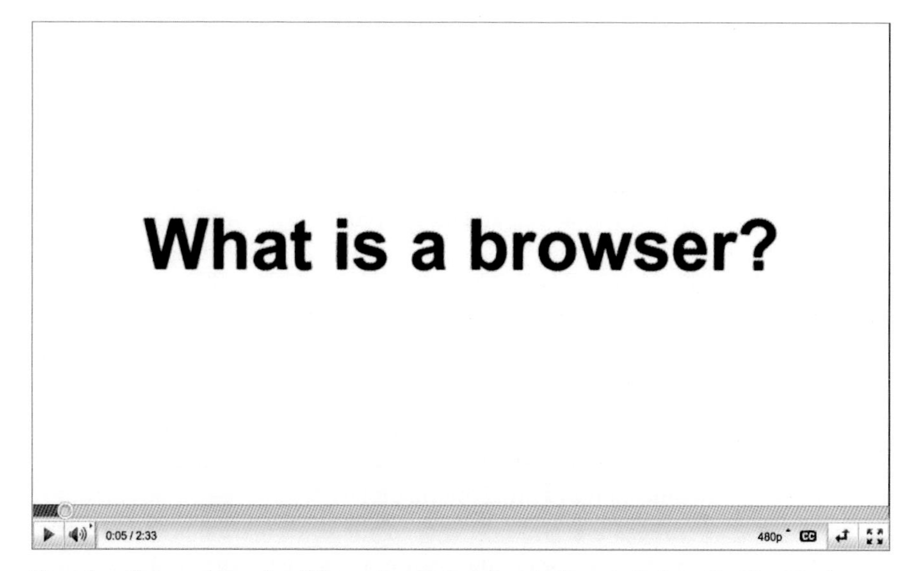

Figure 6 – 1. If you want to see how little people understand about the internet, check out this video: What is a browser? (`http://www.youtube.com/watch?v=o4MwTvtyrUQ`)

You'll use it when deciding what information to group together (people talk not only about objects but also concepts and groups – something we go into deeply in chapter 10), what to call your navigation items, and how to phrase ideas in content. You'll need it if you're creating an A-Z list or tweaking your search engine.

I can't stress enough how important this is. Well, actually I can – I'm going to continue to talk about it right through the book!

Collecting information about people – how to

Before you start – what do you want to learn?
Before you start the process of learning about people, think about what you want to learn and why you want to learn it. This will help you decide who will be involved, the types of activities you will do, the size of your research project and whether you run it as a formal research project or something quite informal.

User research can help you find out a range of things – from learning broad patterns of behaviour to help you identify opportunities for new products, to getting a detailed understanding of how people do a particular activity. That's why it's so important to figure out exactly what you want to learn. If you don't prepare, you'll run around in circles later wondering what the point was, and may not collect what you actually need.

What questions to ask
I've described some of the things you can learn from user research. Now you'll need to think about which of those things you actually need to know. You may not need to know which content people use most often – you can look at your web analytics for that. But you may want to know what they feel is missing, or how good the quality of the existing information is.

For some projects I've been interested in what people do with a particular type of information, and sometimes how they use information within their working day. As you can imagine, if I hadn't thought of what I needed, I may not have asked the right questions.

Sometimes, when brainstorming with a client, I play a modified '5 Whys' game[2]. Start with something you know about users, and ask 'why do they need/want that?' until your answer is 'I don't know'. The idea is that you can usually figure this out within 5 steps.

Case Study: UX Australia

5 whys for UX Australia

For example, thinking about the UX Australia website:

1. What is something we know people want from the website?: They want to see what presentations will be at the conference
2. Why do they need to do that?: So they can make a decision about whether to come
3. Why do they need to do that?: Because there are a lot of conferences they could attend
4. Why do they choose one over another?: I don't know

Aha! Now we have a research question (and in only 4 whys too) – to find out how people decide which conference to go to.

As you could imagine, knowing that could help us express our information in a way that will help people make that decision – even if they decide our conference isn't for them .

[1] http://en.wikipedia.org/wiki/5_Whys

[2] By the way, I haven't researched this as I only thought about it while making up this example, but now I probably will.

How much research to do

The biggest decision you'll make is how much research you actually need to do. As I said, I do some user research for every project, and I'm always glad I did because I always learn something interesting and important. But that doesn't mean I do extensive, in-depth research for everything. Sometimes I just look at existing web analytics and customer queries, and then chat with a few people already using the site. And that may be enough to let me know who I'm designing for and what their main issues are.

But sometimes I'll run an extensive research project, involving a range of people from different roles and demographics who are all trying to do different things.

Some key factors when making this decision:

- How much do you already (really) know about your audience? Do you hang out with them all the time, or have you never met them before?
- What are the consequences of getting it wrong? If you make a mistake from a lack of information, can you fix it up pretty quickly (change a label, move some content around) or will it be a major change (a complete revision of the IA)?
- How much money is involved? Again, if you make a mistake from lack of information are you throwing away a few hours work or millions of dollars?
- How quickly do you get feedback? If you do something silly, will you hear about it immediately (and be able to fix it immediately) or will you lose thousands of customers before you even know what's happened?

If it's a low-cost project where you already know your audience well, and you can get quick feedback and changes made just as quickly, you can probably get by with just a small amount of research. Or you may decide to work flexibly with users throughout the project.

But if you've never met one of these strange members of your audience, are working on a project that will end at delivery, that costs lots of money and may lose the business a lot of money...well, I think you can guess the answer to that.[4]

Personal blog

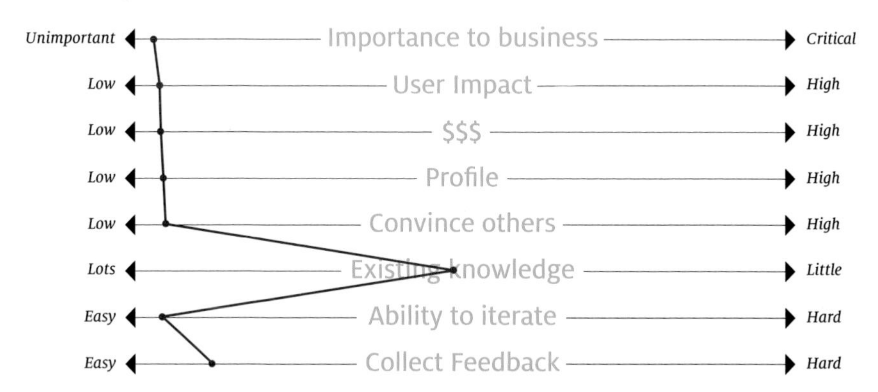

Figure 6 – 2. When looking at whether to do user research - for a personal blog, you don't need to do much

Enterprise application

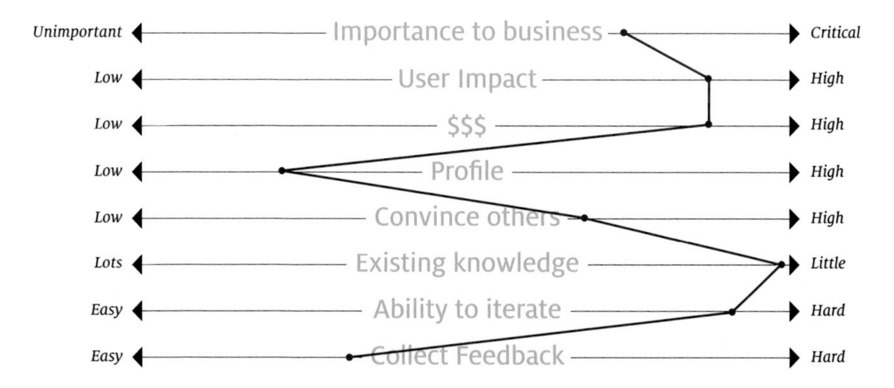

Figure 6 – 3. For a million dollar enterprise application, user research would be a good idea

[4] For a more thorough explanation of some of the attributes that may go into the decision on how much research to run, see `http://maadmob.net/donna/blog/2008/user_research_decisions`

When you're thinking about how much to do, remember that you can do user research more than once. My favourite way is to study existing information, talk to a few people and then decide whether I know enough or need to continue. I may find I've identified the key points already, or I may need to do more research.

Who to research

One of the first questions to answer is just who you need to learn about. If you're trying to make improvements for existing customers, you'll want to talk to them. If you're trying to attract new customers, you'll want to find potential customers and talk to them. If you're working on a corporate intranet, you may need to talk with people from a wide range of roles and areas across the organisation.

One common mistake, particularly in corporate projects, is talking only to managers. That's fine if you're designing something only the managers will use. But if non-managerial staff will use it as well, you'll really want to talk to them. You won't get the same type of information by talking to their managers.

How to find them

After figuring out who you need to involve, the next step is to find them and arrange for them to be involved. How you do this will depend on the amount of research you want to do and how well-connected you are to your audience. Here are some ways to go about it[5].

Formal recruiting

Market research companies have long lists of people interested in being involved in research. You give the market research company a detailed description of who you want to talk to – age, income, role, location, etc. – and they'll find people for you and schedule them. You usually pay per-head according to how many

[5] I've assembled some resources on recruiting here: `http://delicious.com/practicalIA/recruiting`

participants you need to involve. Many companies will also hire out facilities such as meeting rooms.

If you're going down the more formal path, you should seriously consider this option. Although it may seem more expensive to begin with, don't underestimate how much time it can take to contact people, invite them and follow up to make sure they turn up. Believe me, you'll only do it yourself once.

Informal recruiting

Informal approaches to recruiting usually involve asking people you already know. Talk to family and friends, ask on Twitter, look for Facebook groups around your topic. See if you already have mailing lists of people you can contact.

An informal approach is a particularly good way to find people for intranet work. You can call for volunteers, phone people from across the organisation or ask your colleagues for recommendations.

Online recruiting

If you're working on an existing site, try recruiting via the site. If you have a site or product that people already like or depend on, they may be happy to help you make it better.

Who else to involve

If you are working in a team, try to get as many as possible involved in the research at some point. In particular, involve anyone who'll make design decisions that will affect people – they'll all benefit from meeting some of the people they're designing for. They don't have to attend every research session, but they should be there for at least some of them.

This is a much more effective approach than having people read a research report or attend a presentation – meeting actual customers makes it much more real.

Ideas or numbers (qualitative or quantitative)

Also think about whether you need to collect mostly qualitative research (ideas, behaviours, observations) or mostly quantitative (statistics, counts, etc). This will affect not only how many people you involve, but also the way you collect information. For example (and we discuss this further in the next section) qualitative research is best collected via interviews, focus groups and observation, while quantitative research is better done with surveys or analytics.

You don't need to choose one or the other – using both gives you insights into different aspects of your research question. And sometimes one type of research reveals insights that need further exploration via the other.

A quantitative approach

Steve Baty, Meld Studios

> "*A few years back we were designing a Web-based business application that would be used by front-desk staff to record transactions. To help set the default values and some preset combinations I went and poured through hundreds of transactions and transcribed the relevant data. I then performed a form of clustering analysis on the data to work out the most common combinations of sale, which we fed back into the design.*
>
> *Three preset pairs of values accounted for slightly over 85% of all transactions, with the rest being set through two standard select lists. The result being much faster data entry for the front-desk staffer, and a shorter sales experience for the customer.*"

User research methods

You can learn about your users in lots of different ways. For some you can use information you already have, while for others you'll collect new information. All have their advantages, limitations and things to watch out for.

I always use more than one of these methods. It makes it easier for me to identify the main issues as I'll see them come up from a couple of sources. It isn't hard to use more than one, and it will give you confidence that you are seeing real issues, not just a strange result from some bias in one method[6].

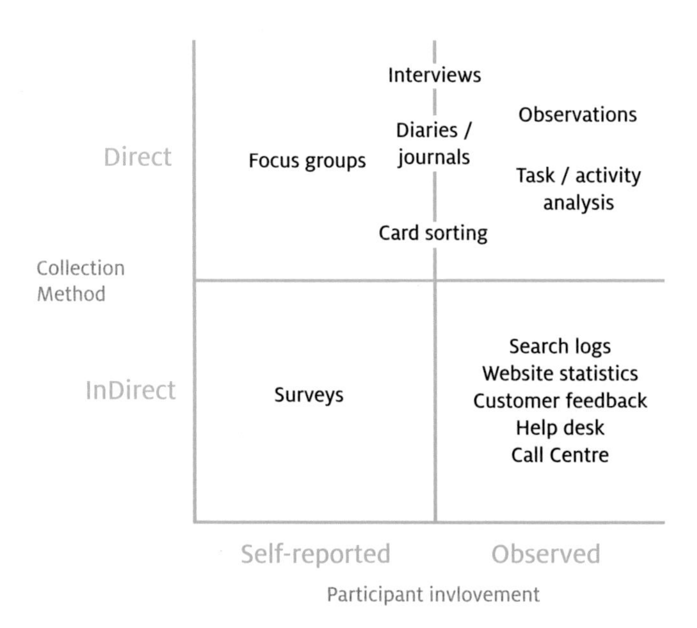

[6] See this article for more about why to use more than one method http://johnnyholland.org/2009/08/20/practical-triangulation/

This diagram shows the methods you can use, depending on to the type of involvement you have with people, and the way you collect the data:

- Direct collection involves some type of face-to-face activity between you and the research participant. The biggest advantage of all direct research methods is that because you're with the participant, you can explore any issues of interest as they arise.
- Indirect collection is done without any face-to-face contact with the participant. These methods often have one big advantage: they can collect a lot of information.
- Self-reported methods rely on the participant telling you what they think they do. These methods can involve a big bias because people aren't particularly good at knowing how or why they do something (or even what they do).
- Observed methods involve seeing how people actually do something, and their biggest strength is their authenticity – all the behaviour is real.

The different aspects are why I always use more than one method – each from a different part of the diagram.

So finally...on to the methods.

Interviews

Interviews are one-on-one discussions with people, usually conducted in their normal environment. They may also involve watching people going about their normal tasks.

Interviews are a great way to gather rich, targeted information about the issues affecting your project – the context people work in, their tasks, their skills and their information needs. Interviews can also be very flexible, letting you explore issues and tangents as they are discussed. It's a good idea to conduct them in the person's normal location so you can combine the discussion with examples. They can quickly show you what they are describing to help you understand their needs.

Interviews don't always need to be face-to-face. You can often do them remotely with screen-sharing technology and a phone call.

If you would like to make interviews more practical, and less of an abstract discussion, include practical activities such as brainstorming, card sorting (see below) or other design games[7].

The main disadvantage of interviews is they can be time-consuming – to organise, run and analyse.

Focus groups

Focus groups are small group discussions with people, usually conducted somewhere outside a normal work environment such as a meeting room or research facility.

Focus groups are good for eliciting feelings and opinions about an issue, but not so good at getting practical details, unless you include activities designed to get more realistic information.

Focus groups need to be moderated carefully. It's very easy for people to follow paths raised by other participants and get involved in some group-think. It can be useful to have people do some 'homework' before the session – it helps them to think through some issues, and they're more likely to discuss and defend their ideas if they've thought about them up front.

One advantage of focus groups over interviews is that you can involve more people in a fixed amount of time.

Observation

Observation is all about watching people doing their normal tasks. It is particularly good when you can't talk to someone while they're doing something – for example, call centres, data processing centres or situations that move at a very fast pace.

Observation sessions are usually more immersive than interviews, and you may spend a lot more time learning about a situation. You can combine the observation time with an interview so you can ask about things you have observed.

[7] http://designgames.com.au

The advantage of observations is you get to see how things really happen, which can be quite different to how people say they happen. But some things you want to learn about may not occur during your observation time, and you may need to arrange another way to collect that type of information.

Diaries and journals

Diary studies are a way to get information about things people do, without having to be around to observe them. Figure out what you want to learn, and come up with a way of asking people to record that information. For example, if you are interested in learning what types of things people search for on an intranet, you could ask them to jot down what they were looking for and why every time they do a search. If you're interested in learning how people conduct research before making a big purchasing decision, you could ask them to make a note every time they collect information.

Diary studies can be good for getting big picture insights for a project, or for collecting detailed information you couldn't get during an interview.

The key to a successful diary study is making it easy for the participants, and also making sure they understand what you want to collect. Because there's so much potential information to collect, it can be hard to tell them what will be important before it happens.

Card sorting

Card sorting[8] is a practical way to get information about how people think about content and categories. You provide participants with index cards on which content ideas are written and ask them to group the cards in ways that make sense to them. When they finish, ask them to write a short description of each group of cards.

[8] For a detailed explanation of how to conduct a card sort, see this article: `http://www.boxesandarrows.com/view/card_sorting_a_definitive_guide` or my book Card Sorting: Designing usable categories (2009, Rosenfeld Media)

From this, you can learn about how people think about groupings within content, and what content goes well together. This will help you later on when you are designing the information architecture.

Surveys

A survey is a set of questions you ask people to complete. The questions can be quantitative (with closed questions that can be statistically analysed), qualitative (with open text-based questions) or a combination of both. You can use them to collect information about how people use something, what they may need in the future and other issues of interest.

Surveys are good for gathering a large number of responses with little effort. You can also use them to compare before and after by asking the same questions.

The disadvantage of surveys is the data you collect can lack richness, even if you ask for open-ended text responses. Surveys don't give you the opportunity to probe more deeply about a particularly interesting comment, or to ask the respondent to show you an example. You may learn what is of interest or problematic, but not always why it occurs.

I use surveys a lot for website user research. Again, I don't use them as my only source of information, but to support other methods. I usually ask the following open questions (using big text fields):

- Why did you visit the website today?/What do you usually visit the website for?
- What information do you use most often?
- What do you use that information for?
- Were you able to find what you were looking for?
- Does the website usually have the information you need?
- Is there any information, feature or improvement you would like to see?

The first three questions are the most useful – collecting, in the users' words, what information is used, why and how.

Existing data – *site statistics, search terms and internal knowledge*
You can learn a lot about people without talking to them. Here are some information sources you may already have access to – and they're free.

- **Website statistics** can give you data about the content people are already using, the most popular areas of the site, and the content people aren't using.
- **Search terms** (from an internal search facility and external search sites) can give you an insight into key information needs and how people describe their needs.
- **Customer emails, letters, forums, call centre logs** and **help-desk queries** can also give you useful information.

They can, however, contain bias. Customer emails, call centre logs and help-desk queries often over-represent new or inexperienced people. Website logs only show what happened, not why it happened.

On most of my projects, this is where I start user research – by looking around at everything we already know. It's a great way to get to know some of the main issues, and to think about what we may want to learn from other research activities.

Tips for collecting research

Here are some tips for collecting user research:

- Have a go at it. Even if you've never done it before, don't be scared. You don't have to run an academically-rigorous research program. You just want to learn some interesting stuff about your audience, and not make stupid design mistakes.
- If you do interviews, focus groups or observations, record them with an audio recorder (or video if you like). Later, create a lightly edited transcript of the session (one with the 'umms', 'ers' and personal comments removed). It is important to capture the interviewees' words as they say them – if you try to take notes, you'll change the terminology into your own or interpret what people have said as you write it.

- For other techniques, capture the data as close to its raw form as possible. For example, collect individual survey responses (not aggregated statistics), detailed search terms (not just the top 20) and full email messages (not just subject lines).

If you want to learn more about user research, including how to plan it in more detail, how to run sessions and much more, I recommend Mike Kuniavsky's book *Observing the user experience*. It's very thorough, and a great guide.

And if you can't do research...

Sometimes it's genuinely hard to do user research. You may have trouble getting to potential users, the cost-benefit may be very small, or you may already be part of the user community and don't need to do formal research.

Even if you don't do formalised user research, you can still keep users in mind when working through the design process. It's not enough just trying to keep user needs in your head as you work – they will slip and change as you go. Instead, take some time to write down what you already know about users, and the types of things they need to do. See the chapter on communicating user research for ways to describe users so you'll remember them.

	Interview	Focus group	Observation	Diaries/journals
What it is	One-on-one discussion with someone	Small group discussion / workshop (6-12 ppl)	Watching people work, not asking them about it	Ask people to record an aspect of whatever you are studying
Good for	Collecting realistic, rich information Exploring an issue Following tangents	Collecting opinions Getting larger numbers of people involved	Situations when you can't interrupt (call centres, critical situations) When you want to absorb a lot Real life	Learning context Seeing behaviours you may miss in interview/observation
Tips	Conduct in context Ask 'show me' Prepare a guide, not rigid questions Audio-record & transcribe	To get more practical input - Ask people to do some preparation - Use activities, not just discussion Audio-record & transcribe	Watch then discuss Some situations may not happen during the session – remember to discuss	Make it straightforward and low effort Provide clear instructions
Time	Can be time-consuming to arrange. Interview time per person	More time effective than interviews	Similar to interviews – time with participant may be longer	Need time for participants to respond

Card sort	Survey	Web analytics	Other people
People group content ideas in ways that make sense for them	Prepared set of questions	Usage information for an existing website	Other people already know about your users
Learning about groups and terminology	Collecting from a large number of people Quick response	Identifying popular content, terminology, entry points, usage trends	Getting an initial understanding of users based on internal knowledge
This is a good activity to run with other methods	Ask open questions (rather than closed) to get more useful information	Analyse regularly Do before other user research	Talk to staff from call centres and help desks
Needs time for preparation. Can be run online to reduce collection time.	Can take a while to prepare the survey. Responses come in quickly (if online)	As needed	As needed

Chapter summary

User research is an important input to an IA project and helps you learn:

- what people need
- what they do with information
- where they use information
- what they know about the topic and technology
- what terminology they use

Planning for user research involves figuring out:

- what you want to learn
- how much research to do
- who to research
- who (from your team) to involve

Common methods for collecting information are:

- interviews
- focus groups
- observation
- diaries and journals
- card sorting
- surveys
- using existing data

There are loads of resources around about conducting user research. Try some of the following.

Books

Kuniavsky, M (2003). *Observing the user experience: A practitioner's guide to user research*. Morgan Kauffman.

Young, I (2008). *Mental models: Aligning design strategy with human behaviour.*

Articles

See the list of articles at `http://delicious.com/practicalIA/user_research/`

7

Analysing user research

Okay, so you've taken my advice and collected some user research. I bet you spotted some interesting things along the way.

Congratulations!

The next step is to dive in and analyse what you've collected so you can identify the key issues and be confident about what you've learned.

Surprisingly, a lot of people forget this step and just run with top-of-mind observations. If you don't analyse your information it's really easy to just spot the things that were most important to you (such as something unexpected), or to see patterns that don't exist[1].

The main reason people forget to analyse the research is it can be very daunting. You can end up with a huge amount of detailed data and feel overwhelmed about tackling it. (The other reason is it's much more fun doing research and detailed design than analysing research).

But don't worry. This chapter will help you to make sense of all that data.

The purpose of analysis

If you watch crime shows, you've probably seen one where the investigator writes notes on the whiteboard, stands and stares at it until the pieces fall into place (often while talking aloud). When analysing user research, we're trying to do the same (though not quite as dramatically).

Like the hotshot investigator, we want to:

- identify consistent issues
- identify patterns of behaviour
- figure out which issues you are going to tackle
- keep track of insights and ideas

[1] Word of the day: This is called apophenia: `http://en.wikipedia.org/wiki/Apophenia`

Analysis steps

Any analysis process can be broken down into these parts[2]:

- Prepare: Get your data and materials ready.
- Deconstruct: Pull the data apart so you can look at it outside its original context.
- Manipulate: Once you have deconstructed your data, it's easier to identify patterns by playing around with it. As you manipulate it, you'll see patterns and issues more easily.
- Identify: Gain insights, start to generate ideas and check that the data supports your ideas.
- Summarise and communicate: Write down what you learned and tell other people.

Preparing for analysis

When you plan to collect user research, make sure you schedule in some analysis time. You may not need a lot, but having it in your schedule means you'll be less likely to forget.

Then get all your data in order. Depending on the method you use (we discuss a few methods below) you'll need to do different things to prepare the data.

If you're working with a team, it's a great idea to do the analysis process together. Involving key people during the process is easier and more effective than telling them what you learned. And the experience of talking through the analysis makes it much more real. This is especially important if the person designing the IA and page layouts was not involved in the user research. Being involved in analysis is much better than reading a report from someone else.

[2] Steve Baty, in the following article, outlines more detailed steps for the 'identify' part http://johnnyholland.org/2009/02/17/deconstructing-analysis-techniques/

Methods

Just as you should use more than one method for user research, it's good to use more than one method for analysis. They each offer a different way of learning about what you have. Here are five different methods you can use.

Exploring the data

One of the easiest analysis methods is to just immerse yourself in the data and explore it a little. This gives you a feel for the type of information you have and the very high-level patterns.

	A	B	C	D	E
1	**Source**	**Tag**	**Tag**	**Comment**	**Search frequency**
2	Interview1	schedule		I looked at the conference schedule a little bit	
3	Interview1	reporting back		I asked my team to find out sessions they want me to attend	
4	Interview1	social		done a lot of unrelated to the conference background prep	
5	Interview1	touristing	food	researching restaurants	
6	Interview1	money		I called my bank and let them know I'm travelling	
7	Interview1	schedule	printed	I downloaded the program and I probably will take it with me on the plane	
8	Interview1	sessions		will probably look at the conference schedule and do a rough plan	
9	Interview1	workshops	description	looked descriptions for the workshop	
10	Interview1	workshops	presenter	I also used my personal understanding of people to choose a workshop	
11	Interview1	blogging		I also got a username sorted out for the blog. I'll use that a bit	
12	Interview2	schedule		Haven't looked at the schedule yet	
13	Interview2	sessions	decide close to time	I think I will decide in the morning	
14	Interview2	sessions	slides help	to see the slides of the presentation, it helped me a lot	
15	Interview2	flights	company booked	My company booked the plane for me	
16	Interview2	accommodation		And I booked a hotel – not the conference hotel	
17	Interview2	touristing		I'm planning on staying two more days in city after the conference is finished	
18	Interview2	touristing	city important	so it is great that the IA Summit is in city It is a great opportunity for me to go to the conference and see the city.	
19	Interview2	workshops	description	I just read the description and the titles of each workshop	
20	Internal search	schedule		program	26
21	Internal search	costs		costs	21
22	Internal search	schedule		timetable	15
23	Internal search	accommodation		hotel	14
24	Internal search	blogging		technorati	12
25	Evaluation survey	structure	plenaries	The plenary speeches were very good ways to start and end the conference	
26	Evaluation survey	sessions	how to	The how to sessions were the most interesting	
27	Evaluation survey	sessions	visionary	I am an experienced ia so the 'future' / 'vision' sessions were interesting.	

Figure 7 – 1. Exploring the data with a spreadsheet

My favourite way of doing this is to drop everything into a spreadsheet with columns labelled *source, tag* and *comment*.

First I go through and record lots of stuff in the comments column. This is the start of deconstructing the data – identifying the individual pieces. Each row represents one thing from the research. Yes, I know 'thing' isn't a very helpful description, but this isn't a precise method. My 'things' are usually individual sentences from an interview transcript, search terms from internal search, comments made during a card sort, answers from a survey response. Each is an independent idea I may want to look at individually. You don't have to record every single sentence from every single interview – a lot of it will be irrelevant – but record anything you think could be useful for your project.

After I've recorded a pile of stuff into a spreadsheet, I start coding the data with simple tags (keywords). Tag each line with whatever comes to mind. Don't worry about creating a complete or consistent set of tags – you can go back later and revise them. I usually have to go through mine twice and fix up some tags in the earlier data to match how I've tagged data later in the spreadsheet. I usually need two columns of tags – one to record the topic of the line item, and the other to record something like how people use the data. Don't worry too much about my way though – let your data guide you.

Now, start exploring the data. Sort it by tags so similar ideas are grouped together. Look at each one for basic patterns and interesting issues. You'll be able to identify key information needs, the issues mentioned most frequently, how people described similar needs (they may have done it in different ways) and whether there was consistency between sources.

Term analysis

Term analysis is a technique used to learn about terminology and understand how people describe ideas.

Choose something you want to know about, and use your research notes to see how they describe it. Look for:

- words used to describe the concept
- synonyms (words with the same meaning)
- antonyms (words with the opposite meaning)
- related concepts
- broader and narrower terms
- concepts frequently mentioned together

You can use the outcomes from this simple analysis to understand how people describe their information needs. It is also very useful later on as a source of terms for navigation labels.

Affinity diagramming

Affinity diagramming is a great team analysis activity. To start, each person in the team goes through the research (transcripts, spreadsheets etc), identifies issues they find interesting and writes them on sticky notes. What is an interesting issue? Like my list of 'things' for the data exploration, it will come from the research.

Figure 7 – 2. An affinity diagram (thanks to Alastair Simpson for sharing it)

It may be something that surprised you, or something confirmed by the research. It may be a particularly insightful quote from a participant, or something you heard over and over again. And it will include lots of simple things that made you stop and think, 'Oh, that's interesting'.

When the team has a pile of sticky notes, start discussing the issues. As you discuss, start grouping the notes by similarity (or affinity) on a big wall or table. Shuffle the notes around, move them between groups, even make new groups, but keep discussing them. As you progress, talk about questions such as:

- What is important about this group of notes?
- Why does this happen?
- What is this group of notes about – what is the underlying idea?

The actual sticky notes and the resulting groupings aren't important, so don't feel you need to keep them (though I usually take a photo in case I need a reminder). The real value is the team discussion about the issues.

The trickiest part of affinity diagramming is determining what issues to include in the initial activity. Some things may only become interesting when there's a lot of them. After the first discussion, check the user research to see if there's anything you missed.

2x2 matrixes

Start as if you were doing an affinity diagram – by writing down interesting ideas on sticky notes (you may decide to colour-code them by participant or some other demographic as an extra level for this technique). Take a first pass through the sticky notes and identify two different dimensions to use – these will come out of the data, and could include things like:

- How often the participant uses the site
- How experienced the participant is with the product
- How familiar the participant is with the content
- How they looked for information – searching or browsing
- Type of task: Were they getting a quick fact or exploring in detail?
- Is the issue about a positive or negative experience?
- How much content would they need to answer their question?
- Any sort of demographic of the participant

Plot out the sticky notes according to where they fall on the scale for each dimension, and then discuss what you've found. When you've finished discussing it, find two more dimensions and start again.

As with affinity diagramming, the diagram isn't the point. It's the discussion and the ability to look at things in different ways that's important.

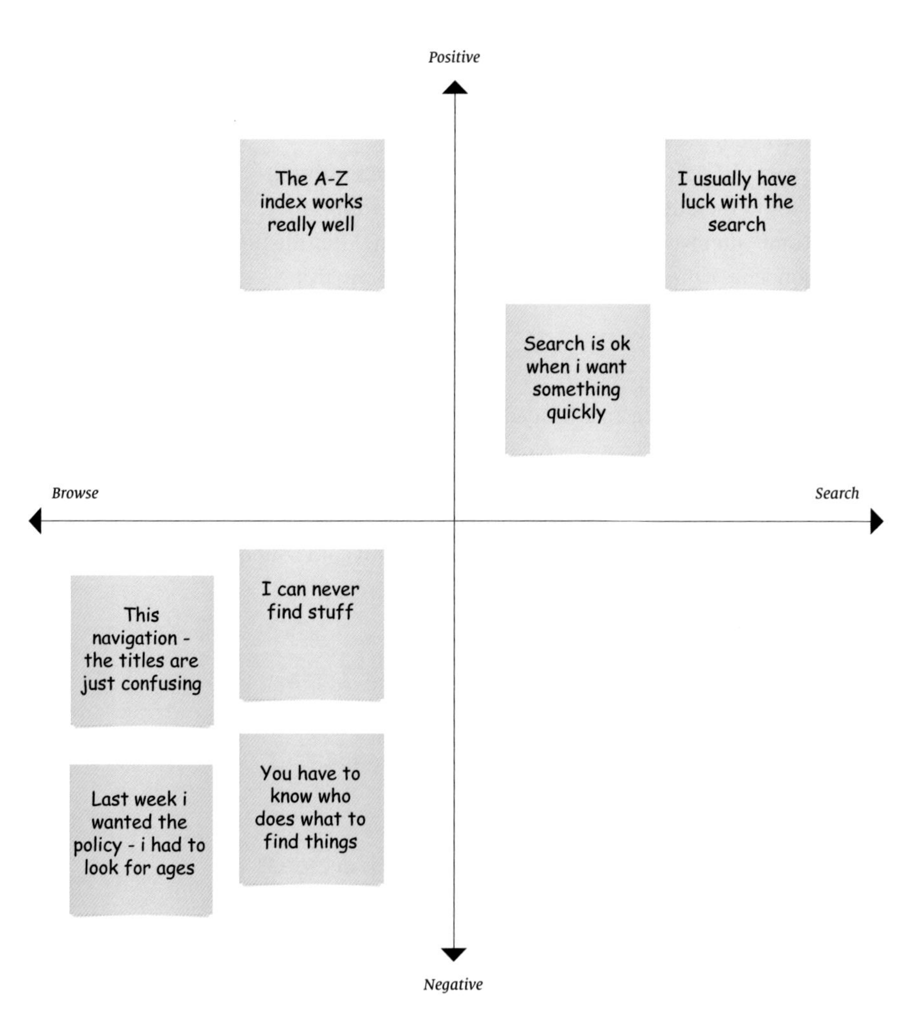

Figure 7 – 3. Plotting the research findings on a matrix

Multi-dimensional analysis

As with 2x2 matrixes, identify a set of dimensions to examine (the ones I mentioned earlier are a good starting point). But instead of plotting sticky notes on a 2x2, discuss each dimension with your team.

For example if you identify a range of familiarity with the topic, look at other aspects and see if there are differences across people. Do people unfamiliar with the domain use different terms to describe concepts or content? Do they need different types of content? What do very frequent users need (are they returning frequently to keep up-to-date?) compared to medium frequency users (who may be after the same content over and over) and infrequent users (who may just need a fast answer)? Think about how people's needs and experiences differ.

When you've examined all you can for one dimension, start over with another. The discussion about people's experiences and needs for each dimension may also suggest new dimensions to examine.

This may be less of a diagramming activity and more of a discussion. It can feel a bit directionless for a while, but as you discuss each idea, you'll gain a deeper understanding of what's going on.

Tips for analysis

Here are some tips for doing any sort of analysis:

- Don't settle on the first pattern you see. Re-arrange your data using one of the methods above and see if you can find something new.
- Allow time for the patterns to form. Don't just look at it in one sitting – sleep on it and review it the next day.
- These methods are designed for analysing qualitative information, so you won't get statistics from it. This process is all about understanding the most important issues for your users.
- As you go, keep a note of important issues that come up during the conversation. You may even assign someone to take notes of your discussion.
- For any conclusion, make sure it is actually supported by the data. It's easy to come up with something that isn't real.

Chapter summary

After collecting user research, make sure you spend time analysing it to identify the key issues you've learned.

After preparing your data, use some of these methods to learn what you learned:

- Exploring the data: to get a general idea of patterns and insights.
- Term analysis: to understand the terminology people use.
- Affinity diagram: a team approach to identifying patterns.
- 2x2 matrixes: another way of looking for patterns by identifying 2 dimensions to explore.
- Multi-dimensional analysis: exploring the data against more than two dimensions.

Further reading

For more information about analysing user research, see `http://delicious.com/practicalIA/user_research_analysis`

8

Communicating user research

You've done your user research, and analysed the data to identify the key things you discovered. The next step is making sure you document what you've learned, and communicate it with others.

I know documentation is a bit of a dirty word these days, with many web people recommending low-level documentation for projects. I'll talk about communication a few times in this book (for content, IA and navigation design). But out of the four things I suggest you document, user research is the most important (to me, at least).

I've worked on projects where the team ran big research projects, spent hours with people, and then never wrote up what they learned. I think this shows disrespect for the research participants. We should treat them as our most precious resource and do whatever we can to minimise the impact on them.

Two other problems with not recording user research outcomes are:

- The insights effectively live in the head of the person who did the research, and so they have to be the continual champion for the users.
- Next time a similar project is run the research will start over, covering much of the same ground.

One of the biggest benefits of recording research and sharing it around is more people get a good understanding of the audience and their needs. This will help in all sorts of situations:

- When developers have to make decisions about something in the interface (no matter how well you document the IA and navigation, decisions still need to be made) they are more likely to do it in a way that is good for people.
- Managers are less likely to say "My wife/husband/best friend really likes feature x, can we put that on the home page" as they'll have a better picture of the real people using their site.
- People in the organisation will become more focused on real needs and behaviour.

I also find that writing up the research results helps me verify that the findings from the analysis step are real. As I commit something to paper, I check the raw research findings to make sure the issue is real. It's easy to 'make up' findings if you don't have to write them down!

Documenting also helps explain why something has been done a certain way. For example, you can use the 'evidence' to show that when someone looks for particular information they use particular terms.

User research documentation doesn't have to be a big scary report that no-one reads. I'll show you some methods that can be easy to produce and easy to consume, which will help other people learn from them.

But before I jump into those, let's talk about what you want to get out of documentation.

Type of document

When deciding what to include in your documentation, and which method to use, you first need to think about your audience – who it's for. Of course you may need to write for more than one audience, which will mean using more than one approach. (This should be the case for every document you produce.)

For example:

- For future projects, you may want to produce a detailed report about all your findings. While no-one might want to read it now, it could be used when a similar research project starts in the future.
- Managers may just need an overview, and you may choose to do something simple and visual.
- If people in your organisation (or your client) have particular opinions about what users want, you may want to focus more on things that will highlight the accuracy or inaccuracy of these opinions.
- If your organisation is full of detail-focused people who like to read, provide detail. If it's full of people who are very person-focused, provide stories.

- If this is the first time user research has been presented, and people are sceptical, choose a more conservative type (a report) over a more touchy-feely type (personas, described below).

So be user-centred about your documentation. Find out what people are actually interested in from the user research and communicate that.

Communication methods

When choosing a method, consider what people will need from the information. But also let your research guide you – don't decide up front how you are going to communicate. And don't be tempted to use whatever approach seems to be popular at the moment (personas have been pretty trendy in the past few years). Use the method that works best for your readers and content. And feel free to ignore my suggestions and make your own up.

But now, over to the methods...

Simple research report

One of the simplest ways to document research is as a basic report. It's not sexy, and not many people will read it, but it's a great way to make sure you've recorded a lot of detail. Include background information like the following (which all provide credibility and context):

- How the research was conducted
- How participants were chosen
- What participants were asked to do or talk about
- How many people were involved

In the main findings section, include things like:

- Key insights (obviously)
- Things that were consistent across everyone
- Any differences you noticed between audience groups

I like to include a set of detailed quotes from research participants, sometimes as an appendix. It makes it feel very real.

Personas

Personas are representations of individual audience members. They provide a rich description of your audience, and are a great way to keep people in mind during a project and communicating with other team members. As personas represent real people, team members can easily empathise with them and over time will talk about them as they make decisions about design elements.

Personas focus on people's goals and describe their needs. In this way, they're quite different to market research demographics, which segment people according to demographic criteria. Personas segment people based on behaviours, goals and needs. For example, two people can be in quite different demographic groups but have the same underlying behaviours and goals.

Personas are also different to roles – they are not job descriptions or career roles. Just as with demographics, two people with the same role can have quite different goals. They may have to do the same tasks, but may approach them quite differently.
It's important to base personas on user research and not just make them up. (A lot of people make up personas instead of doing actual research.) Because they are so powerful – people can really empathise with them – people forget you don't actually know the users. You may not spot your mistakes because the team is so enamoured with a particular persona.

Example persona

Jennifer is a sales rep for an upmarket kitchenware manufacturer in Sydney. She spends her days driving to clients' retail stores to check their stock and place orders for them. The office gives Jennifer the schedule of customers to visit each day. As customers have different timetables for visits, the schedule is never the same. Her first job of the day, and the most frustrating, is sorting out the most efficient way to get to the clients. She is familiar with the customer's locations as she visits them frequently, but not as familiar with the best route between them. Sitting in traffic all day is not Jennifer's idea of fun. She hates being late to a scheduled customer, and hates having to rush and arrive flustered.

A friend told her about a in-car navigation computers. She said that some let you put in all your locations and get a map of the best way to get there, then talk you through the directions. They can also get around traffic jams. Jennifer is not sure about getting one – it is already hard enough to drive around Sydney without a computer babbling at you. She also worries that she won't be able to use it. She can't even set the clock on the video! How will she set all the locations and know that she's done everything right?

Figure 8 – 1. An example persona from an in-car navigation system project

When analysing your research data, focus on identifying key goals that people have. The original persona methodology[1] focused on three types of goal:

- Life goals: personal aspirations of the person, usually beyond the product being designed
- Experience goals: how the person wants to feel while using the product

[1] Described in Alan Cooper's book *About Face 2.0: The essentials of interaction design* (2003, Wiley). There have been more approaches developed since then

- End goals: actual outcomes from using the product
- For most systems, end goals provide the most input, experience goals are important and life goals provide a broader context to remember.

When analysing user research, try to identify different goals. Think about why people behave in a particular way, and what they ultimately want to achieve. Goals include end results of things people want to do, their underlying reason for undertaking a task, and their feelings and concerns about something. Whenever you hear someone say "I want to" you are hearing a goal. Often asking why a user wants to perform a particular task can reveal the broader goal behind it.

Identify the different goals and start grouping them according to similarity. This is the trickiest part – figuring out what goals are 'similar' and whether to put them together or keep them separate. Combine research participants into individual personas based on similar goals and behaviours, not on demographic characteristics. Try to identify a small set of personas that represent different groups of people. For most systems you won't need a large set of personas – people may differ in the information they need or tasks they perform, but overall goals usually aren't so diverse.

When you're ready, write a description that incorporates the goals. You can write a narrative description like the one above, or a set of bullet points. Some organisations don't like narratives – they can be too touchy-feely – but are okay with a list of key features. Add only enough personal information to fill out the persona – don't let them get in the way of the underlying message. Add experience and life goals relevant to the site you're working with so people understand why you've included them.

Photographs can also be useful, but use stock photography rather than photos of actual research participants. A persona is a representative user, not a real person.

Personas are only part of the documentation picture – they describe the users' goals, but don't give you enough information to do detailed interaction and interface design. For that, you need scenarios.

Scenarios

Scenarios are short stories that describe someone using a product.

They don't describe the nitty-gritty detail (e.g. the person clicks the 'submit' button), but instead describe the important steps, actions and decision points. They're written before interfaces are designed, so they're independent of an interface.
Scenarios often describe the system being used as a day-in-the-life so important context is clear. They will usually focus on:

- Where will the product be used: Will it be on a fast computer in the office? A handheld device on the street? A child's shared computer?
- Frequency and length of use: Is the task one short, infrequent process (e.g. taking a screen shot of a website and copying into a document)? Many short processes (e.g. reading and answering individual emails)? A long process (e.g. quality checking an insurance claim form)? An ongoing process (e.g. creating an artwork using a software tool)?
- What else is the person doing: Are they checking the status while working on something else, or focused with everything else turned off? Are there a lot of interruptions? Do they have to get up and do something in the middle of the process (system timeouts are terrible in these situations)?
- What other products are being used: Does the person need to copy information between products? Do they need to read a document while filling out a form?
- What are the main activities that need to be done?
- What is the expected end result of the task?

Example scenario

Jennifer gets the list of client calls by email at home before she leaves. She enters the addresses of all the places she has to visit today. She notes that one of them must be done at 11am and one at 2.30pm and asks for her route to be shown.

She looks at the sequence the computer has calculated. It looks good, but there is one client she would like to see in the morning instead of the afternoon. She moves this, recalculates her route and gets going.

For the first client, she doesn't need directions. She turns it on after the first client and hears the directions as she drives. It is quite clear but she occasionally looks at the screen when there is too much noise.

The system shows her the distances she needs to travel, so she can plan when to get petrol. She has time after her 2.30 client, so shows the nearest petrol station and heads there, then shows the nearest ATM to grab some cash (the route recalculates for her).

This system is turning out to be much more useful than she thought. It is saving her time and petrol and making her day much less frazzled.

I'm often asked what the difference is between scenarios and requirements. In my experience, requirements describe what must be built and are great for software development processes where it's important to trace everything back to requirements.

Scenarios can help describe the requirements in a way business stakeholders understand. They're great for making requirements come to life and understanding the full consequences of decisions. Building scenarios with your team can really help prioritise requirements for the project.

Research quotes

A simple way to communicate user research is to assemble actual quotes from the research into a document, presentation or poster. Use the actual words from participants, without editing. Group them according to similarity. And make sure they're balanced – include positive comments, criticisms and requests for features and information needs.

Experience map

An experience map is a visual representation of one customer's (or aggregated customers') experience/s with a product.

These diagrams don't have any particular guidelines, but most that I've seen and used have the following characteristic:

- Time: One of the main focuses of the diagram is how a customer interacts over time.
- Touchpoints: This diagram often shows how a customer interacts with different parts of a business (website, sales, customer service etc) and how they connect.
- End-to-end: It usually shows and end-to-end experience.

An experience map can be done as a before and after. Use one to show how people currently experience your product, service or website (based on your user research) and another to show how they may do it in an ideal future.

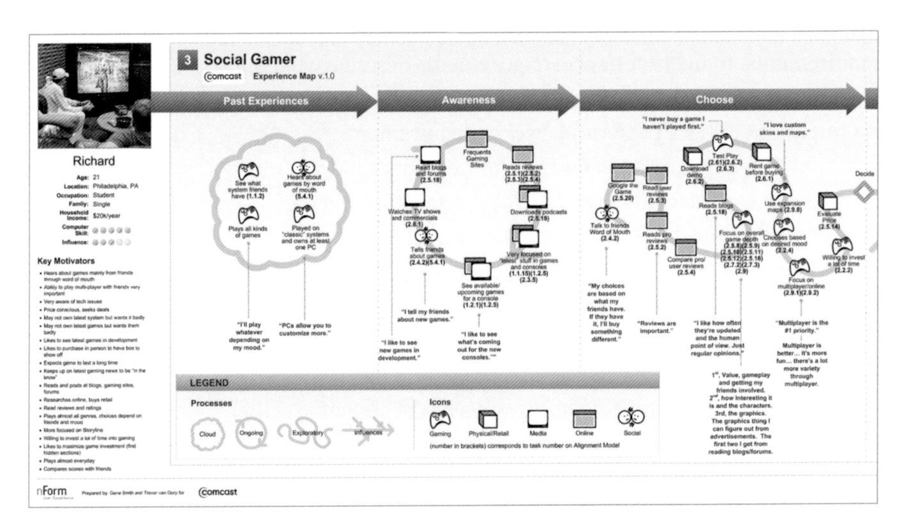

Figure 8 – 2. Part of an experience map (thanks to Gene Smith from nForm). Read more about this example at (`http://nform.ca/blog/2010/02/experience-maps-cross-channel-experiences-deliverable-for-gamers`)

Other diagrams

- The top half shows people's needs, grouped according roughly to topic (the colour-coding shows where information came from)
- The bottom half shows content for each topic.

This diagram quickly shows what people were interested in and what was available for each topic. In some cases there were user needs but no content, and content without any clear user need (not shown in my diagram). This was a very useful diagram for discussing the outcomes of user research with individual content providers, as they could quickly see how their work connected with the needs of real people.

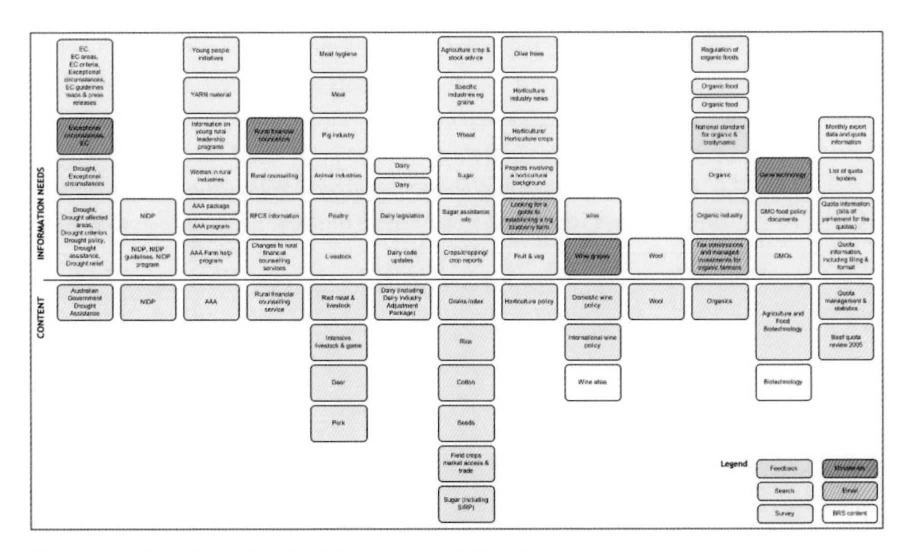

Figure 8 – 3. Information needs and existing content, plotted together

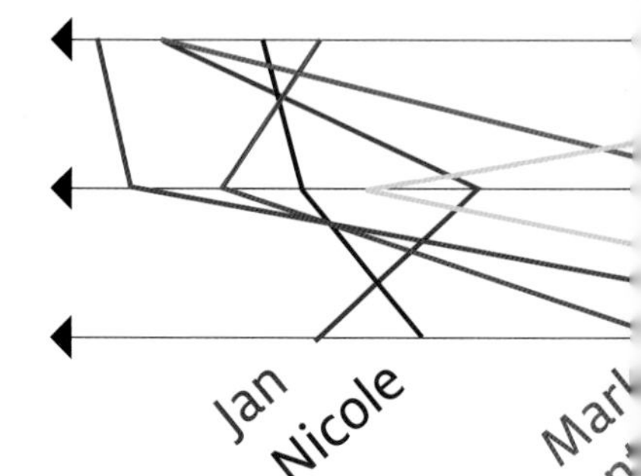

Figure 8 – 4. Diagram showing how people engage with TV

Another diagram I created aligns with the 'multi-dimensions' analysis method I mentioned in the last chapter. Here I identified a number of dimensions from the data and then plotted each user, showing where they fell for each of the dimensions. This quickly showed there were two different sets of behaviours. I've used this type of diagram a few times to show how individual research participants are similar in some respects and different in others. So keep an open mind about how to best represent what you learned. I'm always interested in new ways of showing things, so please share yours with me.

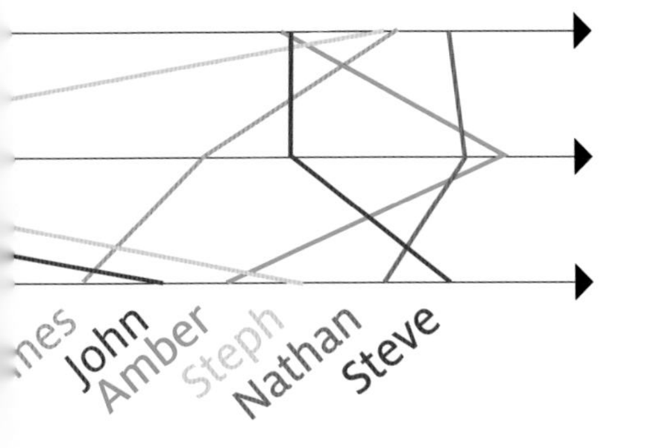

Social/watch with someone

Planned/know what's on

Watching/immersed

Chapter summary

The next step in user research is to communicate it to other people. This ensures everyone is thinking about the people you're designing for.

Commonly used communication methods include:

- a user research report
- personas
- scenarios
- quotes from research participants
- experience maps
- other diagrams you may invent

Further reading

For more information about communicating user research, see `http://delicious.com/practicalIA/communicating_user_research`

9

How people look for information

This chapter is a bit different to the first three chapters in this part. It's not a 'how to' chapter, but rather about how people go about looking for information, and what you need to consider when designing for different behaviours. (Think of it as background information about your users.)

You may have heard the myth about how people either search or browse, but never both. That is, some people will always search while others will always browse. I don't know where this myth came from, but plenty of people have told me about it. And if you've ever been in a meeting where someone said "Why do we need to bother with all this information architecture stuff? Let's just put a search engine in", then chances are they've also heard the myth – and believe it.

You can tell where I'm heading with this. It's simply not true. There isn't a soul out there who will only search or only browse. Oh, people definitely have preferences. If they've always had good luck with search on their intranet, they're more likely to try that. On the other hand, if they've had terrible luck searching for information, they're more likely to browse. And the more people use Google and have good search experiences, the more they expect from it.

The decision to search or browse has much more to do with the information task people are trying to perform.

In this chapter I introduce you to different types of information behaviours, outline their core features, provide tips for designing for these behaviours, and show some examples.

Finding known items

One of the most common things people use the internet for is to find known items. When you have a known-item task, you:

- know what you want
- have words to describe it
- may have a fairly good idea where to start
- know that there is an answer
- know when you see the answer

Depending on exactly what you are doing with the information, you may be happy with the first answer you find and may not care where the answer comes from. It's also unlikely that the task will evolve while you're finding the answer.

Examples of this type of behaviour include:

- finding out what 'apophenia' means
- checking the title of the new Stephen King novel
- getting a copy of the travel form
- checking the price of a product (a single product in a single store – more than that and it becomes a compare task)
- seeing what films Cate Blanchett has been in
- finding out what galangal is

This is a very common behaviour on the internet. I haven't actually counted, but I must do this at least a dozen times a day – jump into a website to find out something, get the answer, and then leave.

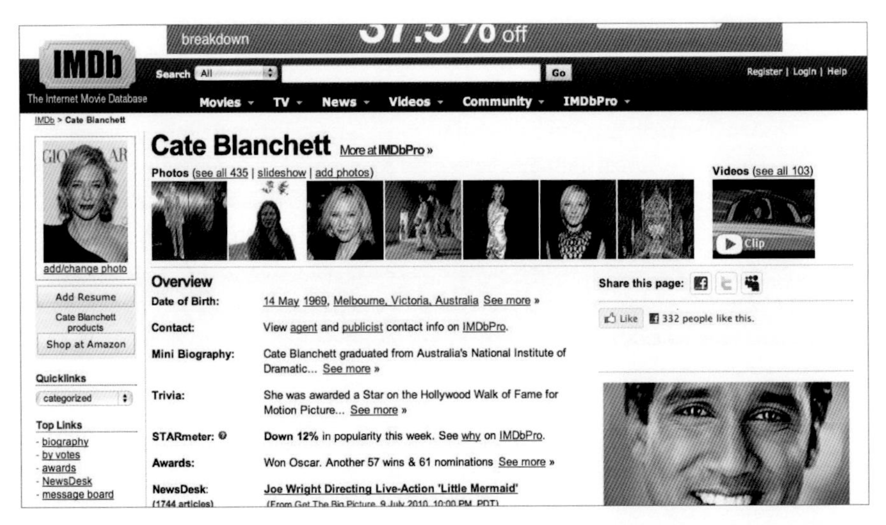

Figure 9 – 1. Finding out what films Cate Blanchett has been in is simple - type her name into IMDB (`http://imdb.com`)

The best design solutions for this behaviour are **search** and **A-Z indexes**. Both can give you an answer very quickly, either by typing your key term into the search box or by scanning a list for it. People will occasionally browse for this type of information, but only if they feel the answer isn't far away.

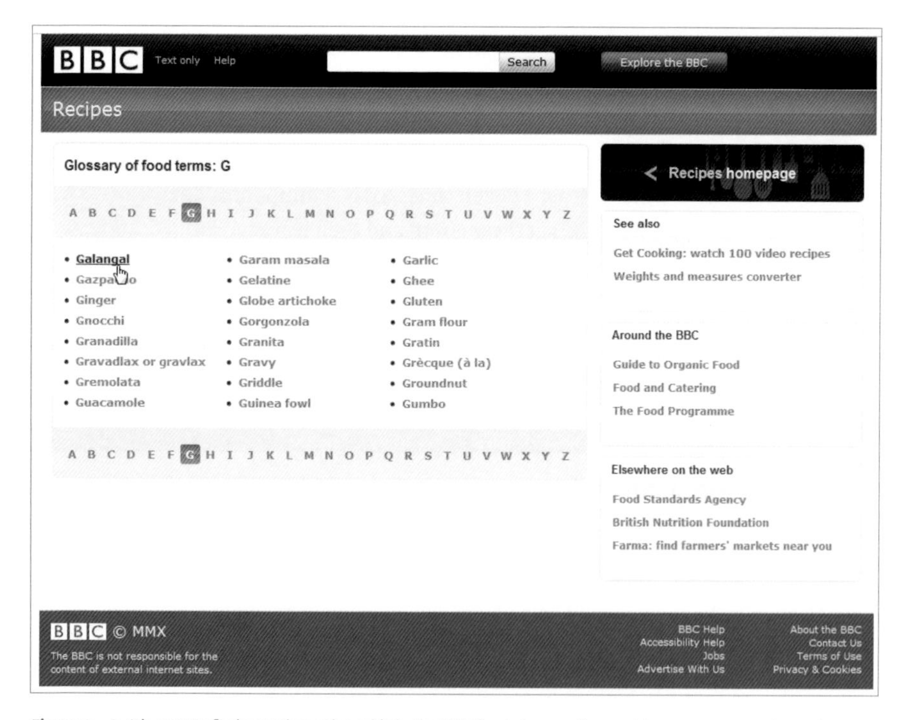

Figure 9 – 2. It's easy to find out what galangal is in the BBC food glossary (`http://www.bbc.co.uk/food/glossary/`)

Exploring

Exploring is the complete opposite to finding known items. When exploring, you:

- have some idea of what you need to know
- may or may not know how to articulate it
- may not yet know the best terminology to use
- may not know where to start looking

These 'explorations' don't necessarily end. You may find enough information to get you started, and then discover more later on. In this mode, the information need will almost certainly change as you discover information and learn, and the gap between your current knowledge and your target knowledge narrows.

As an example, a few years ago I was looking for information on the cognitive mechanisms that allow people to navigate the physical world (I was comparing the concept of online and physical navigation). I knew what I wanted, but couldn't describe it ('navigation' in a search engine gave me results for web navigation), and had no idea where to start. I tried a number of places, but didn't succeed at all. Six months later I stumbled across some 'wayfinding' papers, and realised it was the term I needed.

Other examples of exploratory tasks include:

- learning how people use card sorting in their work practices
- finding examples of sites with complex forms laid out using CSS
- locating music I like (which for me never ends!)

Because this task is so broad, I don't have particular recommendations for design solutions. Needless to say search rarely helps with this one – in a lot of cases you don't have the terminology to put into a search box. Links between relevant content pages will help people move between things, and build up knowledge.

If you're in a situation where someone is pushing for better search, look at your user research and see what types of tasks people are doing. If a lot of people are exploring, particularly if they're trying to learn something new, find some good examples to show why search may not be the ideal solution.

Refining and narrowing

Refining and narrowing happens whenever you have a large number of items to choose from, and you want to narrow down to just those of interest.

In this situation, you will usually have some criteria in mind when you start, and you should be able to recognise products that meet that criteria. In some cases, you may do some exploring at the start to learn about what's important and to set your criteria, then find a set of products and narrow down.

This behaviour will sometimes be followed by a comparison task, which we discuss below.

Examples include:

- You have thought about what is important for your next car, but are not sure which brand and model you want.
- You have ingredients for dinner, but no recipe yet.
- You want to buy a birthday gift for your 5 year old nephew, and know that he likes trucks.

The most appropriate design solutions are **filters** and **faceted browse.**

A filter lets you select a number of criteria, and displays results for those criteria. Good filters let you to play around with the criteria and update results as you do so. Poor filters make you set all your criteria up front and submit them to display results. (It's poor because you can easily get a zero result, but have no idea which criteria caused the zero result).

Faceted browse let you refine a set of results one click/criteria at a time. The best faceted browse systems let you determine which criteria you start with and which sequence you use. You never get a zero result as facets aren't displayed where they're not valid. (I discuss faceted browse more in the section about navigation.)

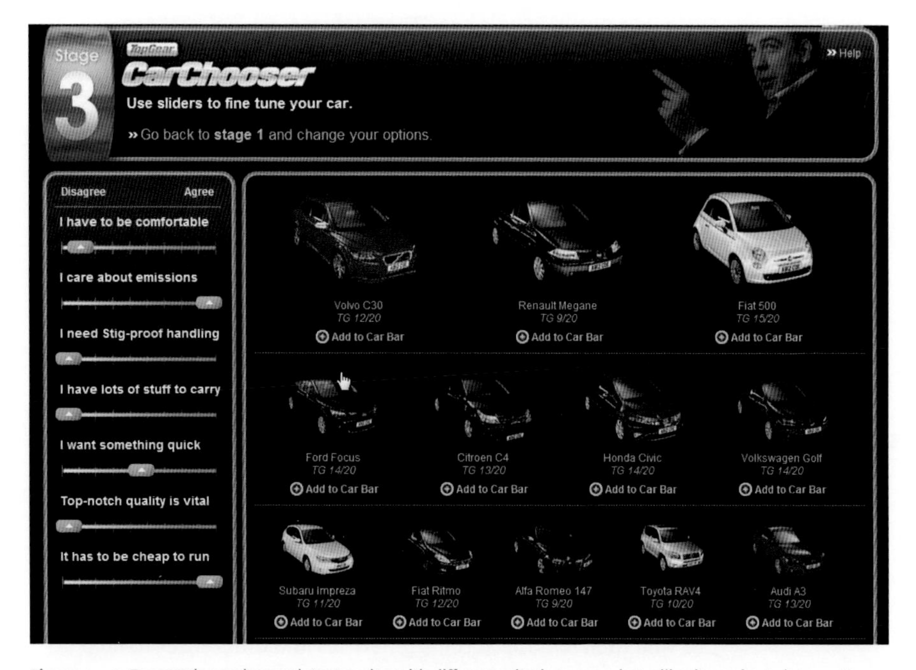

Figure 9 – 3. Top gear's car chooser lets you play with different criteria to see what will suit you best (`http://www.topgear.com/au/car-chooser-launch`)

Figure 9 – 4. Wine.com lets you filter into the content one criteria at a time (`http://wine.com/`)

Comparing

Comparing is all about finding 2 or more things you're interested in, and then looking at the similarities and differences to help you make a decision. As I mentioned earlier, you will usually compare after you've narrowed down to a set of things you're interested in. But if there are only a small number of products (for example, three different software versions), you may compare without narrowing.

Examples of when you would want to compare items include many shopping situations, when there are slightly different versions of a product, features for a new school or university – the list is endless.

If you are going to design an interface that lets your users compare, you'll need a few things to do it well:

- a very good understanding of what criteria and features are important to people
- a very good understanding of how people make final decisions (this may not be the same as their initial criteria)
- content with enough structure to display things side-by-side
- a great filter, to let people narrow (if appropriate for your content)

Comparison interfaces are hard work. I can't stress enough the importance of knowing what's important to your audience to do this well. This is one place where user research, iterative design and usability testing are critical to the success of the site.

When you have this right, you'll then need to figure out how to display the results so people can easily spot the similarities and differences and make a decision between items. This is where people decide – to buy, or to leave.

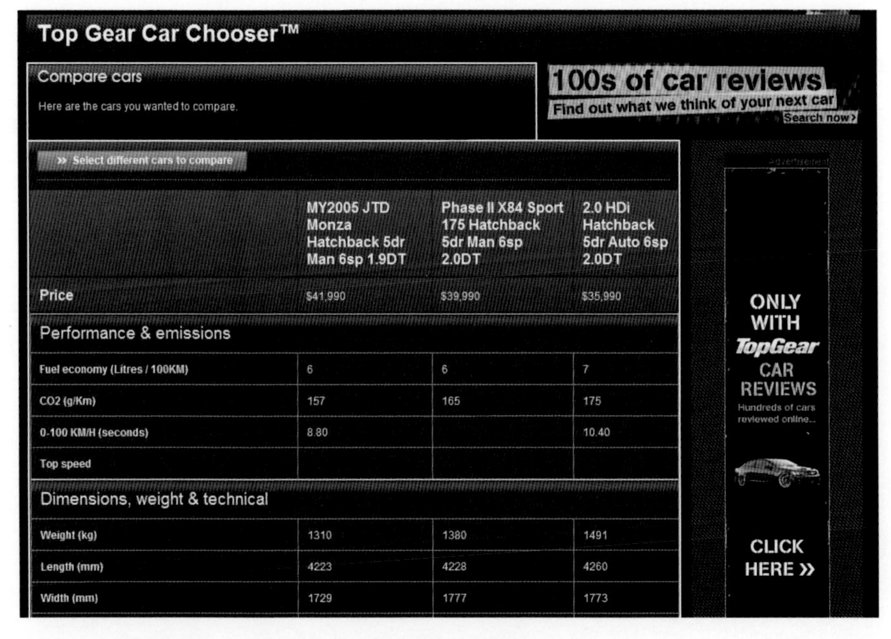

Figure 9 – 5. After filtering, you can compare car features side by side (`http://www.topgear.com/au/car-chooser-launch`)

Getting a broad idea

This is quite different to some of the other tasks I've mentioned. Sometimes you'll learn that your users just need some basic information about a topic. (This could match a known-item or exploratory task – they aren't mutually exclusive.)

I mention this one because I've seen it go wrong on many websites with detailed content, particularly Government sites. A lot of websites I've worked with in the past few years contain fantastic, detailed content. But they forget to provide high-level overviews. People get very frustrated when they want just the main ideas, a summary or the big picture, but have to dig around in detailed content first.

The solution is simple: make sure you provide summaries of detailed content. Depending on what you're presenting, they could be bullet points, diagrams or even videos that communicate the main ideas easily.

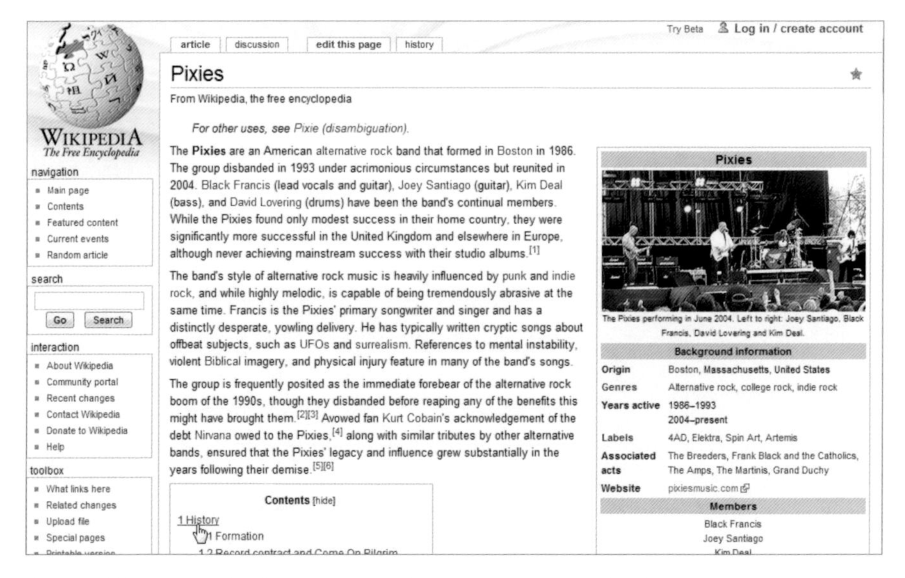

Figure 9 – 6. Many wikipedia articles provide a good summary before diving into detail (`http://en.wikipedia.org/wiki/Pixies`)

Diving into detail

While some people want just a broad overview, other people want detail – and lots of it. This is another situation where your user research will be particularly helpful. In situations where people need a lot of detail, you'll need to know just how much 'a lot' really is. You may not be providing enough information, causing people to go elsewhere. Or you may be still providing far more than people need.

A good design solution that balances both these needs is to create layers of information. Start with some good overview information, and let people who need to dive into the next layer for more detail. If it's still not enough, provide another layer with even more detail. The layering stops it overwhelming the people who don't need as much detail.

Discovering unknown things

Have you ever gone to a website for one thing and found yourself spending ages looking at other things on the site? If so, chances are the site does a great job of helping you discover things you didn't know existed, but were interested in.

This behaviour isn't one you undertake deliberately. I doubt many people[1] go to the web just to 'surf' or look around for things that might be interesting. Or I could be wrong.

Two reasons this will come up when you're designing:

- Your business goals involve encouraging people to stick around – to sell them product they are interested in but didn't know about, or maybe to expose them to more advertising.
- You learn through user research that people visit your site with one thing in mind, but actually need something else.

[1] with the exception of my 11-year-old daughter on YouTube

To design well for this behaviour, you'll need to understand your users. But more importantly, you'll need to understand the relationships between your content items, so you can show people 'related' things. And you have to provide links to them – it is all about capturing their attention and making it easy for them to explore. If you can get this right, people really will stick around and look for more. But if they can't get around easily (with good links), they'll go elsewhere.

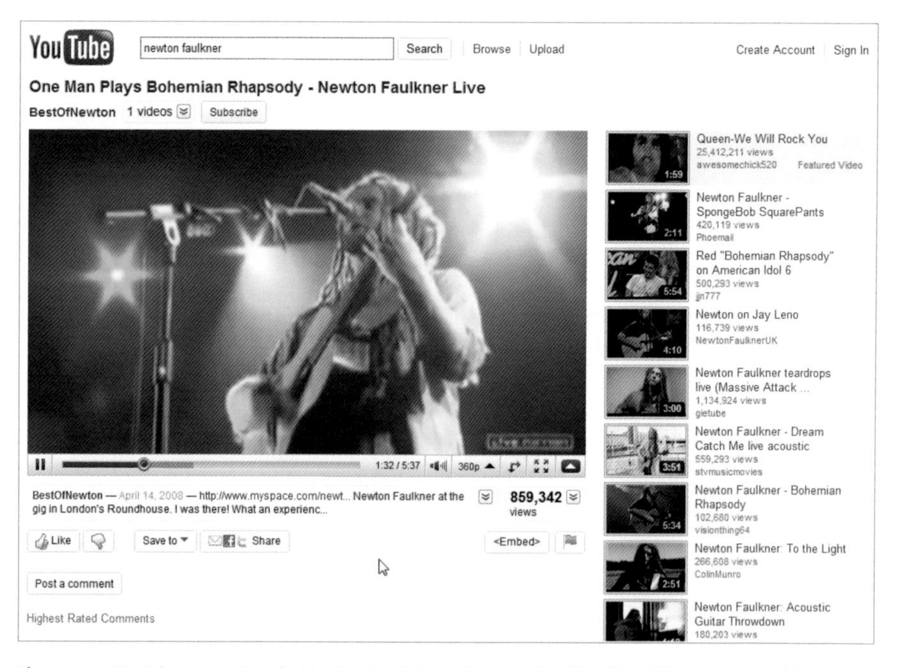

Figure 9 – 7. YouTube appears to calculate its related videos based on the title of the video you are watching - simple but effective (`http://www.youtube.com/watch?v=n_k8_HSA1-o`)

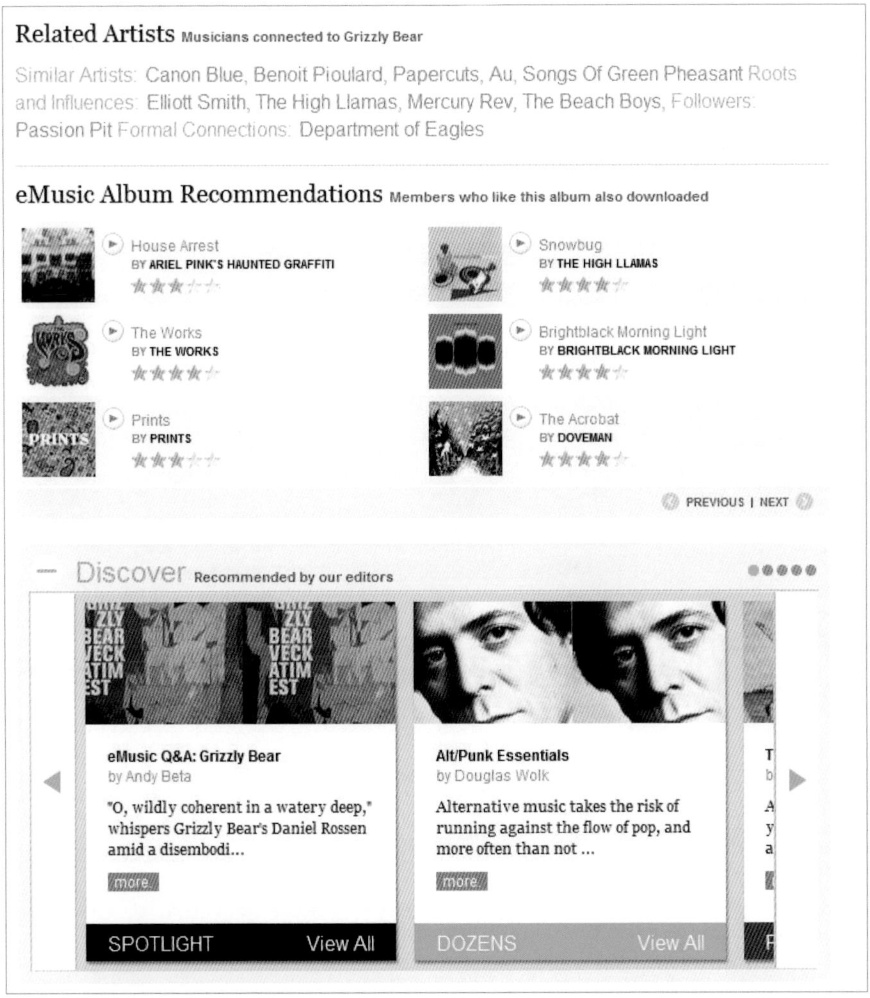

Figure 9 – 8. emusic provides suggestions based on connected musicians, member downloads and editorial recommendations (`http://emusic.com/`)

Keeping up to date

People often want to keep up to date with what's happening within an industry or topic, but aren't looking for a specific answer.

Figure 9 – 9. Google anaytics lets me keep on touch with my website activity (`http://google.com/analytics/`)

Re-finding

This mode is relatively straightforward – looking for things they've already seen. They may remember exactly where it is, remember what site it was on, or have little idea about where it was.

Four common ways to implement re-finding are:

- services explicitly for re-finding (e.g. bookmark managers like delicious.com)
- when you are signed in, you can save items (e.g. to a wishlist)
- when you are signed in the site pays attention to what you look at without you needing to save
- items are saved without you signing in

These are all good for different situations. Again, you'll use the user research to find out what people most likely need to do, and design features to let them do it.

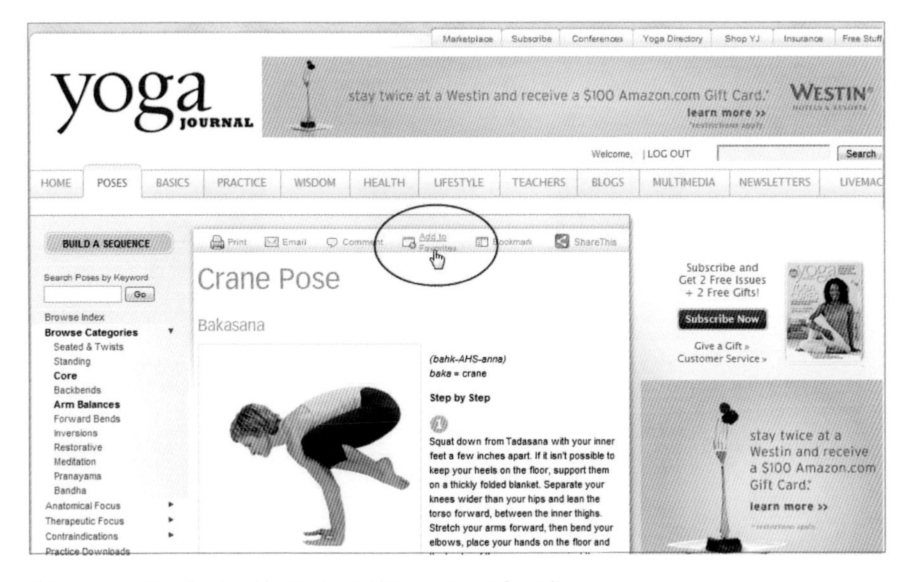

Figure 9 – 10. When I'm signed in Yoga Journal lets me save my favourite poses (`http://www.yogajournal.com/poses/468`)

Recently Viewed

Browse
Albums - Alternative/Punk - Indie Rock

In The Reins
by Iron And Wine / Calexico

Alligator
by The National

Veckatimest
by Grizzly Bear

Figure 9 – 11. emusic keep track of what albums I've looked at (`http://emusic.com`)

More Items to Consider

You viewed — Customers who viewed this also viewed

The Girl Who Kicked the Hornets' Nest Kindle Edition by Stieg Larsson **$11.99**

The Girl with the Dragon Tattoo Kindle Edition by Stieg Larsson **$7.50**

The Girl Who Played with Fire Kindle Edition by Stieg Larsson **$11.99**

› View or edit your browsing history

Related to Items You've Viewed

You viewed — Customers who viewed this also viewed

Hetty Feather Kindle Edition by Jacqueline Wilson **$11.99**

Lacuna, The Kindle Edition by Barbara Kingsolver **$11.00**

Elegy for Easterly, An Kindle Edition by Petina Gappah **$10.70**

› View or edit your browsing history

Figure 9 – 12. Amazon keeps track of what I've looked at even when not signed in (`http://amazon.com/`)

Chapter summary

People don't have an in-built preference to 'search' or to 'browse'. Instead, the behaviours they use to find information depend on the type of task they're doing at the time.

Some common information-seeking behaviours include:

- known item
- exploratory
- refining and narrowing
- comparing
- getting a broad idea
- diving into detail
- discovering unknown things
- keeping up to date
- re-finding

Further reading

For more information about information-seeking behaviours, see `http://delicious.com/practicalIA/information-behaviour`

10

How people think about categories

This chapter is a little like the last one. Instead of a how-to chapter it has more background information - this time on how people think about categories. For IA work, this is very important, as a large part of what you'll be doing is grouping content into categories.

So what exactly is a category? A category is an idea or a concept that represents a collection of things. You see categories everywhere. We even think in categories. We don't think about individual, discrete objects, but rather groups of objects and abstract ideas. And because we think in categories, our language is built around them.

In this chapter I'll describe some of the key features about how categories work in our brain, how we think about them and why they are important to us.

Oh, and if you think categories sound a lot like the groups we've been talking about up until now, you're right. So don't worry about the new name. You already know what they are.
So now for an example.

A category: Sports

I sent out a tweet asking followers to send me the names of 5 sports (that's all – it wasn't a trick question). This is what came back:

Figure 10 – 1. A word cloud of sports

This simple example illustrates some important characteristics of categories, which I've outlined below.

All about categories

The most important thing to know about categories is they don't exist independently in the world. They exist in the human brain. They're formed over time, based on our experiences with the world. And because we all think differently, we all have different ideas about categories.

There are consistent patterns. And individual communities, cultures and workplaces will even use categories that are similar. But no categories (or at least very few) will ever be universally understood.

There is no 'right' answer

One of the things people ask me most about categories is how to figure out what set of categories are 'right' for their content.

This holy grail of categorisation doesn't exist. There is no right way to categorise a particular set of information. In most situations there's more than one way to categorise a given set of information, and the 'right' answer will depend on things such as:

- what people already know about the information
- what they will be using information for
- how they think

So why do people ask me about the 'right' set of categories? Because someone told them there's no need to do user research for a project and understood how people think, so they should just organise the content the 'right' way. And often this 'right' way is the Department structure or a similarly technical aspect of the content.

Category boundaries are fuzzy

In workshops, I often ask people to brainstorm and write down five 'games'. Every time I've done this, someone has included sports in their list (which, by the way, is fine). In the workshop situation, there's usually some discussion about whether sports are actually games or a different thing altogether.

Category boundaries are fuzzy. They aren't clear, well-defined and universally understood. They're messy, and the edges blur and overlap with other categories.

Categories overlap

The games and sports example illustrates another aspect of categories – their boundaries overlap. If I asked people to give me the names of five sports and five games, there would be some that end up in both categories, and quite validly too.

You'll definitely find this in IA work. When you create a set of categories and assign your content to it, some content will definitely fit in more than one place (though if it happens a lot, it may be a sign you need to think more about your approach).

Family resemblance

A category can be filled with items that don't share a single set of attributes (in the category literature this is called 'family resemblance'). For example, if you look at the sports diagram, there's no characteristic that fits them all. Soccer, cricket and basketball are all team sports and competitive; rock climbing and yoga are individual sports and non-competitive

Contents change over time

Category boundaries aren't fixed – they can change over time. For example, as new types of sports emerge they will become part of the 'sports' category.

Dependent on context
I asked the sport question just before Christmas in the middle of the afternoon Australian time, late evening US time and before most of Europe woke up. Can you imagine how different this would be if I asked it in the middle of the Olympic Games? It doesn't change what a sport is, but certainly changes what people are thinking about.

Some things belong better than others
Another attribute is that some objects fit in a category better than others – that is, there are central and non-central members. For example, cricket, soccer and baseball were mentioned more than anything else – certainly more than yoga and beer pong. These things are a better fit for the 'sports' category.

You'll find a lot of these when you create categories for your web content. Some things will be easy to place in the category and people will expect to find them there. Other things will never quite fit, no matter how hard you try.

Some categories are hard to define, but still real in our brains
Most sets of content will have a set of items that are *miscellaneous, other, general*. This is a real category in our brains. We think of all the things that fit into various categories, and will usually have things left over.

We should expect this to happen. Again, because categorisation occurs in our brains, boundaries change over time, and some things fit better than others. We should expect a pile of things that don't fit.

Our problem isn't usually the category of miscellaneous stuff, but what to do with it in IA work where our job is to help people find information. Usually I end up putting these types of things in a category where they best fit (even if that fit is poor) or create a single-item category (which is fine). But I keep an eye out over time as more content is created, and modify the categories as needed.

More than one level – subcategories
In all my descriptions above, I've talked about categories as if they are a single level. But they're not. Categories contain sub-categories and sub-categories contain sub-categories and categories can be grouped into broader categories until they make a whole hierarchy of categories. We'll talk about hierarchies and their different types briefly below, then in much more detail in chapter 16 (IA patterns).

Basic level categories

If I asked what you were sitting on right now, I expect you would more likely say *chair* than *furniture* or *office chair*. If you were researching how to make your house more energy efficient you may tell me you were interested in finding out about *saving water* rather than *sustainability* or *under-floor rainwater tanks*.

These examples represent an important concept in language and category theory – where we think and talk.

I mentioned above that all categories can be broken down into subcategories and aggregated into broader categories.

Even though this does happen, we tend to think and talk at a particular place in the category hierarchy. In categorisation literature this is known as the **basic level category**.

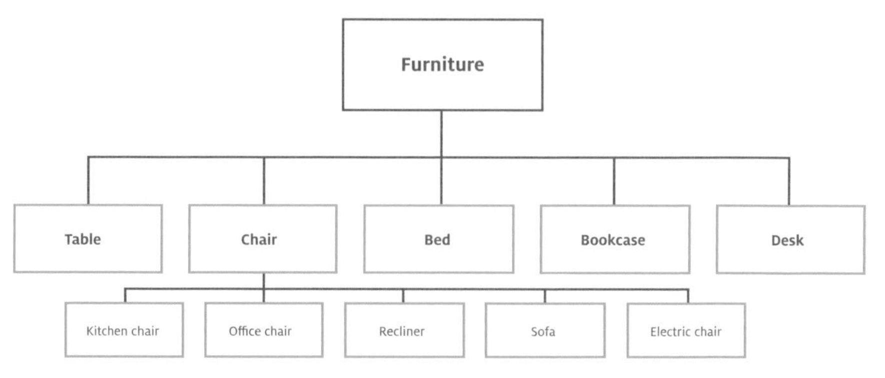

Figure 10 – 2. A simple hierarchy for furniture

There's a lot to this, and lots of interesting research if you're into categories as much as I am[1]. But given you're probably not, here are the two main implications of it.

We think about 'topics'

When we're researching and looking for information, we mainly think about the topic we're interested in. For example, I might be researching how to save water, reduce waste or reduce my energy use. These are all topics. I don't think "I'm looking for information" or "I'm shopping" or "I'm a water-wise gardener". I think "I want to know more about rainwater tanks".

This has important consequences for the type of classification scheme you choose for your content. We'll discuss this more in chapter 15, but it's almost always better to arrange content around topics than around tasks or audiences, given this is where people think.

People think at different levels depending on their experience

I mentioned before that categories don't exist independently in the world, but are formed in our brains. One important thing, which relates to the idea of basic-level categories, is that people think at different levels of a hierarchy depending on their experience and knowledge about the topic. You can imagine talking to the salesman when looking for a new bed – you'll be talking about a 'bed' (the category you use) but he'll know and think about the different types of bed.

This happens a lot when I talk to subject matter experts. They think at a more precise, more detailed level. Sometimes the people who will use their information will be thinking at a much broader level. Your IA job is to bridge the gap between the two – not always an easy task. But armed with a better understanding of why it happens, you'll be better prepared for it.

[1] The main work in this area is George Lakoff's *Women, Fire and Dangerous Things: What Categories Reveal About the Mind* (1987, Chigaco Press). It's a hard read!

Chapter summary

Categories are such a key part of IA work that it's good to know how we think about them. Some key features of categories are:

- They don't exist independently in the world, but in the human brain
- There is no right answer
- Category boundaries are fuzzy
- Categories overlap
- Items in a category have a family resemblance, but may not have a set of features in common
- Contents change over time
- Some things belong better than others
- Categories such as miscellaneous are real in our brains, but hard to use in IA
- Categories and sub-categories form a hierarchy

We also think at a particular level of a hierarchy – the 'basic level category' – though people can think at different levels depending on what they already know. For many types of information, the basic level is like a topic – which is how we naturally think.

Further reading

Books

Lakoff, George (1987). *Women, Fire and Dangerous Things: What Categories Reveal About the Mind.* Chigaco Press

Part 3

Understanding Content

In chapter 1, I described how a good IA balances the needs of people, the context (including project goals) and the content. We discussed context in chapter 1.5, and people in part 2.

Now we'll start looking at the content side of things – content being the stuff you'll provide via your site. In these chapters we'll talk about finding out what you already have, identifying what you need, communicating, and planning and prioritising for release. And in the last chapter we'll talk about classification schemes and when to use them.

Content you need

Communicating about content

Content planning

Classification schemes

11

Content you have

Most people I talk to are working on redesign projects – redesigning websites and intranets, updating applications, or adding new types of content (such as video and user-generated content) to an existing site.

When redesigning, one of the first steps on the content side of the project is to understand what you have already. If you're working on a new project with no content, jump to the next chapter, which is all about figuring out what you may need.

For any content-heavy project, you need to have a good understanding of the content before you even think of tackling the IA. If you don't, your IA and content just won't fit together later.

Note: when I talk about content, I'm not just talking about words. I'm talking about everything you make available to people – words, video, audio, downloads, files, feeds and functions. These are all content.

Learning what you have

Learning what content you have will help you:

- Understand the subject: If you're working on a new site, or a subject you don't have much experience with, this step will help you to learn about the subject – essential for creating an effective IA.
- Look at it with fresh eyes: If you're working with something you already know, it's a great refresher and gives you another chance to look at your content.
- Clean up: You'll get a chance to clean up old, out-of-date and inaccurate content.
- Migrate it: If you're migrating to a new IA or a new content management system (CMS) you'll need to know what you have so you don't lose anything in the migration.
- Manage progress: As you work through a project, you'll need to keep track of things like what content has been rewritten, what needs deleting, and what has been migrated.

How you go about learning what you have will depend on how much content you have. As you can imagine, the process for a 100-page informational site is different to a product catalogue with hundreds of thousands of items.

The three common approaches are:

1. Full content inventory
2. Partial content inventory
3. Content audit

Full inventory

A full content inventory lists out everything on your site. It's the most useful approach because you get a complete listing of everything, which means you'll completely understand the content when creating the IA.

Of course a full inventory isn't always possible. I've taken an inventory of a site with 30,000 pages, but it took two of us more than a month to do. It was incredibly useful, and the IA we based it on was very solid. But it was only possible because we built time into the project to create it.

A full inventory may include a list of:

- all 'pages'
- all downloadable objects, such as PDF files, documents, spreadsheets, executables or other files
- all embedded objects, such as video or audio
- other content, such as reader comments

Partial inventory

If you can't take a full inventory, take a partial inventory. This usually collects information for a particular number of levels of the site, though it may show some parts of the site in more detail. It is a good practical approach for very large sites as you still get a good understanding of the overall content in a reasonable time.

> *"An Intranet I recently worked on had over 85,000 pages and no consistent IA. In this instance we convened a team of about 8 people, conducted an inventory only down to a certain level and identified common content types. We then selected specific, high priority, areas of the site to receive more in-depth inventories, which will be conducted with subject matter experts as part of the evaluation of content for migration to new system."*
>
> Kirsten Hall, User Experience Consultant, www.kirstenhall.ca

A partial inventory is also appropriate if you'll be writing all content from scratch. You won't need a list of everything, but you'll get a good idea of the main types of content that already exist.

Content audit

A content audit collects less information than either of the inventory approaches, and is more a sample across the site. It may collect details for the first couple of levels of a site, then details for different page types in each section.

A content audit is most useful for product sites. You may not need to list out every item sold on the website, but you still need information on a good cross-section.

As with the partial inventory, you may want to create a more detailed inventory for some parts of the site.

What to collect

What information you collect for each page (or content item) will vary depending on the type of project and the type of content you have. The idea is to collect only what you'll need for your project, and nothing more.

Here's some of the information I usually collect:

- Link name: The label used in navigation
- Page name: The main heading on a page. This may be different to the navigation link name and is handy to see if the navigation and page names are different
- Page URL: The full URL of the page
- Content type: e.g. is it a publication, FAQ, how-to, product, brochure, report, specification sheet, article or something else?
- Resources: Are there PDF or Word documents, images or other downloadable files attached?
- Status: Is it current or out of date?
- Date updated: When was it last updated?
- Owner: Who owns it? (For sites with distributed authors)
- Comments: Anything else you want to note

Before you start listing out all your content, read this and the next three chapters and decide what you'll need to collect. Of course you may not know ahead of time what you'll do, so don't be afraid to create a basic listing and expand it later.

Where the 'content' comes from

In most cases, you'll use the current site. But sometimes you'll want to scout further:

- If you're working on an intranet, you may want to find out where else people get information (e.g. network drives or document management systems). You may want to also look at how people store information. I've seen lots of cases where people don't have a good place to store information and create work-arounds, such as email folders and local drives. These can be handy to know for your intranet redesign.
- If you are combining multiple websites, make sure you list content from all of them.
- Find out if you have any customer extranets to see if they contain content relevant to a broader audience.

Taking an inventory

I always use spreadsheets to record content inventories. I like them because they're so flexible – I can vary what I collect for each project, add new information as I need to, and easily share them with other people. You could use a database, but in 10 years of doing this I've never felt the need to use anything other than a spreadsheet.

	A	B	C	D	E
1		Navigation title	Page title	Comments	
2	0.0	Home	no page title		
3	1.0	UX Australia 2009	no page title	Page title is long description	
4	1.1.0	About	About UX Australia 2009		
5	1.1.1	Promote	Help promote UX Australia 2009		
6	1.2.0	Program	UX Australia 2009 Program		
7	1.2.1	Main conference	UX Australia 2009 presentations: A-Z		
8	1.2.2	Conference audio	UX Australia 2009 conference audio		
9	1.2.3	Pre-conference workshops	UX Australia 2009 pre-conference workshops		
10	1.2.4	Social	Social program		
11	1.2.5	Call for proposals	Call for proposals		
12	1.2.6	Guiding principles	UX Australia 2009 program – Guiding principles		
13	1.3	Reviews	Reviews and posts for UX Australia 2009		
14	1.4.0	Speakers	UX Australia presenters		
15	1.4.1	For speakers	For UX Australia 2009 speakers		
16	1.5	Why attend	Why attend UX Australia		
17	1.6	Pricing	UX Australia 2009 pricing		
18	1.7.0	Sponsors	Sponsors		
19	1.7.1	Partners	no page title	Needs page title added	
20	1.7.2	Sponsorship opportunities	Sponsorship opportunities for UX Australia 2009		
21	1.8.0	Venue	Conference venue		
22	1.8.1	Accommodation	Accommodation		
23	1.8.2	About Canberra	About Canberra		
24	1.8.3	Canberra food	Canberra restaurant suggestions		
25	1.9	Crowdvine	UX Australia	Link to crowdvine domain	
26	2.0	UX Australia 2010	no page title	Page title is long description	
27	2.1	About	About UX Australia 2010		
28	2.2.0	Program	UX Australia 2010 program		
29	2.2.1	Guiding principles	UX Australia 2010 program – Guiding principles		
30	2.2.2	Call for proposals	UX Australia 2010 program – Call for proposals		
31	2.2.3	Call for reviewers	UX Australia 2010 – Call for reviewers		
32	2.3.0	Sponsors	Sponsors		

Figure 11 – 1. UX Australia content inventory

1. Semi-automatic

If my client has something similar to a content management system I ask them for a listing of everything in the system. If I'm really lucky this will:

- Have details about every page and object (not just titles, but links, date updated, owners etc)
- Show the basic structure of the site (if it's a hierarchy)
- Only show content available publicly

If I'm not so lucky (and I rarely am), I can often get a list of all the files on the file system. This isn't fantastic as I still need to do a manual inventory, but it does give me an idea of what's available. One thing I usually discover is a pile of orphaned files sitting on the server – nothing links to them, but internal search can often find them. My clients usually don't know they're still available, and we can get started on a tidy-up process by deleting them. (Don't tell anyone, but I love cleaning up and deleting garbage – there's something therapeutic about it.)

The third way to get an automated listing is by using a program to follow the website links and produce a list of pages. If you know how, you can also write a script to do this. As with the CMS file listing, you'll get a list but it won't show you how the site is currently structured.

Even if you can get a start with an automated listing, you'll probably need to do manual work to create a listing that shows current structure.

2. Manual

Sometimes, though thankfully it's becoming less common, there's no way to create an automatic listing. In this case I have to create the inventory manually by clicking through every page and listing it in the spreadsheet.

I know this sounds really tedious, but looking at every page of the content gives you a very deep understanding of the content. You don't get the same depth of knowledge looking quickly at the site or reading through someone else's inventory.

Here's how I create a manual inventory for a hierarchical website:

- Start at the home page. In the spreadsheet, list out the main navigation items, plus anything not included beneath one of the main navigation items (e.g. contacts, site map, A-Z index, disclaimer, copyright and privacy pages).
- Go into the first navigation item and list out the direct sub-pages for that item.
- Start at the first sub-page and list out any sub-pages of it.
- Continue going down the first path as far as the structure goes.
- Go back one level and continue.
- Keep going down branches and listing out everything beneath before going up a level. This will help you keep track of where you are up to so you'll know you've covered everything.
- At each step just list the basics – link name, page name, hyperlink and maybe whether there are downloadable files. Don't worry about anything else yet.

After you've listed the basic information, go back and add more detail where you need. I do this as a second step as I find trying to list out everything the first time around breaks my flow.

Content inventory tips

One of the most important aspects of an inventory is the relationship between items. If your site is a hierarchy, make sure the hierarchy is reflected in the sheet – look at the numbering system and indenting I use in my example. This makes it much easier to understand what you have.

One question people ask all the time is where to include cross-links in the inventory – beneath the page they link from, or within the section where they live structurally? I usually include only the structural aspects or the inventory gets messy. I try as hard as possible to list each page (or resource) only once. If you think it's worth knowing what pages cross-link to each other, create a separate column for it, or make a note in the comments column.

I list out all pages, but not always all resources on the pages (e.g. the video, audio or downloadable files). If you're keeping pages as they are, you may not need to list out all the resources. But if you'll be using a more automated system to produce your pages in the future you may want to list all the resources.

Other tips:

- Use two monitors, with the site on one and the spreadsheet on the other. It will save you countless mouse-clicks swapping between the two.
- I have a keyboard with browser back and forward buttons beneath the space bar. This too saves a lot of mouse clicks. (If you don't have one of these you can use the backspace key in most browsers instead of the back button).
- Use standard keyboard shortcuts for copy and paste.
- Stop regularly and stretch. This is one of those tasks that keeps you at the keyboard 'just finishing one more section' for far too long.

Don't forget: there's no right or wrong way to create an inventory. It's a tool for you to use, so feel free to modify my suggestions so it does what you need it to.

Chapter summary

The first step to working with content is to understand what you already have. This will help you:

- understand the subject (if you are new to it)
- look at it with fresh eyes (if you already know it)
- clean up out-of-date and inaccurate content
- prepare for migration
- manage project progress

This is normally done via a content inventory – a full or partial inventory, or a content audit. The inventory lists all content and shows main content relationships. You may be able to do it at least partly automatically, or you may need to do it manually by clicking on every page in the site.

Further reading

For more about taking a content inventory, see `http://delicious.com/practicalIA/content_inventory`

12

Content you need

Whether you're working on a redesign or launching a brand new site, you'll need to spend time thinking about what content to include on the site.

The content you choose should not only meet the needs of the people using your site, but also achieve your project goals.

Sometimes the choice of content is easy and obvious, especially for small sites. For larger sites, it's not hard to come up with content ideas, but it can be a nightmare to figure out what to keep. (Have you ever tried telling someone you're deleting their content because no-one needs it?) On top of that, you need to figure out what you can maintain with your available resources.

We'll talk about prioritising more in chapter 14. For now, let's look at ways to identify potential content. Three places to start getting content ideas are:

- current behaviours
- user research
- your own ideas for content (or your client's)

Current behaviour

One of the easiest ways to get ideas for content, or to confirm what you should include, is to look at what's being used already.

If you have web statistics for current content, use them to identify the most popular content. Don't just check the most recent statistics – some content may be more popular at different times of the year. Also check what happens when new content is added – does it peak and then never get used again?

In most cases you'll keep your popular content, though you may want to make it easier to find. Think about why people like this particular content, and whether you can create more like it. Also think whether you can use it to help people find other things. For example, you may be able to provide better links to related content.

Popular content is only popular because people can find it. If you have good content but your statistics show that it's rarely used, think about why it might be happening. People may not be finding it because it's in a strange place in the site, or has a poor title. It may be very important, but only to a few people. Of course it may not be important to anyone, in which case you may be better off deleting it entirely.

Even if you're working on a brand new site, you can still get some ideas about what people are interested in. You can visit websites like digg.com or delicious.com and see what's popular in your field. If you have competitors, or sites that are similar to yours, see if they display 'top articles'.

User research

In Part 2 we discussed ways to collect information about people's information needs. One of the main reasons was to help you understand what they need and want, so you can include the right content for them. User research is a great source of information about the types of content you can provide.

Go through the research (you may have already done it in the analysis step) and identify everything that indicates a content need.

Some information needs will be obvious:

- "I go to this site to download the latest research report"
- "The page I use most is the canteen menu"
- "I use this A-Z of yoga poses a lot to see how to do a pose or to refine how I'm doing it"

Some will be less obvious. For example:

- "I skim the news headlines every day and read articles that look interesting" tells you someone is interested in the news, but you'll need to dig further to find out which stories are most interesting.
- "I need to convince my boss to let me attend the conference" tells you they need something, but not what will help them convince their boss.

When you're going through the user research, also pay attention to needs for functional items such as calculators, templates and tools.

Content brainstorm

The easiest way to generate a list of content ideas for a new site is to brainstorm content ideas. You should do this for an existing site as well – you will probably come up with ideas for new features.

Simply brainstorm with your team. Start by thinking about the types of content you could include. Use your user research and business goals to guide you.

At this stage it's good enough to brainstorm the types of content you'll need. In chapter 14 we'll discuss content planning, where you'll elaborate on what these content ideas actually mean and set priorities for producing them.

Competitor analysis

When you start thinking about content, it's a good time for competitor analysis – seeing what your main competitors provide and how well they do it. You obviously won't want to copy them, but this process may trigger some ideas that didn't occur to you. Again, check they meet both the needs of your audience and your project goals before including them on your list of potential content.

Chapter summary

The next step in content planning is to think of what you may need in the site. For a redesign, you can use the current content and how it's used as a starter. Add in user research findings and a brainstorm with your team to create a list of content ideas.

13

Communicating about content

This chapter describes different types of documents you can use to communicate with authors and your team about content, and offers tips on working with content authors.

When you talk about content, you inevitably talk about the IA as well, as the two are so intertwined. In this chapter, I'll just discuss what you may need to communicate about content before the IA design starts.

For content authors, you may need to:

- show them what content exists
- discuss what should be deleted and rewritten
- talk about priorities for updating or adding content
- discuss content responsibilities

In the project team you may need to:

- keep a record of content ideas
- manage project activities such as content updating and migration

Content inventory

In chapter 11 I described how to create a content inventory spreadsheet. Although I described it as a tool to learn about content, it's also very useful when you're talking with content authors and your team. It may not be pretty, but it's functional, flexible and easy to work with.

I sometimes combine the content inventory with website analytics data to visually show how people use it. I colour-code rows of content according to how much people use it. It's a powerful way to help people see the content being used most often (and the content *not* being used).

Depending on what you want to communicate to your authors, you can also create summary charts and diagrams.

	A	B	C	D
1		Navigation title	Page title	Comments
2	0.0	Home	no page title	
3	1.0	UX Australia 2009	no page title	Page title is long description
4	1.1.0	About	About UX Australia 2009	
5	1.1.1	Promote	Help promote UX Australia 2009	
6	1.2.0	Program	UX Australia 2009 Program	
7	1.2.1	Main conference	UX Australia 2009 presentations: A-Z	
8	1.2.2	Conference audio	UX Australia 2009 conference audio	
9	1.2.3	Pre-conference workshops	UX Australia 2009 pre-conference workshops	
10	1.2.4	Social	Social program	
11	1.2.5	Call for proposals	Call for proposals	
12	1.2.6	Guiding principles	UX Australia 2009 program – Guiding principles	
13	1.3	Reviews	Reviews and posts for UX Australia 2009	
14	1.4.0	Speakers	UX Australia presenters	
16	1.5	Why attend	Why attend UX Australia	
17	1.6	Pricing	UX Australia 2009 pricing	
18	1.7.0	Sponsors	Sponsors	
21	1.8.0	Venue	Conference venue	
25	1.9	Crowdvine	UX Australia	Link to crowdvine domain
26	2.0	UX Australia 2010	no page title	Page title is long description
27	2.1	About	About UX Australia 2010	
28	2.2.0	Program	UX Australia 2010 program	
29	2.2.1	Guiding principles	UX Australia 2010 program – Guiding principles	
30	2.2.2	Call for proposals	UX Australia 2010 program – Call for proposals	
31	2.2.3	Call for reviewers	UX Australia 2010 – Call for reviewers	
32	2.3.0	Sponsors	Sponsors	
34	2.4	Pricing	UX Australia 2010 pricing	
35	3.0	Contact us	Contact us	
37	4.0	Blog	no page title	List of recent posts
38	5.0	Register		Not visible until 1 May

Figure 13 – 1. Colour-coding according to popularity helps you spot patterns in content use

Case Study: UX Australia website content

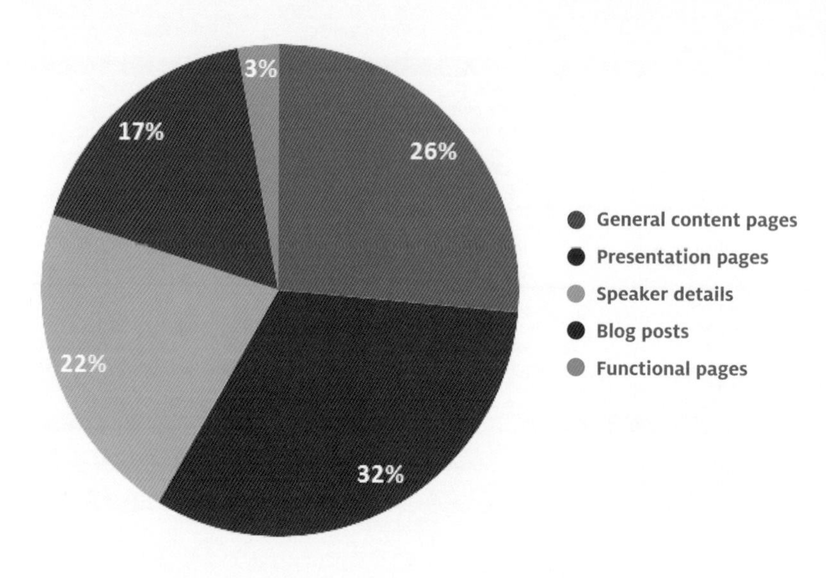

Figure 13 – 2. Content types for UX Australia

Site map

If your website is small, or you want to communicate about the top few levels of a large site, you can draw the content inventory as a sitemap (a diagram of the content – see examples in chapter 19). It's much easier to look at than an inventory spreadsheet. Unfortunately it doesn't scale well to large amounts of content.

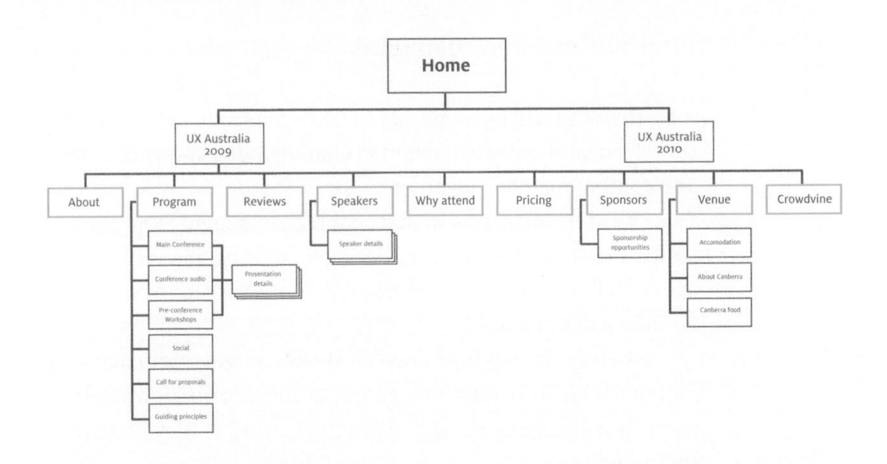

Figure 13 – 3. A sitemap is good for showing details of small sites

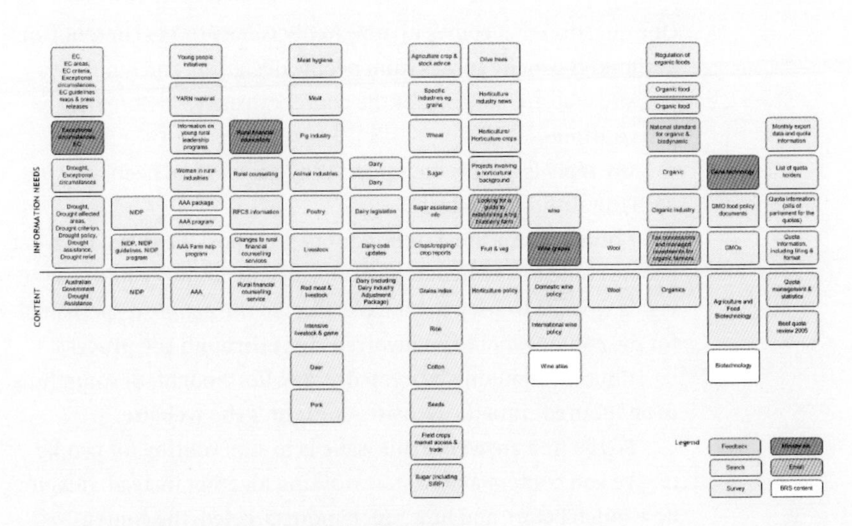

Figure 13 – 4. Diagram showing user needs and content

Information needs diagrams

A great way to talk to people about content is to match it up with user needs. I showed a diagram in chapter 8 that shows user needs and content matched together:

Any of the diagrams in that chapter can benefit from showing content ideas against the user needs. It helps people see how the content will be used, and whether there are gaps or content without a defined need.

When you're talking to people about content, particularly authors, make sure they have access to any information about users. It will help them keep the users in mind as they prepare the content.

Liaising with content authors

One question that comes up repeatedly is how to 'get content from authors'. It usually comes from people designing and building a website who are 'waiting for the content to arrive' before they can continue.

My reply is always the same: "Why haven't you been working with the authors all along?"

Content is the most important part of most websites. It's what people come for – whether it's text, video or audio. People rarely visit a website to see what it looks like. So the people responsible for the content should be involved **right through the process.**

Content shouldn't be treated as an afterthought, or something to be "poured" into the website. **Content *is* the website.**

So the first answer to this issue is to stop waiting for people to give you content and to start working together instead. Imagine how much better, and how much more targeted, the content would be if the authors were involved in the user research from the start. And think how much better the IA would be if you involved the people who know the content best.

But what if you haven't done this? You can't turn back time, and so you're waiting for the content. In my experience, here's what may have happened:

- Someone has been told to 'write the content', but it's low on their list of priorities.
- The content author doesn't know what they're really meant to produce, and aren't where to start.
- The content author has been given the IA and told to write the content, but they don't understand what should be written.

Again, the answer is to involve them more. Make sure they understand all the background to the project, including a good understanding of the users. Help them understand the information architecture, and what should go where. And if they're having trouble fitting the content into the IA, listen to them and adapt the IA.

Chapter summary

You may need to communicate with authors and your team about content:

- You can use your content inventory, or graphs and charts, to talk about what you have already.
- A site map can show the main parts of the site as a diagram.
- You can extend the techniques to communicate about people to show how the content meets their needs.

And don't forget to work with authors throughout the project, not just when you want content for the IA.

Further reading

For more about communicating content, see `http://delicious.com/practicalIA/communicating_content`

14 Content planning and priorities

With a good understanding of the current content, and solid ideas for future content, it's time to take the next step. You need to define the content in more detail, think about what you need to provide, and prioritise and plan for its release.

Defining detailed content

I often get asked to fix a brand new IA that someone else has designed. (Yes, you read that correctly. I get called in to fix brand new IAs, usually before they're even released). In every case, the IA needed fixing because the content ideas were too vague. When my client tried preparing the new content, it didn't quite fit into the IA. (Sometimes it didn't even come close!)

You should expect the IA to change as you prepare content – some things run longer than you expect, some shorter. You may end up with a paragraph where you thought you'd have a page. But when the content and IA don't fit together at all, it's usually because no-one properly analysed the content or defined it in enough detail to begin with.

When you brainstorm content ideas you'll usually come up with high-level content types. Before drafting an IA, you'll need to know exactly what the content will be. For example, in brainstorming for a conference, we might say we need:

- a description for each presentation
- a bio for each presenter
- a map of the venue
- a list of nearby accommodation
- information for people coming from out of town

Defining the content in more detail isn't hard. But it is important. Make sure you've thought about what the content actually is and how it can be used. (You'll finish thinking about how it can be used as you design the IA.) Do this for current content as well – it will help you identify opportunities you may not have thought about yet.

Now, consider the following aspects.

Content format

For each type of content , think about the format it will be in. For written material you could produce a publication, how-to, brochure, report, specification sheet, article, FAQ or just a plain old content page (or something else – this isn't an exhaustive list). Maybe you'd be better off with a downloadable file, an audio clip, video or a diagram. It may even be appropriate to offer multiple formats – you may want a video, written instructions and a quick reference for mobile use.

Figure 14 – 1. Yoga journal has basics, articles and videos for many poses

Look at your user research for clues about the best format for people to use for different tasks or contexts. I've worked on intranets full of dense policies and guidelines, and a lot of our work involved pulling out the pieces that people most wanted and putting them into formats that were easier to digest.

Also consider whether your site is the most appropriate venue for communicating. I know that sounds strange, but I've worked on projects where a poster in the workplace or a short training course would be a much more effective way to communicate than the intranet.

Content length

When you create the IA and page layouts for a site, you base it on a given volume of information. If one thing contributes to my designs failing, it's not estimating the length or volume of content correctly. I usually underestimate, but sometimes what I thought would be a page of content ends up taking a paragraph.

And then there's the other side of the coin. I've worked on projects as an IA and content writer where someone arbitrarily decided how much content would be in a given design. They'd say things like we could only have 5 top level categories, a 30 word excerpt, 200 word page and no more than 6 links in a sidebar (or the design would implode in a puff of dust). Talk about frustrating!

Make sure you know how long your content will actually be. If you're working with existing content, check the longest and shortest pieces of a particular type. Look at which content you might combine and see how long it's likely to be. If you're working with brand new content, draft a couple of core content pages to get an idea of the length.

And then design for the content – don't squeeze or pad the content to the design.

Audiences

Check to see if there's any content aimed at particular audiences.

If there is, go through everything you have and identify who it's for. When you go to design the IA this will help you decide whether an audience scheme is suitable (see chapter 15 for more about this), and what audiences and content you'll use.

I've seen a website with content clearly written for a scientific reader, even though the website was for the general public. I've found content obviously written for children buried in a dense government site where kids would never discover it. In both cases I think they may have forgotten this step.

And don't forget your user research. It will come in very handy here, particularly if you have two or more audiences with different understanding of the subject and different needs. You may decide to write content specifically for each audience, or to provide overview material for one and detail for another.

Tasks

If your users have defined tasks to do (such as booking travel or reconciling their bank statement) see what content is available for each task. This will quickly show content gaps, and is a very important process if you're writing technical support material. It may also reveal some high-priority tasks that need prominence in the IA, or even guide you towards using a task-based classification scheme (which we'll discuss in the next chapter).

Accuracy

If you're migrating content from an old IA, spend some time assessing how accurate the current content is, and what you need to do about it. In most of my IA projects I've faced the problem where a lot of the content has become out-of-date. If you're facing the same problem you may need to get it up-to-date before you can finish analysing it. Otherwise you may well be making decisions based on the old content, not the new.

Changes over time

Find out how often new content will be added, and what type of content it will be. This will have a significant impact on the IA you develop, as you don't want the content to outgrow the website.

Structured or unstructured content

One of the most important things to figure out for each type of content is whether it's structured or unstructured (and whether you'll use the structure in the IA).

No, you haven't missed anything. I haven't talked about structured and unstructured content yet, so don't panic. But this is a very important aspect of content, and we need to discuss it.

With **structured content** every item of a particular type is made up of the same pieces. You can look at one item and know that all the others of the same type will be similar. If you've ever worked with a database you'll know what I mean – everything in a database is structured content. All content of a particular type has to fit into the same structure.

Unstructured content is where every item in the website is different (structurally). As one of reviewers for this book said "unstructured content is stuff that only occurs once in a website".

Case Study: UX Australia

For example, for the UX Australia conference website the following content types were structured:

- Presentation details: Title, short description, long description, presenter, time, slideshow (embedded), audio (embedded)
- Presenter: Name, organisation, URL, bio, presentations
- Blog posts: Title, post, categories
- Sponsors: Name, description, logo, URL

These things were unstructured:

- About the conference
- Why attend
- Price
- Venue details
- Links to reviews

You need to know this because it will be a significant input to how you design your information architecture.

The advantages of structured content are:

- You can design a standard page for the content type, enter the content in a structured way, and then use the system to generate pages. You don't have to create each page manually.
- When anyone adds new content, it automatically gets included in lists that link to it (such as index pages).
- You can create different views of the content and store it once. For example, with the presentation information I could create an A-Z list of titles, a schedule, and a list containing only content with embedded audio and slideshows. And when I add a new presentation, it appears in the right place without an extra step.

But structured content takes more work. You need to define its pieces, and then decide how you are going to use it. And every item has to fit into the structure. So only create structured content when you'll be using the structure to automatically generate content, or to generate different views of it.

Setting content priorities

Depending on the size of the project you're working on, and whether there's any time-specific or seasonal content, you may need to decide when to release certain content.

You're likely to do this after drafting the IA, but I've included it in this chapter because you should start thinking about it while you're analysing your content.

In the olden days of the web, most of my projects were large website designs or redesigns that would be launched when they were complete. These days, most of my projects are released in stages.

The main advantage of releasing in stages is you can release content earlier. Projects that wait until everything is 'finished' get held up by the slowest content. Releasing in stages also acknowledges the web isn't a publication. Your site will always be changing, so there's no need to wait for everything to be finished.

If you *are* going to release in stages, you'll need to know what content will be released when. This probably won't affect your IA design, as you may well design for what the site will look like in the long run. Then again, it might. You may move some information around and change things like top level categories over time.

I use different methods to set priorities depending on the project and content. I've outlined four, though chances are you'll find other ways that better suit your project and content.

Cyclical or seasonal content

UX Australia runs on a yearly cycle, with different information being released at different times. We created a map showing key conference milestones, what content would be released and what sections it would be in:

Navigation & content / Milestone	Launch	Call for proposals	Registration opens	During conference	After
Home	- Basic conference info - Key dates - Location	Add: - Call for proposals	Remove: - Call for proposals Add: - Keynote speaker - Register now	Add: - Overview of schedule Remove: - Register now	- Basic conference info - Links to materials - Photos from flickr - Testimonials - Link to next year's conference
About	- What (about the conference) - Where (city & venue) - When (detailed dates)		Add: - Why attend		
Program		- Call for proposals	Remove CFP Add - Pre-con workshops - Conference presentations	Add: - Presentation guide (something to help people pick what to see – by topic, experience, interest)	Add: - Presentation files
Speakers		- Why speak at UXAustralia (link to CFP)	Remove: - Why speak Add: - Speakers - Tips for speakers	Add info about where to upload files etc	
Social			- What's planned - Call for helpers??	- What's happening - How to get involved	Add: - Links to photos etc
Register			- Registration process - Prices & inclusions		Remove registration form (or close it)
Sponsors	Sponsors: - Why sponsor (deals etc)	Add: - List of sponsors			Change to thank our sponsors
Previous	Previous (obviously not for first year) - Link to previous year sites - List of all presentations (by topic, by date)				

Figure 14 – 2. A plan for when to add particular content

Value vs cost

On another project, we had to decide what content would go first. We plotted the main content chunks on a matrix, with one axis showing the value to the user and organisation, and the other showing the cost or difficultly of producing the content. This helped identify priorities – low value, high cost items wouldn't be released until later.

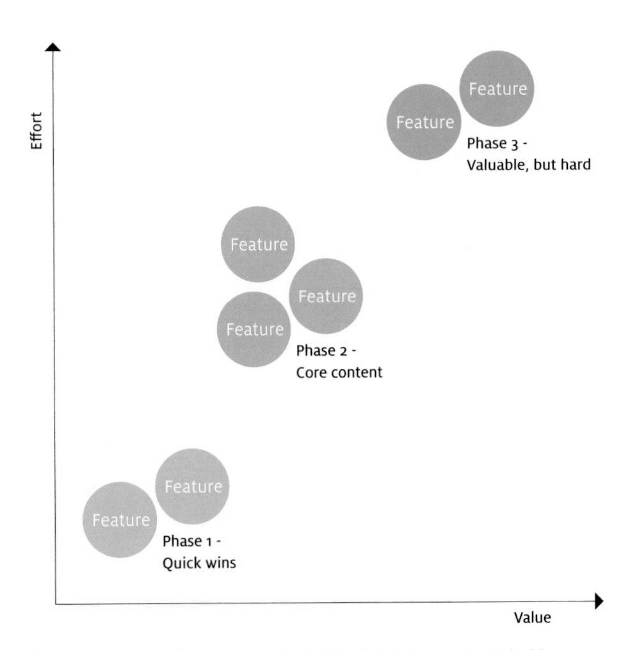

Figure 14 – 3. A matrix showing value and effort helps to set priorities

Scoring system

For one big website redesign, with multiple teams and sections of content, we created a scoring system that included:

- how important the content was to users (1=not important, 10= critical)
- how much of it was out of date (1=out of date, 10=accurate)
- how much content there was (1=lots, 10=little)
- how quickly the authors could get it updated (1=likely to be slow, 10=fast and responsive)

We weighted the first criteria higher (we doubled it) and simply added the scores up. The section with the highest score went first.

> *"A method I've used for connecting personas & scenarios to content & requirements is to create a matrix of the tasks or steps a given persona would perform with the site, and then rank these based on frequency and importance. This plotting exercise can help to reveal what is most important to allocate resources to and prioritize within design."*
>
> Kirsten Hall, User Experience Consultant, www.kirstenhall.ca

Core content first

On a recent project we knew some content was core to the whole site, and a lot of the other content would link into it. We rewrote that content first so authors could link to it as they updated the rest of the content.

Working with authors to prioritise web content

Murray Thompson, Grande Prairie, Alberta

> *"In my organization, I noticed that most groups weren't moving anywhere with their website content – it was essentially frozen from a few years before. So to help them move forward, I worked through a process around developing a road map for their content. I like to call it a "future content audit".*
>
> *The way it worked was to:*
>
> 1. *Get key members of the group together*
> 2. *Talk about who their users are and list them out (prioritizing key audiences)*
> 3. *Brainstorm ideas on content their audiences may be looking for, and messages the group wanted to share (this could be*

helped along with existing personas and other user research deliverables)

4. *Organize the brainstormed items into a structure, including:*
   - *What might need a section, a page, or just a few words on a page*
   - *How items are grouped and related to each other*
   - *What's feasible to maintain and what's not (record "what's not" items, but don't include them in the structure)*
   - *What content belongs to others (and can be linked to)*

During the process, we didn't look at what was in the website already or look at what other websites had. This allowed us to start with a clean slate more easily, avoiding "I just want what they have" thinking or fitting things into a possibly broken or constrained structure.

After the process with each group – which sometimes took a couple of hours, sometimes a couple of days – I wrote up the list of users and structured items for them. In the end, each group had a better idea of who they were making content for and a map of what they were working towards. Many didn't have very much content in the first place, so it was easy to see what was already there and the gaps that existed from the map.

The next step was for each group to take pieces of their map, prioritizing the content they needed to work on. As they worked on the content, sometimes the map changed: a section wasn't needed after all, or something was shifted to a different spot. But at least they had a reference to work with that outlined how it all tied it together. They could see how changes affected the whole picture. For areas that put resources towards it after the initial mapping, it helped them get where they wanted to go.

Going through process helped people in each group realize what they could actually use the website for and see new possibilities. It wasn't someone who told them what they should have, but was built by the group itself based on who their users are.

From the overall website perspective, it also helped identify common patterns and needs that popped-up across different areas, as well as how groups were tied together in their content."

Chapter summary

The last steps in content planning are to define the content in more detail and set priorities for release.

When defining the content in more detail, consider:

- content format
- length
- audiences
- tasks
- how accurate it is now
- what changes will happen over time
- whether it is structured or unstructured (and whether you'll use any structural aspects in your design)

You may release your whole site at once, or in stages. If you release in stages, you'll need to set priorities. You can use a scoring system, determine value versus cost or release core content first. If your site is on a cycle, identify what content is released at each part of the cycle.

Further reading

For more about content planning `http://delicious.com/practicalIA/content_planning`

15

Classification schemes

As I've mentioned a few times, any set of content can be organised in different ways. One of the challenges for an IA project is figuring out what works best for your audience, your content and your project's goals.

In this chapter I'll talk about the different ways you can organise your content, and offer tips on when to use a particular method and how to use it. I'll refer to these as 'classification schemes', which sounds a bit formal but helps me set it apart from the general categorisation ideas we talked about in chapter 10.

This is just background information for you to think about for your content. We'll discuss how to actually come up with an IA in the next part of the book.

But first, a little background on two different types of classification schemes.

Types of classification schemes

There are two common types of classification schemes.

The first is called an **exact scheme**. With an exact scheme you won't have any problem assigning items to individual categories, and the categories themselves may be easy to create. Some obvious examples are time, alphabetical and geographical schemes. As you can imagine, there's no problem figuring out where 'apple' should be categorised in an alphabetical scheme.

Some exact schemes may already have been created (such as geographical boundaries) so you don't have to figure out the starting categories. You just need to decide what level of category you'll use (e.g. what area to use for geography).

The second is called an **ambiguous scheme**. With an ambiguous scheme you may well have to design it from scratch specifically for your situation. (While there are pre-existing categorisation schemes for many situations, for your website or intranet you'll probably make up your own). And when start assigning content to the categories, you'll have to make a lot of judgement calls about what content goes in what categories

– as we discussed in chapter 10, category boundaries are fuzzy. Examples of ambiguous schemes include subject, audience and task.

I'm mentioning this now so, should you decide on an exact scheme, you can skip some of the information coming up about creating categories and assigning content.

And now on to the schemes...

Classification schemes

Here are 8 classification schemes. For each one I'll describe when they are most useful, show some examples and provide some tips on how to use them well.

In some cases the what-they-are-good-for part is pretty straightforward, so don't be surprised when it seems obvious. But the tips aren't as obvious, so they're well worth reading.

Time

Time-based schemes organise content into groups according to when something happens. You can use them for any content where time is a key aspect of the content.

This scheme is most useful when you know people want to access content based on the time or date. For example:

- News
- Weblogs
- History
- TV guides
- Event listings

As you can see, time can be used in two different ways – when content is published at a particular time (news, weblogs), and when time is a key attribute of the content (history, start times for TV shows, events).

Time published is most suitable for content that people will use in real time (or close to it). Think about when people will use your information. Will they be keeping up with it as you publish it (as is the case with most news content)? If so, displaying stories according to the published time will help people keep up-to-date.

But also consider how people will access the content if they've been away for a few days, or want to see what older content is available, or want to find something specific. You may also have to use something like a subject classification scheme to help them. Many weblogs do this particularly poorly, giving users only month-based categories to help them find content later on.

Time-based schemes are so easy to design and implement that you may use one without thinking it through. Check your user research to see if people want to access your information in that way.

For example, let's say you're redesigning a TV guide and you find most users don't watch TV when it airs (they record shows and watch them later). If that's the case, perhaps you should display your TV guide by type of show, subject and alphabetically, rather than by time. And if you run an opinion-based news site you may choose to organise stories around topic and columnist as well as by date.

Time is used in two ways to organise information – as a grouping method and a sequencing method. For example news stories may be sequenced down a page by time, but may not be grouped by it. If you're sequencing content by time, think about whether people need to see it ordered from oldest to newest or vice versa. For news it will usually be newest at the top, but for some other content the reverse order may be best.

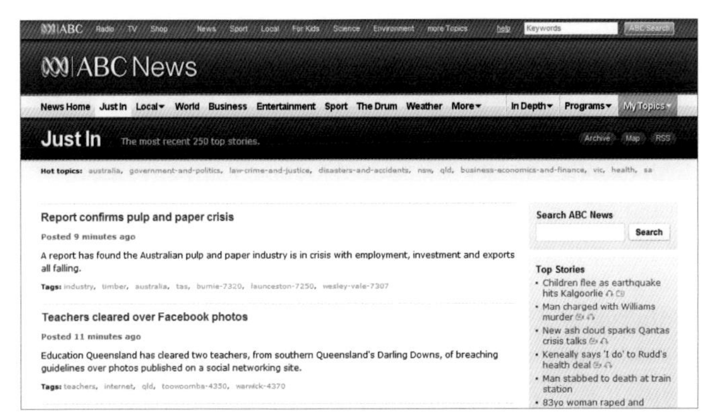

Figure 15 – 1. ABC news has a Just In page - good for keeping up to date with the latest news (`http://www.abc.net.au/news/justin/`)

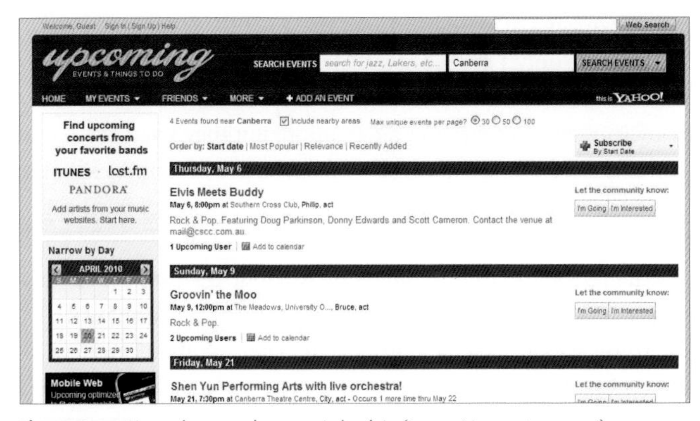

Figure 15 – 2. Upcoming organises events by date (`http://upcoming.org/`)

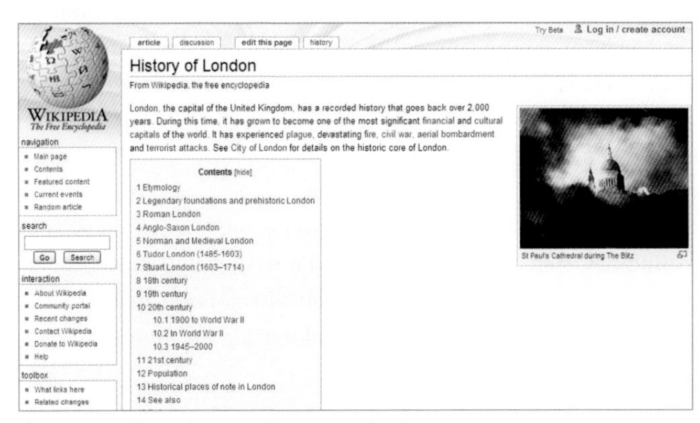

Figure 15 – 3. History is a natural to sequence by time

Alphabetic

As you can probably guess, an alphabetic scheme is also an exact scheme – one where you don't have to make up any categories and can assign content to categories easily.

Alphabetic schemes can be used for practically any type of information – as long as you can give an item a name, you can include it in an A-Z scheme. But that doesn't mean alphabetic schemes are necessarily good for all content.

Alphabetic schemes work best when people know what they're looking for, know how to describe it, and the item labelling matches the words that they're looking for. (Remember the 'known item' information seeking task from chapter 9?) An alphabetic scheme is perfect for this type of task as people can simply scan a list of words and spot the one they're looking for.

There are only a couple of situations where you'd use alphabetic as the main way of organising your content – dictionaries and glossaries come to mind. But they're great secondary schemes to a main scheme. Even as a secondary scheme they can be valuable – I've worked on intranets where people said "Do whatever you like, just don't take away the A-Z".

When people ask me about using A-Z indexes, three questions always come up. I'm not a professional indexer (indexing is an entire profession in itself) so my answers just skim the surface:

- Should I list things twice?
  Yes, list things under two headings where there are two common terms for something, and where you know people will use more than one term. Be conservative though – you don't want to double the size of your index by adding extra terms. Do it only when there is a real need.
- Should I use more terms that are technically correct, or the words people use?
  You'll often find that people use inaccurate, outdated or incorrect terminology. If this happens, and you know they will use these terms, add them to the A-Z index. If you'd like to educate them about correct terminology, include it alongside the more common one.

- Should I list every content page?
  When you'll be using an A-Z index, you usually won't need to include every content page. You'll probably want to include all of your main topical pages or landing pages, though this will depend on your site structure and type of content. For example on an intranet you may have an index item for 'Maternity leave' but probably not for the individual pages on maternity leave.

  Your user research is a great input into the A-Z as you should have a rich resource of the terminology people use.

Figure 15 – 4. The BBC A-Z is a great way to jump to something you know the name of

Figure 15 – 5 Wondering what a macguffin is but can't remember how to spell it? Look it up in the IMDB glossary (`http://www.imdb.com/Glossary/M`)

Geography

Again, geography is an exact scheme – once you have a set of boundaries, it's easy to tell which category or area a particular things belong to.

This is almost obvious, but geographical schemes can be used for any content with some sort of geography as a key attribute. And just like time and alphabetical schemes, the real trick to using it is knowing whether your users want to access information geographically.

I can't tell you how many web and intranet project meetings I've been in where someone has said "We should just include a map on the home page and let people use that". In some cases it's a perfectly good suggestion, but in others it's not so good.

So when is it good? There are two real criteria for a successful geographical scheme. The first is what I've already said a number of times – your audience must want to access information in that way. The second is more important – they must understand the geography you're using, often in quite a lot of detail.

As an example (and I've changed this slightly to protect my client), I once worked on a project to provide information about changes in water volumes over the past 100 years. And of course the inevitable statement came up – that we should just include a map on the home page and let people drill down to see information about their local area. That wasn't necessarily a bad idea – we already knew people were interested in what was happening around them and would want to know this information. The big problem would be narrowing down to 'around them'.

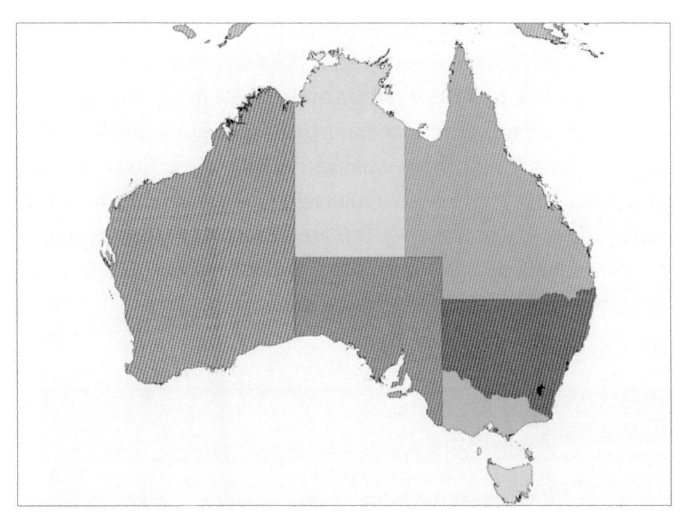

Figure 15 – 6 From (`http://en.wikipedia.org/wiki/States_and_territories_of_Australia`)

Here's a quick introduction to Australian geography. We have 6 States and two Territories.

Every Australian knows what State they're in. But States are big, and this information would have to relate to much smaller areas. So we talked about what we'd do below state level and everyone (on the client side) agreed we would base it on... water catchment areas.

Two big problems with the idea. First, hardly anyone knows what catchment they are in (I wouldn't have a clue). And second, catchments (where the rain falls before ending up in rivers and water stores) don't care about State borders.

I've seen the conversation repeated over and over; "We should use a map", "What boundaries will we use?", "Oh..."

This can happen even at a broader level. While every Australian knows what State they're in, they don't necessarily know what State some of Australia's key tourist attractions are in (me included). This posed a real challenge for a tourism website I worked on, and we had to make sure we offered both geographical and topical approaches to tourist attractions.

Another thing I've experienced is the difference between using a map to display information and using a map to navigate to it. Two quite different uses for maps that can mean quite different things for users. Think about what you're trying to achieve with a geographical scheme/map. Are you trying to show precisely where various objects are in the world? Or are you trying to help people get to content about a particular area. By figuring this out the map's purpose will be clearer, which can be important.

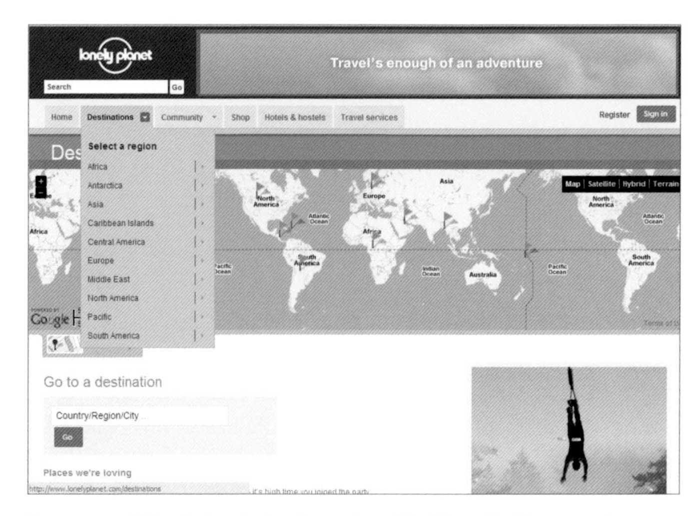

Figure 15 – 7. Naturally, Lonely planet organises a lot of its content by geography (`lonelyplanet.com`)

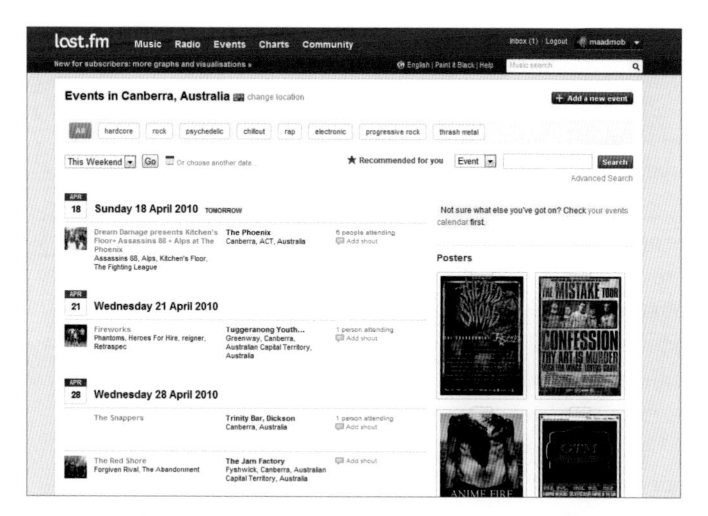

Figure 15 – 8. Lastfm lets me see gigs near my local area, or in other locations (`last.fm`)

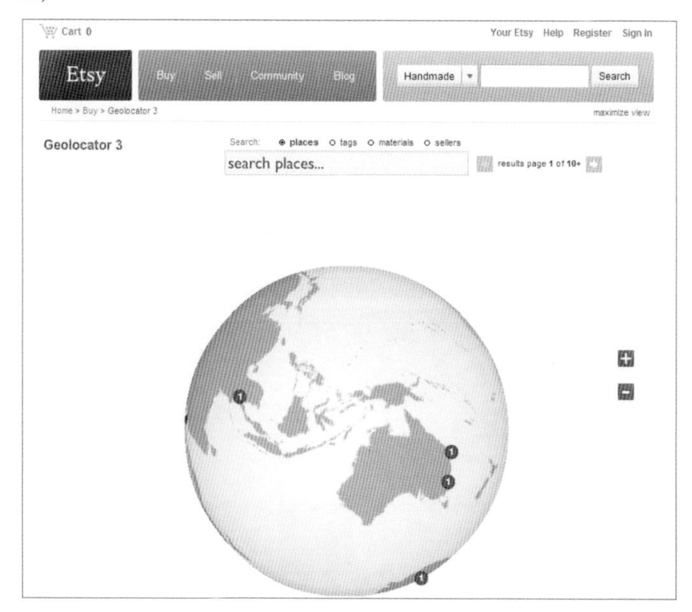

Figure 15 – 9. Etsy lets me search for items by location (`etsy.com`)

(A map for navigation doesn't need to be particularly accurate, but a map for displaying information certainly does.)

As with the previous two schemes, geography may be good as a secondary way to access information, supporting one of the other schemes.

Format

Format is another exact organisation scheme, where you organise your content around the format of the file. This is particularly common on sites such as instructional websites (where they group videos, articles and tutorials) and article websites (where they group articles, interviews and tools).

Again, it's a fine way of organising your content as long as your audience expects and wants to find it like that.

I must admit I have my reservations. I think people think first about what they want to do and then about the format they want to see it in. If I want to find out how to varnish my back verandah (something I did need to do recently) I'll want to find out about varnishing first before deciding whether to read instructions, download a brochure, watch a video or hear a description.

Figure 15 – 10. Bunnings (my local hardware store) has a great DIY section, organised by format of the content. I'd prefer to see the topics, then choose a format (`bunnings.com.au`)

I certainly don't want to look in three different parts of a site to see what's available. But format is a great way to show people the different types of information available once they've found the topic.

Organisational structure

Another exact scheme, and one you'll come across in both intranet and website work, is the structure of the organisation you're working with.

This scheme comes about because it's easy for authors – they can prepare information and put it in 'their' part of the site. And managers can see not only where their stuff is, but also the stuff for their section.

The biggest problem with this structure is anyone who needs the information needs to know who is responsible for it.

So generally, this is a bad way of organising information. Of all the projects I've worked on I've suggested the organisation structure be retained only twice (and both were for intranets):

- In a very small organisation where everyone actually did know who does what. This was supported via user research.
- In an organisation where structure and rank matter a lot. In my situation, this was a Defence Department. I saw little point trying to remove the organisational structure from the intranet as the internal structure was so much a part of how they thought. It didn't mean that staff knew who did what though, so we provided other ways for them to find information (see the Focused entry points pattern in chapter 16)

> *"I was once working on a project for a client in the financial sector where the intranet was categorised by the name of the teams. The problem was that whenever a restructure occurred, no one could remember the name of the team! This was a particular problem for the front-line staff (those facing the customers) as they didn't have time to find a particular piece of information by determining the team name. The additional challenge was that many*

of the teams didn't have easily identifiable names. This resulted in a lot of printed material that got out of date quickly, many excel spreadsheets living on desktops and a heavy reliance on phone calls between teams."

Ruth Ellison, Stamford Interactive, stamfordinteractive.com.au

Task

Task is the first ambiguous classification scheme we'll discuss. Because it's an ambiguous scheme you'll have to come up with the categories first, and then assign content to them.

Task-based schemes are interesting. On the surface they seem to be fairly easy – just organise the content around the main tasks that people do. But whenever I've tried doing this (usually because a client thinks it's a good way to start) we end up with so many and varied tasks that it becomes too hard. Even if we come up with a draft, we often find that most of the time a particular piece of content will apply to more than one task.

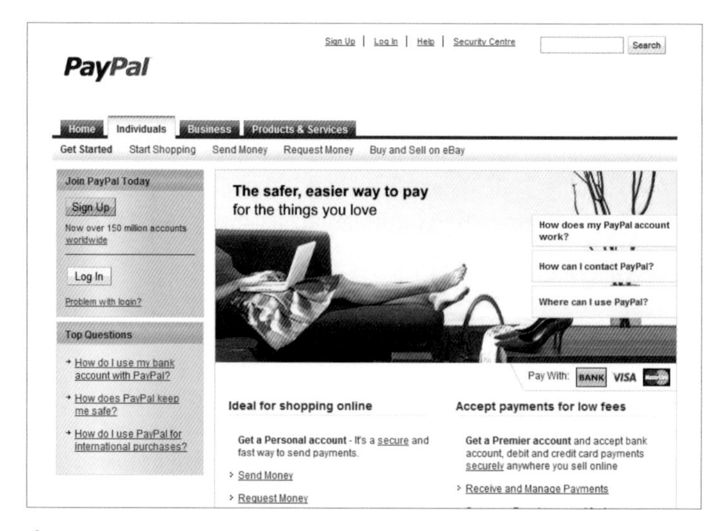

Figure 15 – 11. Paypal starts with a simple audience scheme, then uses a task based scheme at the second level – sensible for them as there are a limited number of clear tasks (`paypal.com`)

I've found that task-based schemes work best when:

- There are only a small set of tasks
- The main tasks have quite clear boundaries
- Your content is easy to allocate to the task groups

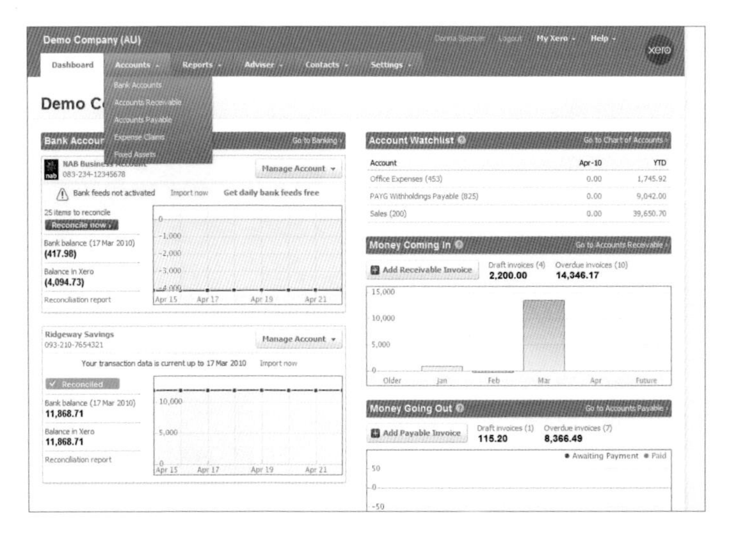

Figure 15 – 12. Even Xero, which is a web-based accounting application, doesn't use a task-based structure, but topic (`xero.com`)

Task-based classification schemes tend to be more suited to things like web applications more than websites and intranets. However, even something like accounting software (which is quite a task-based activity) doesn't fit into tasks, but instead to the content types you'll work on.

When you're looking for tasks in your user research, keep an eye out for phrases like "I need to" or "I do". Whatever follows is usually a task.

Audience

Audience schemes are very much like task-based schemes, in that they often sound like a good approach on the surface but are harder than they look.

Audience schemes are suitable, and only work when:

- You can split your audience into groups, with very clear boundaries
- At any point in time, a user can identify which group they belong to (they may switch groups for different tasks – this is okay as long as they know where they fit each time)
- Your content assigns across audience groups without too much overlap

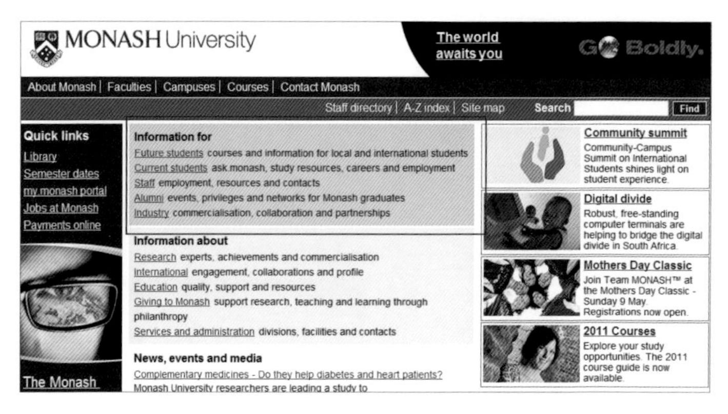

Figure 15 – 13. A lot of universities use an audience scheme. Monash university has information for different audiences, plus information about various topics (`monash.edu.au`)

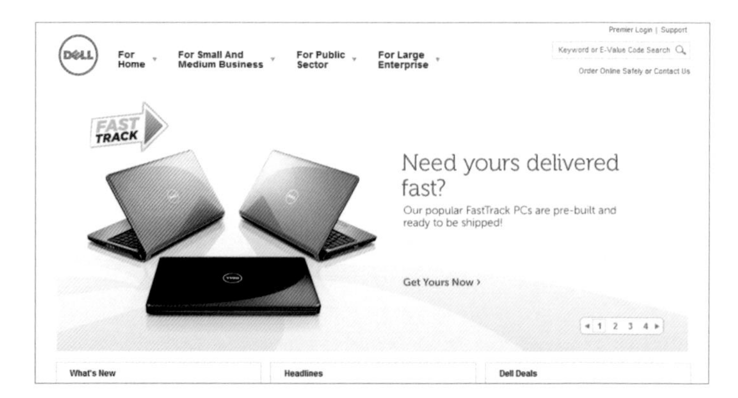

Figure 15 – 14. Dell use audience as the primary scheme for their content. Unfortunately I never know whether I have a home office or small business, and wonder what the difference is (does the 'other group' get different prices?) (`dell.com.au`)

Again, this is much harder than it seems. In most cases when we start along this path, it's hard enough identifying the audiences in the first place - people cross over groups and aren't sure who they are, and a lot of content applies to more than one group. If you have this problem, try a subject-based scheme as your primary scheme and use an audience scheme as a secondary way to help people find specific information.

If you decide an audience scheme is best for your content:

- Make sure the boundaries are clear. For example, don't use small, medium and large – use numbers to describe what they are about
- Label the groups in the same way that your users will talk about them

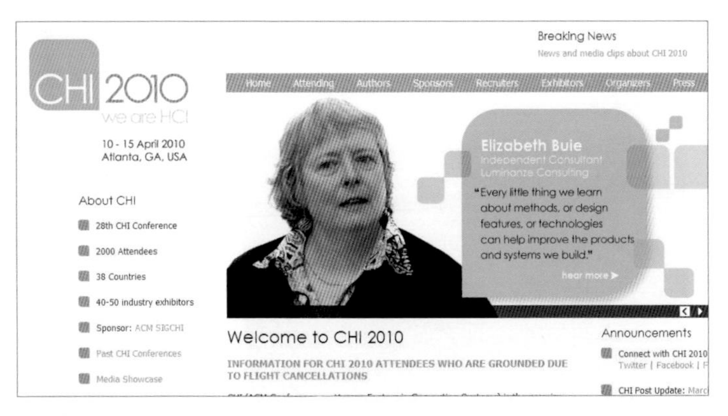

Figure 15 – 15. I was looking for the program and list of speakers for this conference. I assumed 'Authors' was a list of authors - no it was information for authors. I eventually found the program and speaker list under 'Attending'.

If you do decide to use an audience scheme, take care with your labelling. One of the most common mistakes is not being clear about whether a group is about something or for a group of people. For example, are the groups *Students, Parents* & *Teachers* a list of people, or information for these groups. It is usually fairly clear if the whole classification scheme is audience-based, but harder to determine when the scheme is mixed.

One last thing to keep in mind when creating audience schemes: you can potentially limit access to information by audience, or at least make it hard for them to find a full range of information. If your audience groups are sensitive, or it looks like you're restricting access by audience, make sure this is what you intended.

Subject/topic

The type of classification scheme you'll use most often is a subject scheme (or topic scheme – I use the terms interchangeably). And chances are you'll be coming up with it from scratch. A subject scheme groups similar things together based on what they're about.

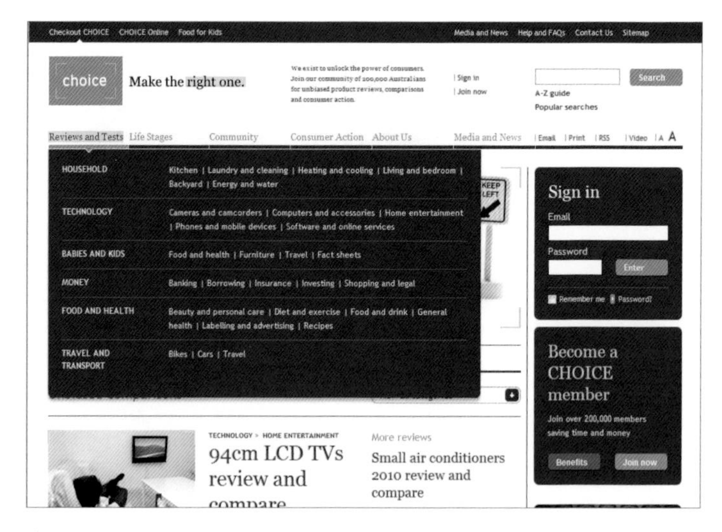

Figure 15 – 16. Choice magazine organises all their reviews and tests by subject (`choice.com.au`)

Figure 15 – 17. A list apart provides access to the magazine articles by topic (alistapart.com)

I'll talk some more about what makes a good subject scheme in part 4, which is about how to actually create your IA. But for now, it's worth knowing this type of classification scheme works well for most content. (I'm yet to meet a set of content I couldn't arrange topically.) And as long as you can do it in a way that makes sense for your audience, it will be suitable for them as well.

Combination schemes

I've described these classification schemes as if they are all independent. In reality you can use a combination.

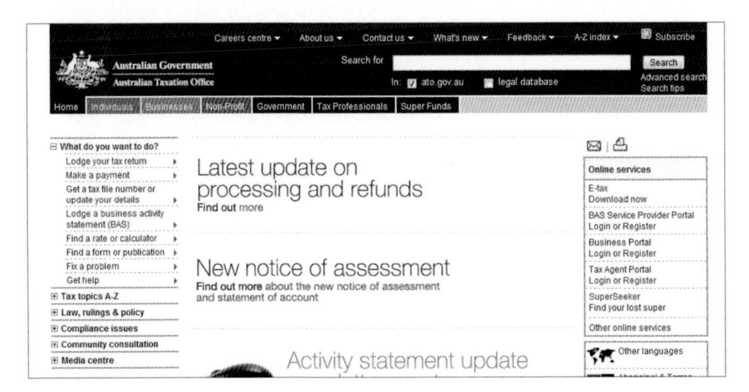

Figure 15 – 18. The Australian Taxation Office provides audience, task and topic entry points on the home page (ato.gov.au)

You could:

- Mix up types at each level
- Start with one type and use a different type at the next level
- Use more than one approach for your whole content set

There are no hard and fast rules. The main things, as I've said, are that it works well for your audience, they expect to access information in this way, and it works well for your content.

Choosing a classification scheme

Often, the choice of a classification scheme, or schemes, is straightforward. As we have seen, some schemes naturally suit particular types of information or user tasks.
We'll talk some more about this in part 4.

Changing classification schemes

Wendy White, Online Projects Developer, Scitech, (www.scitech.org.au)

#1 – Scitech's Outreach Programs website
Scitech is an interactive science centre in Perth, Western Australia. In the early half of the millennium, Scitech's web presence was actually three distinct domains and websites – one for their internal programs, one for their external programs, and one for their planetarium.

About five years ago the decision was made to consolidate these websites into one. Each original site used a different IA classification scheme.

While overall the combination of the three websites made sense, the department running external outreach programs were tough to convince when it came to changing the structure of their navigation from an audience-based to subject-based. They had used the audience-based structure for almost three years, it was familiar to them, and they felt that their audience would be confused if it changed.

Their second concern was not too difficult to address. Based on the information we had, their website's audience tended not to use the site more than once or twice a year, usually to perform a single task. So it seemed unlikely that a large number of visitors would have memorised their routes through the website. We questioned a few users of the website, and even the ones who had visited it in the last month were only able to recall the colour scheme – none of them could recall the path they used to locate information. So "upsetting the users" was not a great concern – unless we made the IA completely clunky and hideous, of course!

The external programs website was divided into three large sections – For Parents, For Teachers, and For Students.

One of the more obvious problems with the original structure was the potential overlap between the parents and teachers categories. If I want a fun activity to do with my kids, will that appear under parents? Teachers? It could believably even appear in the students area. Which itself was also a little vague as to which students it was catering to. It was aimed largely at those in the Upper Primary level, which at the time was the main audience of our external programs.

The content management system being used at the time also didn't allow a page of content to appear under more than one classification. This lead to inconsistent duplication of information between audience areas, with some duplicates being updated and others forgotten about.

A new IA was decided upon in time, however, and our external programs are now ordered by subject – there are career programs, maths programs, science activities designed for ESL (English as a Second Language) students – and this scheme seems to be working quite well. However, in the middle of 2010 Scitech will be conducting a series of site-wide usability tests – then we'll really be able to see how our audience is finding the information they need on our website.

#2 – ScienceNetwork WA changes from geographic to subject
The ScienceNetwork WA website is a government-supported news website which focuses on scientific research and development occurring in Western Australia.

When it was first created, events were organised by time, and news articles were divided up by location – 'Local' (Western Australian), 'National' and 'International'. After that, articles were sorted by month and year published.

Organising the articles by location at some point must have made sense to someone, somewhere. It doubtless came out of the desire to illustrate WA's place in scientific research in comparison to the rest of the world. It didn't make a lick of difference to the website visitors, however.

Another problem with the structure at that point was that many news stories could be classified as both 'Local' and 'National', even 'International' when several universities across the globe collaborated their astronomical research, for example.

After some discussion, it was decided that the news and event listings would be best sorted by subject, then date. We spoke to the journalists, scientists and general audience to find out what labels they used to categorise various areas of science. We found that it was best to first divide news up by broad area of science, such as Space, Agriculture, Technology and so on, which would take you to that subject's page with the latest stories. For specialist users, we then offered a secondary level of information dividing the broader areas into even more specific categories, such as Radio Astronomy, Microwave Astronomy, Astrophysics etc.

Most users are content to browse by the broad categories, but the few users who report an interest in more specific areas, usually the scientist and industry types, use the additional level of navigation to drill down into their areas of speciality. The IA is still undergoing some tweaking, but the subject-date categorisation is far more successful than the geography-date categorisation.

Chapter summary

Any set of content can be organised in more than one way. One of the most important decisions is choosing how you'll organise content so it is useful for your audience.

You can use a range of classification schemes, including:

- Time
- Alphabetic
- Geography
- Format
- Organisational structure
- Task
- Audience
- Subject or topic

Of course, you can use more than one of these, and even mix them up.

Part 4

Designing an Information architecture

So far we've talked about the three inputs you need to make an IA – goals, an understanding of the people, and an understanding of the content. And you've learned some background ideas about classifications.

Here's where we start to pull it all together and create an IA. This section describes IA structures and common patterns, the importance of language and labelling, the process of actually creating an IA, testing it and communicating it.

IA patterns

Labels and language

How to create IA

Testing IA

Communicating IA

16

IA PATTERNS

This chapter is all about IA patterns – common approaches to IA for different types of sites. You can use these patterns as a starting point when figuring out your own IA. Chances are your site will fit into one of the patterns, or maybe a combination of them.

What patterns are

A pattern is a common solution to a design problem that crops up again and again.

The idea of patterns came from architecture[1]. As you can imagine, buildings have common issues that need to be addressed over and over – the relationship between food preparation areas and food serving areas, how people will enter a building, and integrating the inside of a room with the outside, and so on.

Patterns are also common in software development (another place where the same issues crop up again and again) and provide developers with solutions to software design. They are also fairly common in interaction design, providing designers with re-usable solutions to common needs such as login forms and pagination.

One of the key ideas of patterns is that they emerge from real-world use. You don't sit down and try creating a set of patterns for a brand new field. The patterns we discuss below are generated from the wild – from seeing how people come up with common approaches to common problems.

IA patterns

I said earlier in the book that IA is relevant for a range of areas where people need to use information. I'll be deviating from that slightly in this chapter and talking mostly about website IA patterns. These patterns are also relevant for intranets, but may not apply as easily to things like web applications and mobile applications – consistent patterns will emerge for these areas over time.

[1] The most famous architectural work on patterns is Christopher Alexander's The Timeless Way of Building (1979)

I'm also sure I haven't found every different type of IA pattern. If you have a site that is very different to all of these (and you've seen others like it) let me know and I'll add it to the book website.

Below I describe the key features of each pattern, when they are good to use, and provide some examples of sites that use them.

First I'll talk about four simple patterns (hierarchy, database, hypertext and linear) then combinations of the three.

Simple patterns

Hierarchy

We've all come across hierarchies, and indeed we have talked about them already in this book when we talked about groups and subgroups. In a hierarchy, the relationship between items is one of parent and child; broader and narrower. It's about aggregating upwards into broader groupings or splitting downwards in narrower groupings.

Hierarchies can described as broad or deep:

- A broad hierarchy has a lot of items at the top level, but few levels.
- A deep hierarchy has a few items at the top level, but many levels.

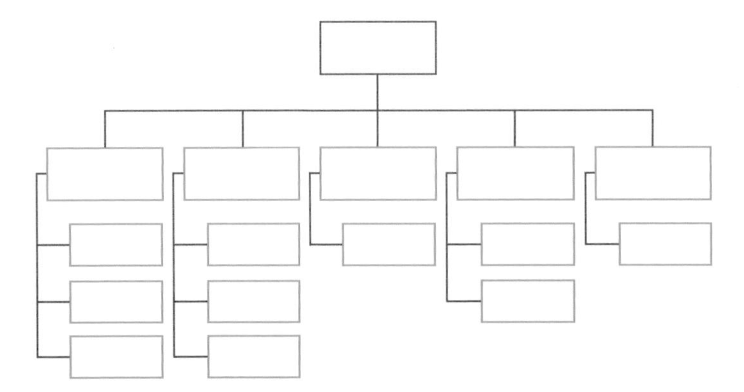

Figure 16 – 1. A hierarchy pattern

A hierarchy can also be described as strict or polyhierarchy:

- In a strict hierarchy an item can be in one and only one place.
- In a polyhierarchy an item can be in more than one place.

Strict hierarchies are necessary in the physical world – after all, it is impossible to put an individual item in more than one place at a time. However, in the electronic world it is easy for us to put things in more than one place. It also copes better with the messiness of real-life categories, letting us place things that people expect to find in more than one place and allowing category boundaries to overlap.

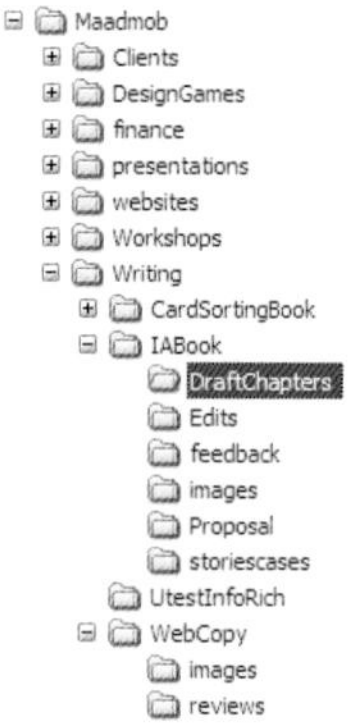

Because hierarchies are a simple and familiar way to organise information, they are suitable for a wide range of content.

They are particularly good for small websites that need nothing fancier than a couple of levels of hierarchy – a top level (home page), some second level pages and maybe a few more detailed pages beneath them.

Although hierarchies are particularly good for small websites, they can also be used for larger sites as well. They are particularly suitable for content-heavy websites where the content is quite varied.

They are also good when your information contains different levels of complexity. For example, you can present overview or broad information first, and allow people to drill down into more detail as they need it.

Maadmob
Clients
DesignGames
finance
presentations
websites
Workshops
Writing
CardSortingBook
IABook
DraftChapters
Edits
feedback
images
Proposal
storiescases
UtestInfoRich
WebCopy
images
reviews

Figure 16 – 2. We've all seen hiearchies - computer file systems are a common example

Everything in 3 clicks?

For many years a web myth stated that everything should be fewer than three clicks from the home page.

For many sites, this is just impractical. To fit everything into a hierarchy like that, there would be so many items at each level it would be impossible to select.

Instead, it's far more important that people can make easy choices at each level, and know they're on the correct or comfortable path. People really will keep clicking if they feel like they are on the right track and learning as they go.

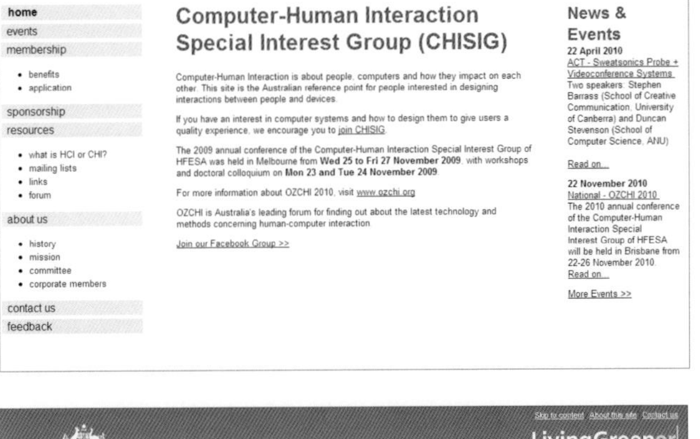

Figure 16 – 3. CHISIG (Computer-Human Interaction Special Interest Group) is a small organisation with a small amount of content. A simple hierarchy is sufficient for their website (`chisig.org`)

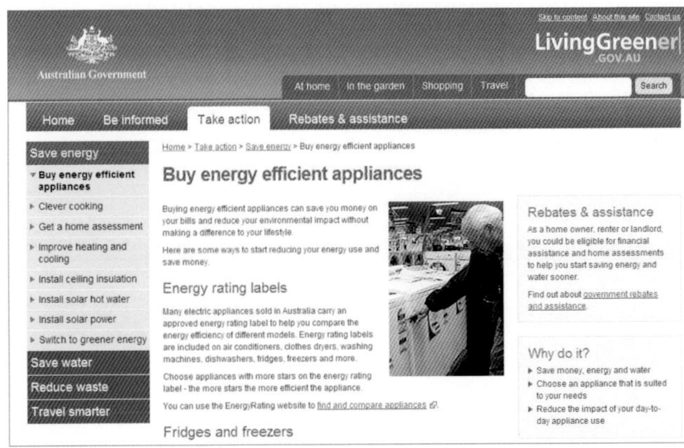

Figure 16 – 4. This content-rich website uses a 3 level hierarchy (`livinggreener.com.au`)

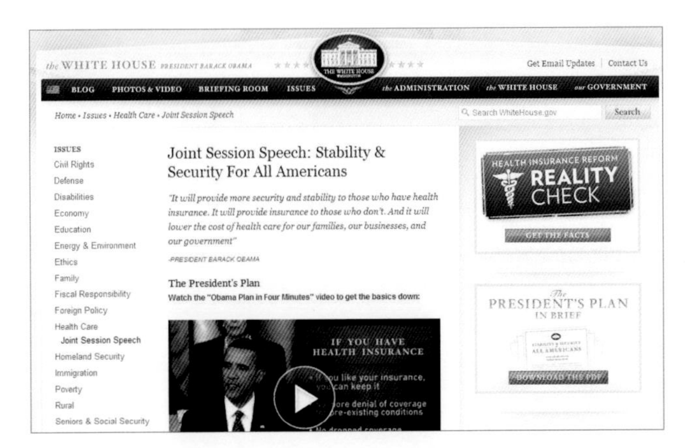

Figure 16 – 5. The White House website has a lot of content, but still uses a basic hierarchy (`whitehouse.gov`)

Database

You've probably come across databases – computerised storage for all types of information. Here I'm talking about a database not as a technical object, but rather as a conceptual pattern.

The common aspect of databases (technical ones) is that there's a planned structure (or model) and all information has to fit into that structure. You can't shoe-horn something into a database that doesn't fit the model.

The database pattern is similar – it's for content that has a consistent structure. The individual pieces of content may have no relationship to one another – they certainly don't have the parent-child relationship that hierarchical content does – but they have the same structure, and are made up of the same pieces.

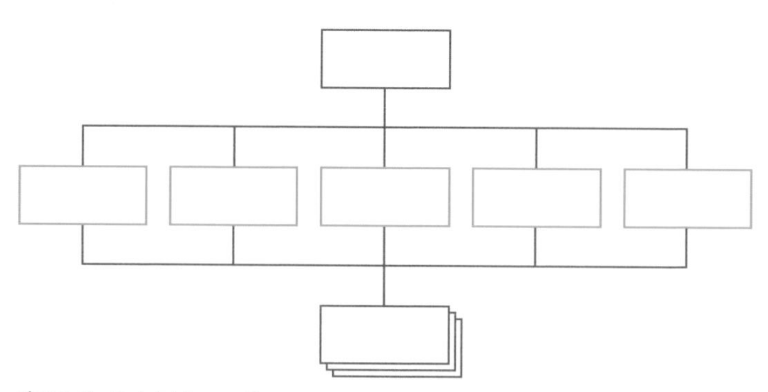

Figure 16 – 6. A database pattern

For example, on a website like etsy, these two items don't really have anything in common:

Figure 16 – 7. A cute crochet beanie (from `etsy.com`)

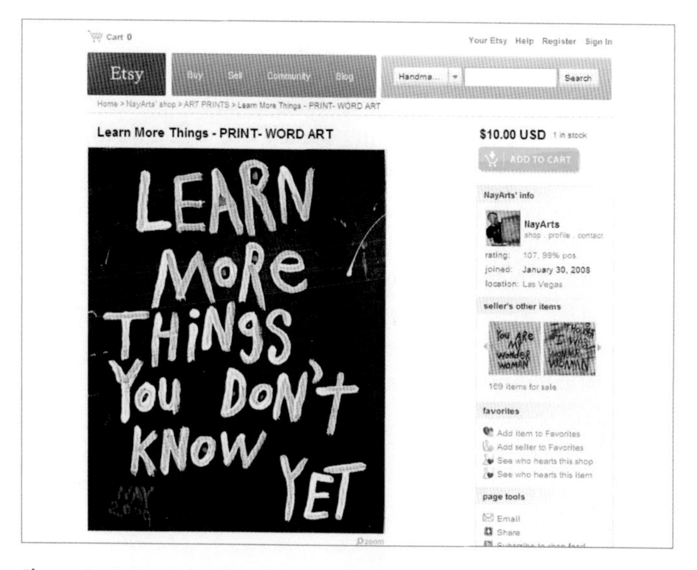

Figure 16 – 8. An art piece (also from `etsy.com`)

But they have the same pieces that make up the listing:

- title
- description
- tags
- materials
- location
- payment methods
- date added
- photograph
- category
- colour

Every product on etsy has to use this same structure.

The database pattern can be used for quite small sets of information, or ones that are very, very large!

One of the big advantages of database structures is that you can store the data once then use the pieces of the structure (the metadata – see the sidebar on page 187) to display information in different ways.

For example, on etsy, you can find content via category (which is a small hierarchy), colour, whether it is local, and even recently added. This gives your people different ways to find content they're interested in. The absolute worst treatment for this type of content would be a hierarchy or any pattern that allows only one way into the content.

Database structures are good for music, product catalogues, books, articles, weblog posts and much more – really, anything where the content pieces have a consistent structure. They are great for situations where people may want to access the content in more than one way.

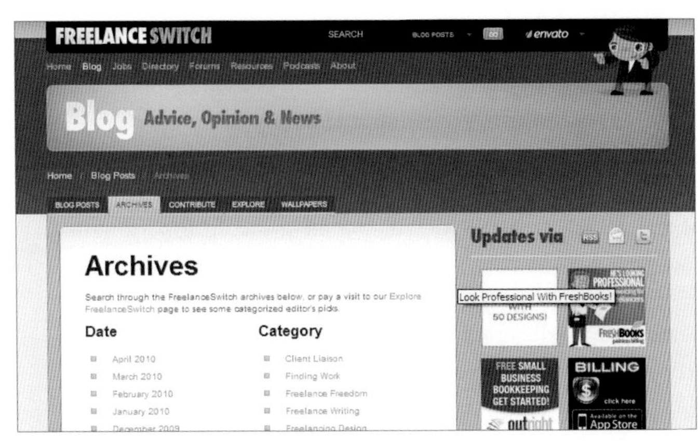

Figure 16 – 9. Freelance Switch allow people to get to articles by date or category (`freelanceswitch.com`)

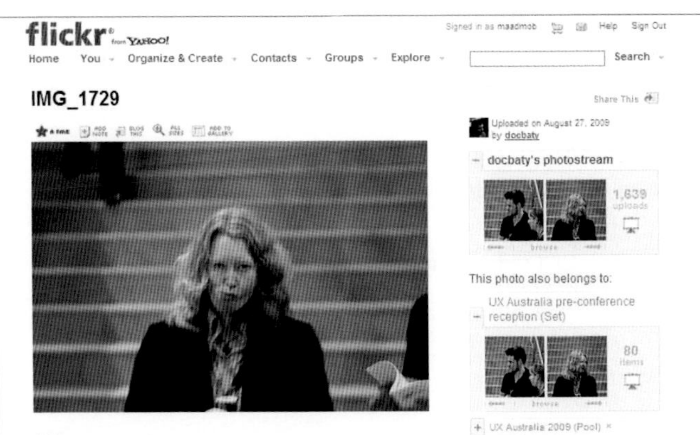

Figure 16 – 10. In flickr, you can find photos by photographer, sets, groups, favourites and tags (`flickr.com`)

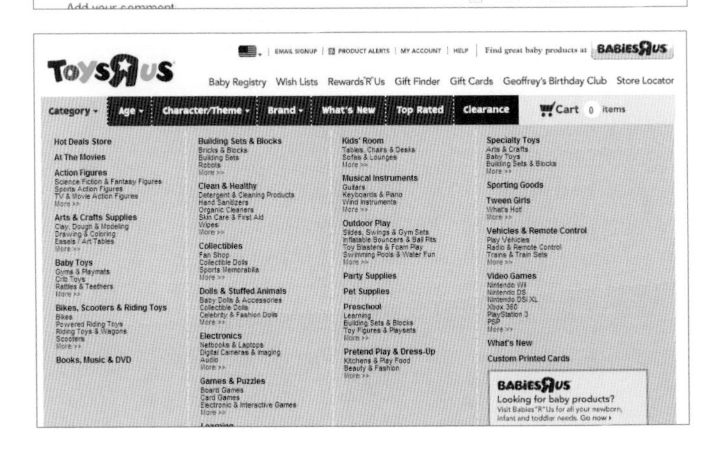

Figure 16 – 11. Toys R Us let you find toys according to category, age, character or brand (`toysrus.com`)

Metadata

Let's not get too technical or scary, but this is where metadata comes into the information architecture story.

Metadata is often defined as 'data about data' (or 'information about information'). It may not be a very helpful definition, but it is an accurate one. Metadata is all of the information that describes or relates to a piece of content.

There are three different types of metadata:

- Intrinsic: What the object actually is
- Administrative: How it is used
- Descriptive: Description of the item

For a weblog like the UX Australia, metadata items may include:

- Type: blog post (intrinsic)
- Author (administrative)
- Date posted (administrative)
- URL (administrative)
- Status: published (administrative)
- Title (descriptive)
- Category (descriptive)
- Tags (descriptive)

This metadata can be used to for two main things:

- Generate lists of particular content (e.g. show all content in the 'Announcements' category)
- Choose what to show on a page (e.g. include title, author, description and category).

That's really all there is to it. The hardest part for a project is deciding what items to collect and what their content is (and so, what categories you will use). We discuss this more in chapter 18.

Hypertext

The hypertext pattern is an interesting one for information architecture as it's almost a pattern of an anti-structure. In this pattern, content pieces are connected to one another simply according to relationships between them. There's no master structure like either a hierarchy or a database – content is just joined together via links.

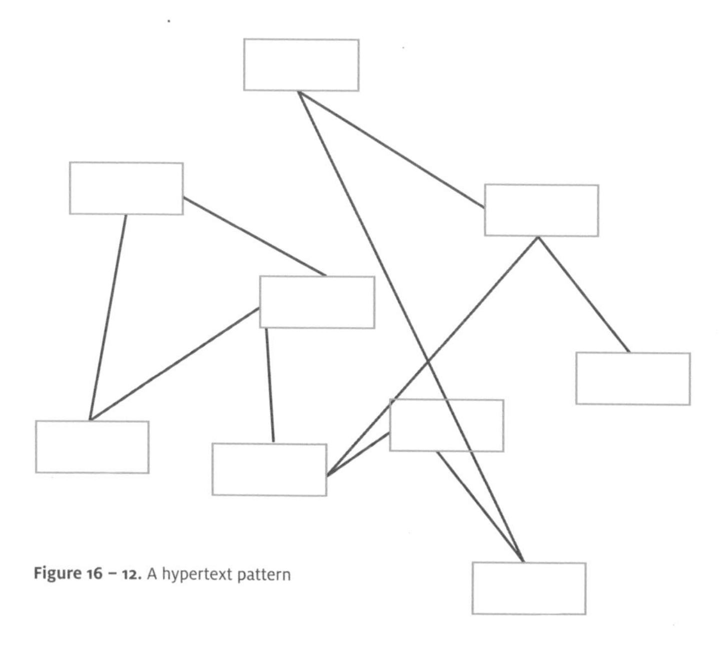

Figure 16 – 12. A hypertext pattern

The best example of a hypertext structure is a wiki. Wikis don't have a pre-planned structure – content is joined by links embedded in the text.

And the best example of a wiki is Wikipedia. It's a perfect embodiment of the hypertext structure. There's no master hierarchy for Wikipedia content, nor is there a strong database structure. (Yes, it is stored in a database, and has some very basic pieces like heading and descriptions. But it isn't a database structure like the ones shown above.) Each page is independent, connected to other pages by associative links.

Figure 16 – 13. Wikipedia pages are connected via links in context (`wikipedia.org`)

Hypertext structures are particularly useful when the content is being developed over a period of time and you don't know exactly what you are going to create. In this situation it would be practically impossible to identify a detailed structure up front, or even to identify a basic pattern for a site. A lot of documentation projects start like this – people write individual pages of documentation as they get around to them and make relationships between them with links.

Many sites that start with a hypertext structure are later reorganised, when the content is known.

The main issue with hypertext structures is their success depends entirely on people making connections between content pieces, and linking them together. Unlike hierarchies where you can see the next level down, or databases where you can display all content of a particular type, hypertext structures don't have the ability to show related content automatically. If authors don't know what's around and don't create links, there is no way for people to find the information.

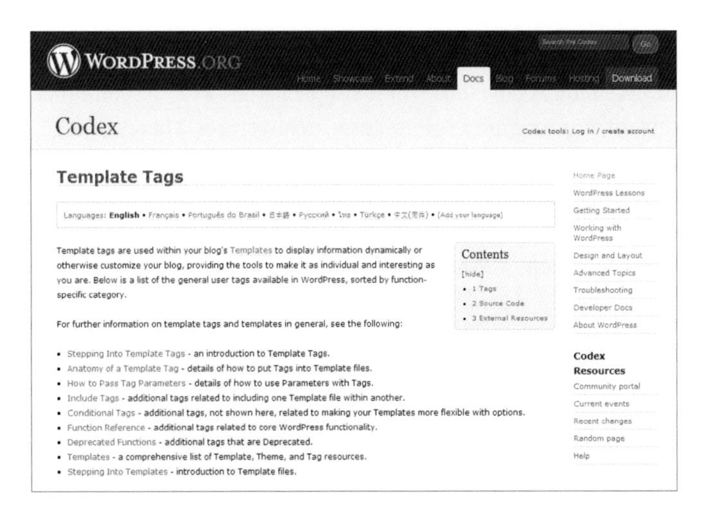

Figure 16 – 14. The wordpress codex (documentation store) is a hypertext pattern – all pages are at the same 'level'. There are some entry pages to help people get started but mostly people will use links to get around (`codex.wordpress.org/Template_Hierarchy`)

Linear

A linear pattern is just as it sounds – one thing follows another in a straight line.

Figure 16 – 15. A linear pattern)

Linear patterns aren't particularly common on the web – we mostly use patterns that let people jump to content in a way that makes sense for them.

However, you can use a linear pattern if you have a situation where people must understand one thing before they move onto another – usually for instructional material. Don't use it unless people really must read things in order, or it will just frustrate them.

Combined patterns

Now let's look at how these three simple patterns can be combined to create more complex information architectures. There's some overlap between these, so don't worry if your site doesn't fall exactly into one or another.

Simple hierarchy + simple database

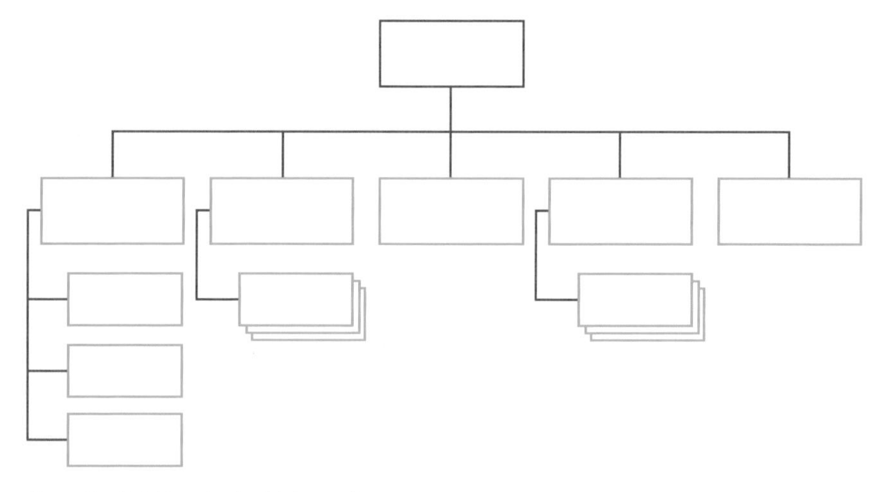

Figure 16 – 16. A hierarchy plus database pattern

One very common pattern (probably the most common pattern on the web) is a combination of a simple hierarchy with some database content.

This pattern is suitable for all sorts of small, medium and large sites. It lets you create hierarchical sections of the website for basic content, and then to use the power of a database to assemble detailed information within a section.

The hierarchy and database pieces may be integrated (e.g. a database structure within one of the sections of the site), side by side (e.g. a database structure as a whole section of the site) or any combination in between.

Case Study: UX Australia

Figure 16 – 17. My conference website does this – some content pages arranged in a small hierarchy (`uxaustralia.com.au/conference-2009/`)

Figure 16 – 18. Presentations use a database structure – this index page shows the title, presenter and short description, sorted in A-Z order. Each links to a presentation page with more detail.

One of the main challenges with this type of pattern is deciding what pieces you'll turn into structured content and what you'll leave as hierarchical. Consider:

- Do you want to re-use something in another part of the site? If you have no need to re-use something, don't worry about structuring it more than necessary – it's just overkill.
- Database structures can help you manage larger volumes of information. If you have a handful of news stories a year, you can manage them as hierarchical content. If you have hundreds a day, you'll probably want to leverage the power of the database structure to automate the display.

Catalog

If the hierarchy + database is the most common pattern on the web, the second most common would definitely be a catalog pattern.

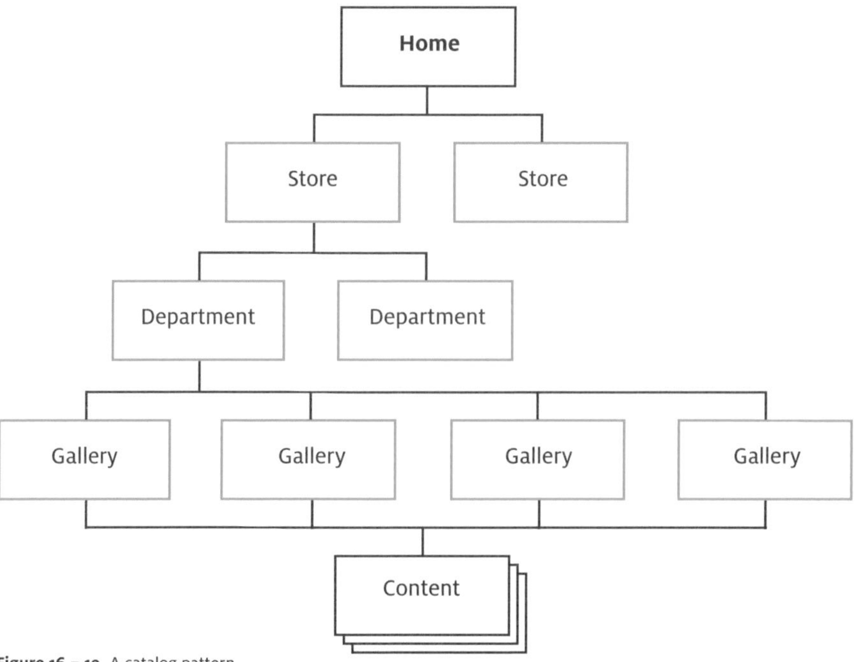

Figure 16 – 19. A catalog pattern

This structure is really just a database pattern, but is worth mentioning because it's so common, particularly in e-commerce. At the bottom level is the content. Above that are up to three levels of hierarchy, depending on the size of the site and type of content.

Jared Spool has written about this pattern extensively[2] and describes three different types of pages between the home page and the content page:

- Gallery pages: these provide direct access to the content pages.
- Department pages: provide access to the galleries.
- Store pages: provide access to the department pages.

How many of these you use depends on how large your site is. As you can imagine, a huge product catalog may use all three.

Jared describes the gallery pages as the hardest working pages on a website as these are the point where people make a decision (or not) to drill down to your content pages.

[1] This pattern is described in more detail in these articles by Jared Spool: http://www.uie.com/brainsparks/2005/11/28/the-8-types-of-navigation-pages/ and http://www.uie.com/events/roadshow/articles/galleries/. It is also described in detail in Jared and Robert Hoekman Jr's book Web anatomy: Interaction design frameworks that work (New Riders, 2010)

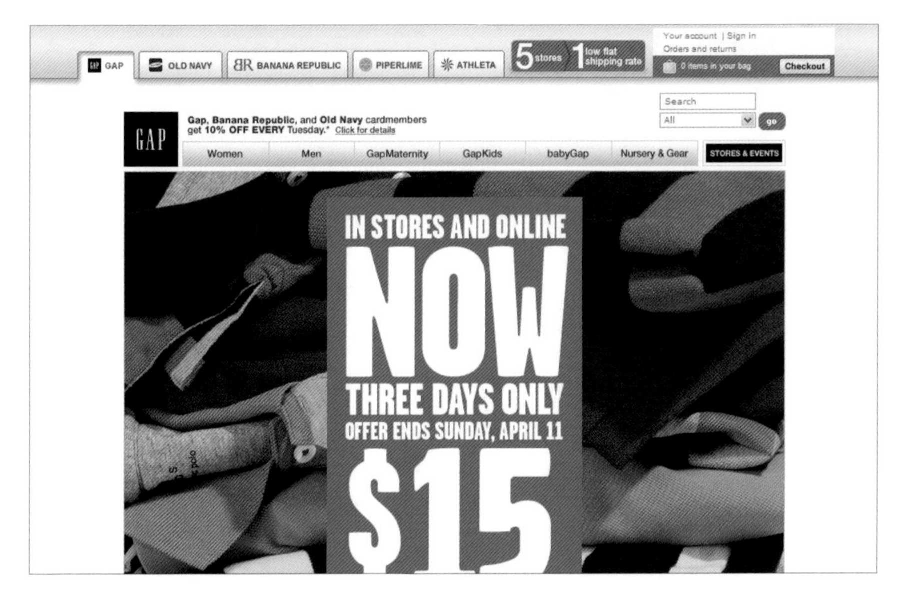

Figure 16 – 20. The Gap home page (gap.com)

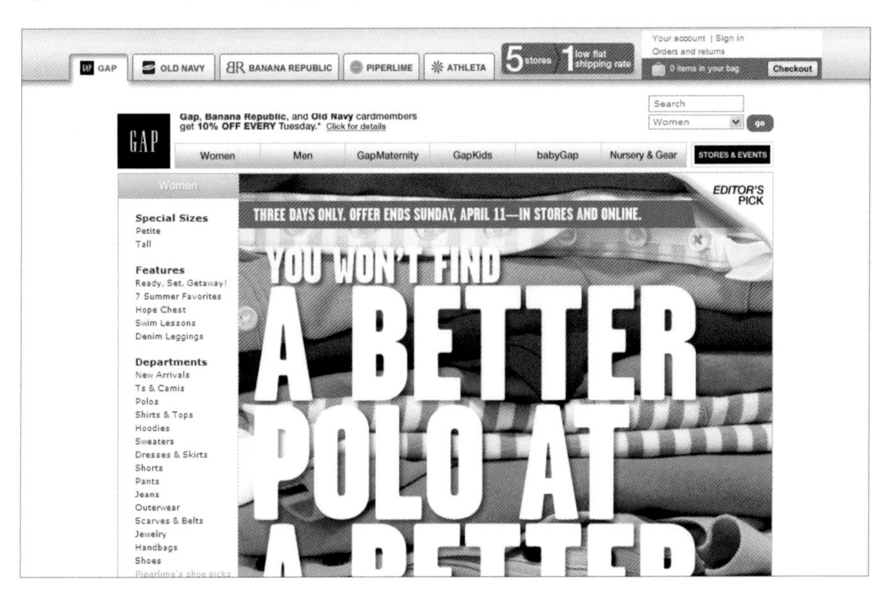

Figure 16 – 21. Gap women

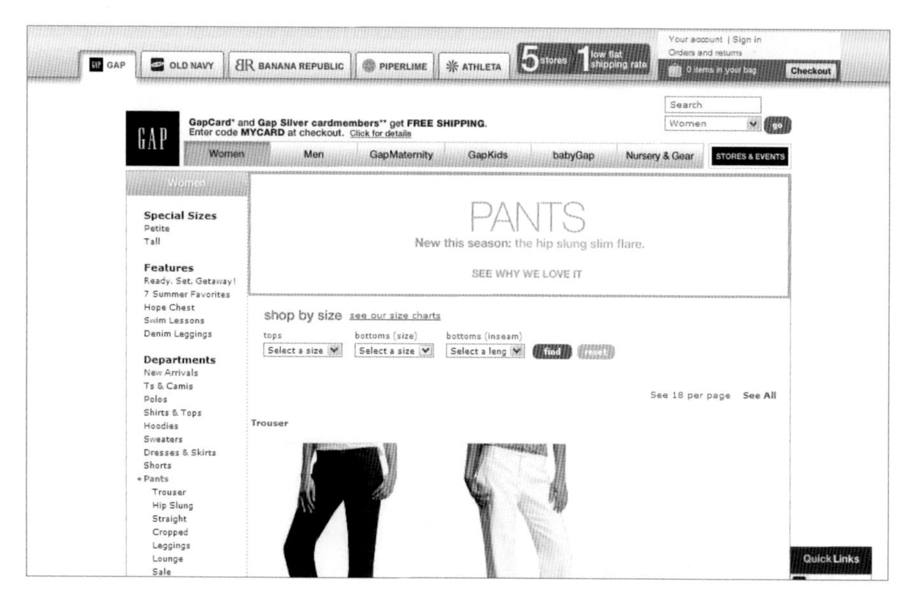

Figure 16 – 22. Gap women's pants

Figure 16 – 23. Gap women's pants, straight-leg

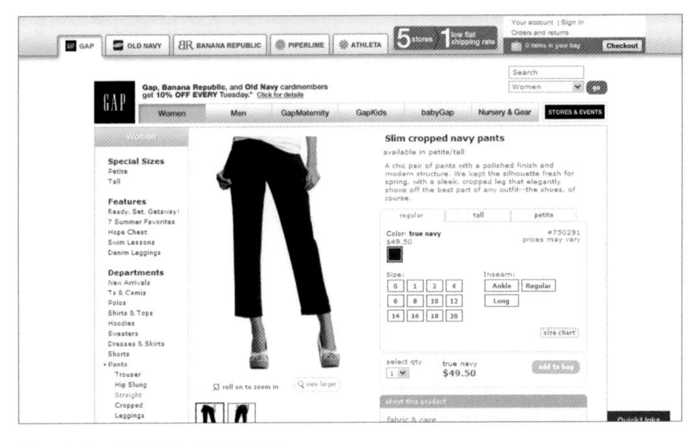

Figure 16 – 24. A Gap content page

Hub & spoke

The hub & spoke pattern is really just a hierarchy. However, it is worth noting as a separate pattern as the way people use it is different to a hierarchy.

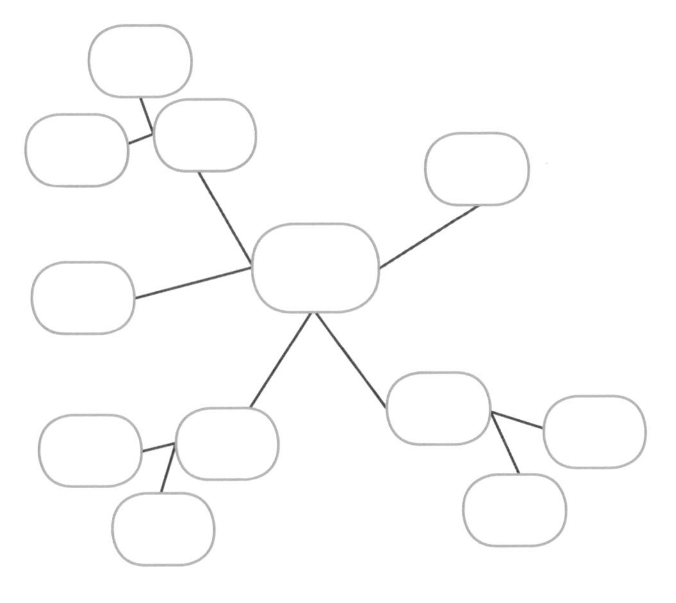

Figure 16 – 25. A hub & spoke pattern

With a hierarchy, people tend to start at a point in it (often the top level) and move down into deeper and deeper content, often sticking within the one branch of the hierarchy. With a hub and spoke, people move down one level into something more detailed, return to the starting point (the hub) then may move to another detailed page, back to the hub and so on.

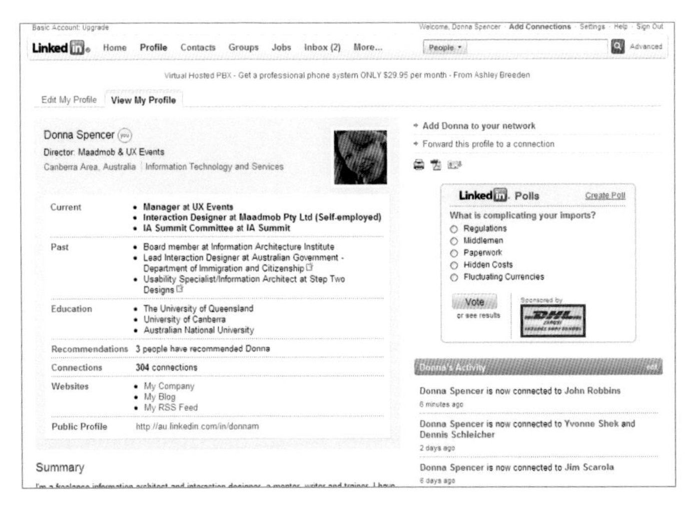

Figure 16 – 26. For LinkedIn, the profile page acts as a hub - it's the place you return to often (`linkedin.com`)

Subsites

I do a lot of work on very large sites – large government sites, large university sites and large intranets. One pattern I've used time and time again is one I call 'subsites' (at one stage people were calling these 'portals' but I haven't heard that term used for a while).

With this pattern the overall site is a series of subsites, held together by a home page or top-level pages. The subsites can use any pattern, and don't all need to use the same one.

In some situations where I've seen this pattern, the subsites all use a consistent approach to navigation and page layout, which

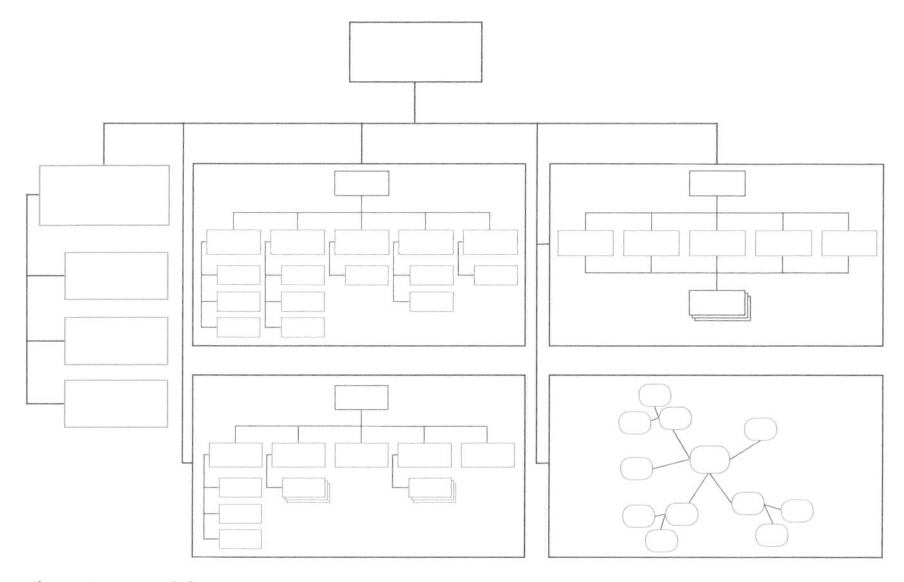

Figure 16 – 27. A subsites pattern

reinforces the idea that the subsites are part of a larger brand. In other situations the subsites have quite different approaches to navigation and page layout as is appropriate for the content and audience, but still use some approach to show they are part of a whole.

This pattern is particularly useful for large organisations that have a range of responsibilities or a range of brands, but still need to represent themselves as a whole. It's also perfect for any situation where, after content analysis, you realise there will be no one-size-fits-all approach to the IA of various sections, and that you'll never be able to force them all into a common approach.

As you can imagine, universities are a perfect example – the university as a whole represents an organisation and brand, the content is diverse, and the individual parts of the university have different communication needs (and people, politics and ego). The same is true for government, big businesses and some intranets.

Example - ABC

As an example, the ABC (Australian Broadcasting Corporation) has a very wide range of TV shows, radio stations (with associated shows), news and other online offerings.

Figure 16 – 28. For the ABC, the home page aims to allow access to the many subsites

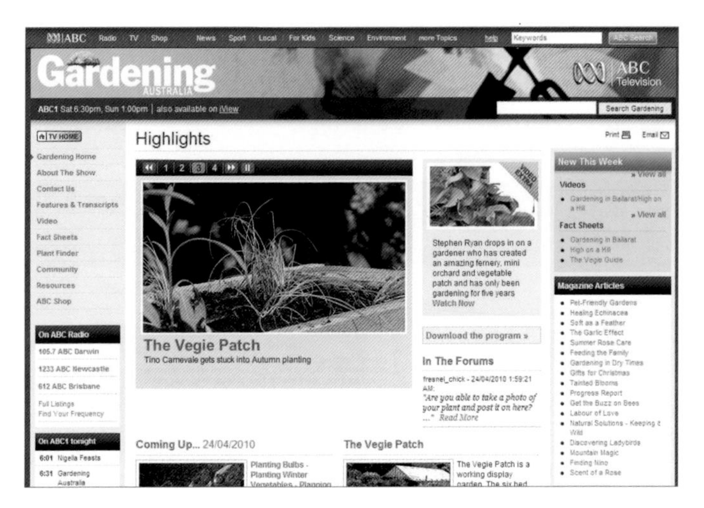

Figure 16 – 29. For the ABC, the subsites each have their own approach to navigation, within the overall brand (`abc.net.au/gardening`)

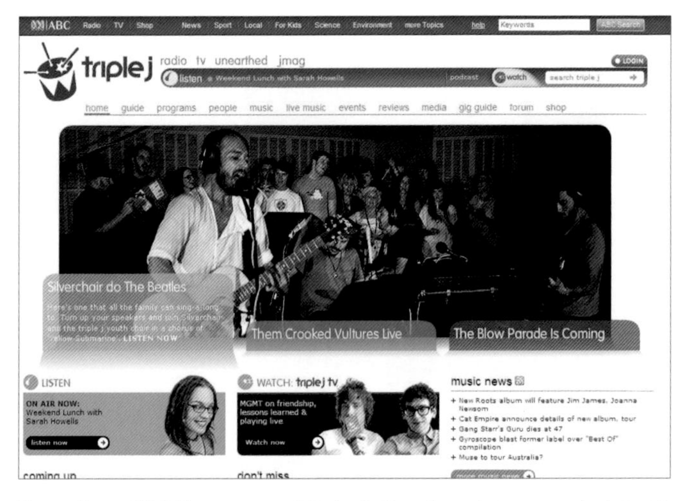

Figure 16 – 30. TripleJ has an approach that suits its audience (`abc.net.au/triplej/`)

Example: Government websites

I use this pattern a lot for government websites. Many government departments (at least in Australia) are cobbled together and have a range of unrelated responsibilities.

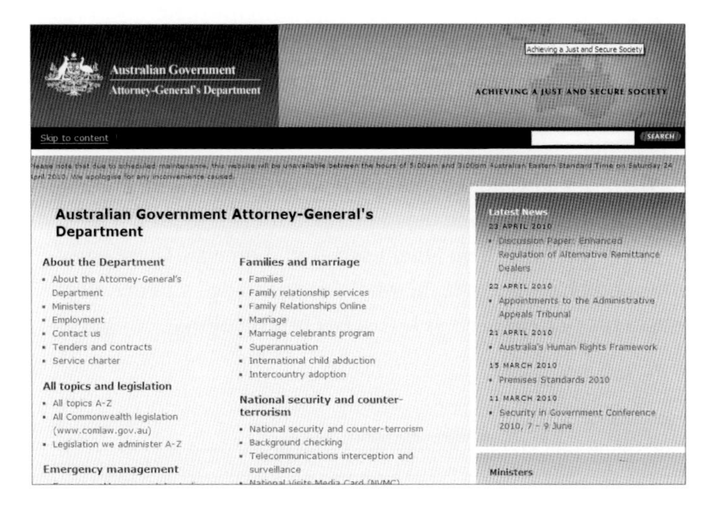

Figure 16 – 31. The Attorney-General's Department is responsible for a huge range of unrelated things. (`ag.gov.au`)

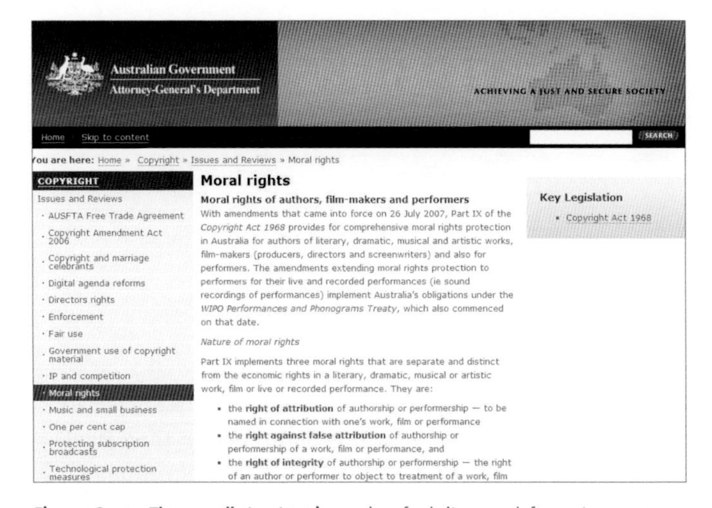

Figure 16 – 32. The overall structure is a series of subsites – each from 3 to 100 pages, in a 3-level hierarchy (`http://www.ag.gov.au/www/agd/agd.nsf/page/Copyright`)

Focused entry points

In a lot of situations (again, mainly for large sites) you'll learn it won't be possible to 'organise' the content in a single way that will suit all the users – usually because they have different information needs and different levels of experience with the topic.

In this situation, I've used a 'focused entry points' pattern. When I use this pattern, I set up the site using whichever pattern best suits the content and the people who need it (usually a hierarchy).

Then, acknowledging that some people simply won't be able to find information using the main structure, I provide a series of 'entry points' that help other users find their way. These entry points don't have to cover the whole site content – you may use them to provide easy access to just key information.

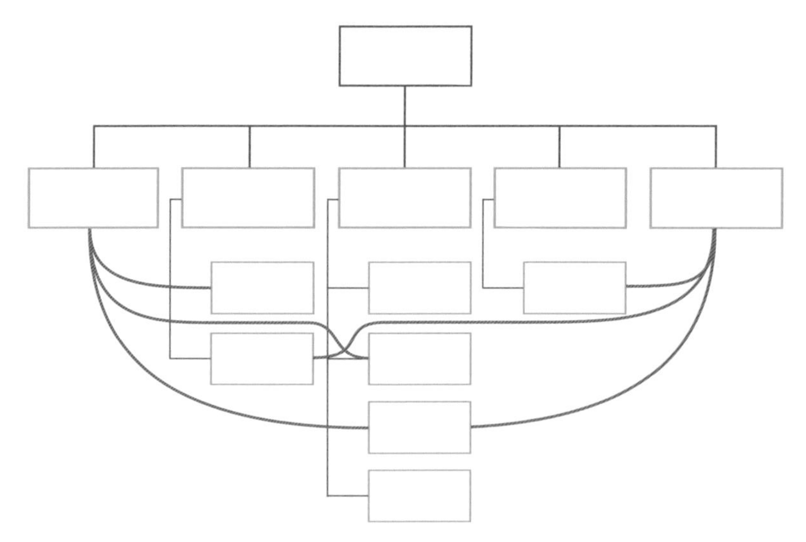

Figure 16 – 33. The focused entry points pattern

In chapter 15 I described some classification schemes that could be hard to use – particularly things like audience and task schemes. I've found these are far better as entry points than as the overall approach to the site structure. For example, you may organise a website with a basic hierarchical structure, then provide entry points for different audiences or tasks.

Example – Australia's Water

The Australian government's water website contains information on Government policies and programs (as many government sites do). The names of the programs and policies are not always obvious – some people know them well (other government folks and the media), and some have no idea (the rest of Australia). Both need to find content deep in the website.

This website is a perfect example for the focused entry points pattern. The main information architecture is a simple hierarchy, organised around the policies and programs:

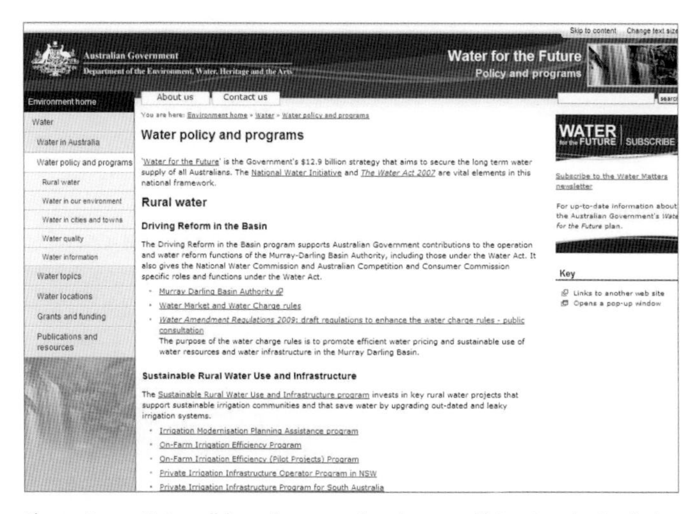

Figure 16 – 34. Water policies and programs, loosely grouped into categories for display (`environment.gov.au/water/policy_programs/`)

Topical 'entry points', like desalination, rainwater tanks and saving water, provide access for people with interest in particular topics:

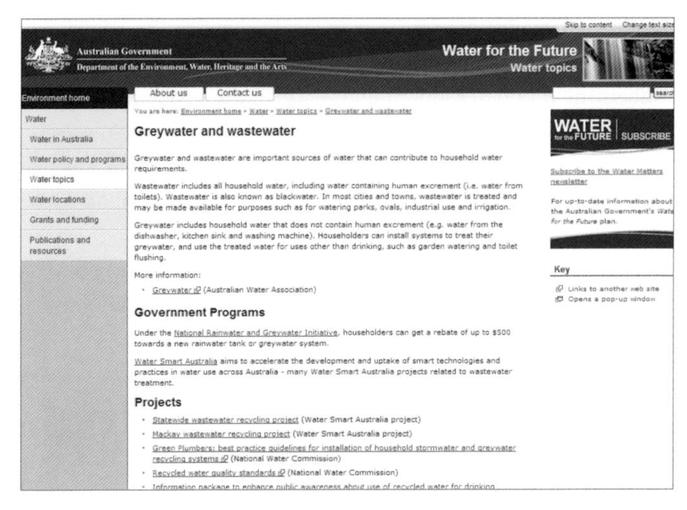

Figure 16 – 35. A topic entry page - this links off to pages throughout the site

Example – Australian National University

University sites often use the entry points pattern as well. Overall, the site uses a subsite pattern, with content is organised around individual schools or faculties. They then provide entry points for particular audiences – particularly for school leavers.

Figure 16 – 36. Study @ANU acts as an entry point, particularly for school leavers (`studyat.anu.edu.au`)

Tagged

A tagged pattern uses either the basic database or hypertext pattern. Each item in the site is 'tagged' with keywords, and those keywords are used to provide access to the content.

The tagging may be done by the original authors of the content, the readers or by some central authority (such as the web team).

This pattern works well for very large collections of diverse content, especially where the content readers will have different ideas what it is about.

It can be useful in situations where people aren't sure what they are looking for or what's around. The tags can help people to explore and find related information.

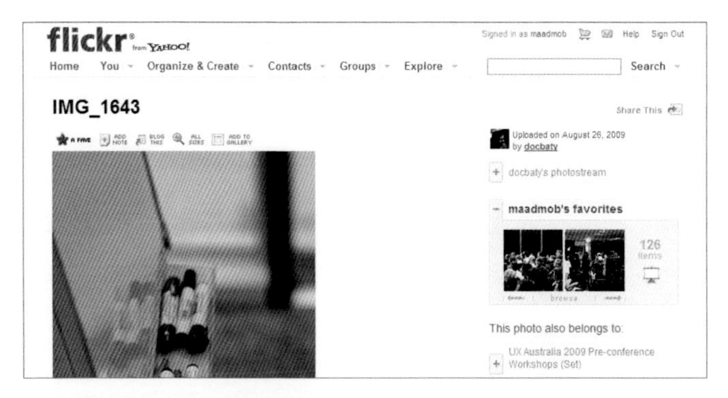

Figure 16 – 37. Flickr includes tags on all photos, letting you find all photos with a particular tag – photographers and visitors can both add tags (`flickr.com`)

Figure 16 – 38. ABC news uses tags - these are added by the ABC (`abc.net.au/news`)

	Suits content
Hierarchy	Small sites Varied content
Database	Content with a consistent structure
Hypertext	Content being developed
Linear	Sequential content
Simple hierarchy + database	General content plus some content types with consistent structure
Catalog	Large sets of structured content
Hub & spoke	Hierarchical content
Subsites	Large corporate and government sites with many independent sections of content
Focused entry points	Any, but usually a hierarchy
Tagged	Large sets of content

Suits people	Challenges & issues
Read broad information and then more detail	Balancing breadth and depth
Want to access content in more than one way	All content must fit the structure Don't collect more metadata than you'll need
Follow links to related material	Authors need to know what to link to You may want to restructure later when the content is complete
When people need to understand one thing before progressing to another	Only use it when people really must read in sequence or people will be frustrated
	Choosing what content to structure and what to leave as unstructured
Finding a particular section then looking at detailed products	
When people will want to return to a central place each time they move to new content	
	Deciding whether the subsites should use the same approach to navigation, page layout and brand
People may want to access it in different ways, and there is no 'best' way	
Find information according to their own terminology. Find related information easily	Who does the tagging, and do the tags come from a central set or generated by the authors

17

Labels and language

Words. In all IA work, everything comes down to the words. No matter how well you group content together or how easy it is to see on a page, the success comes down to what you call things. Words will make your IA a success, or have people staring stupidly at the page wondering what to click on.

Your IA, the words you use (labelling) and how you put it all in front of people (usually navigation) are all deeply connected. I've separated them into chapters for convenience so we can discuss each separately, but they really do all work together. I'm starting with labelling as it will be handy to know what a good label is when you start creating an IA.

What labels do

As we discussed in the section about information-seeking behaviours, people come to a set of information with an idea in their head. It may be a quick task to learn something specific, or a longer research task. Either way, they have some pre-conceived ideas about what they are interested in, what they already call it, and what they hope to see.

If they arrive at your information and immediately see the word that's in their head, they'll click on it, learn something and be satisfied. If they don't see what's in their head, they may look around to see if there is be something similar enough, and may spend a bit of time wondering what each thing is about. But no-one likes to feel stupid (and believe me this is something that makes people feel stupid) – if they can't figure out your labelling pretty quickly, they'll go somewhere else. (And if there's nowhere to go, they'll just be cross at you).

That's why we want to make sure our labels are great.

Where are labels used

Before we start into the characteristics of labels, let me explain better what I'm talking about. Labels are all the things that describe chunks of content. They'll include not only the names of items in your navigation and the hyperlinks you use in content and lists, but also the headings that describe chunks of content.

Characteristics of good labels

The best labels are dull, boring and completely obvious – they just work and no-one ever thinks twice about them. Often when I tell people this they look scared and almost start hyperventilating – they think their labels should be interesting and innovative.

Make your content interesting and your features innovative, but don't try to break new ground with your labels. Keep them simple and stable.

The best labels:

- call things by their correct name
- are consistent
- use terms that your audience uses
- are as clear as possible

As a list, this looks pretty straightforward, but doing it is sometimes a very hard balance. Let's look at each one.

Call things by their correct name

One of the hardest issues you'll come across in labelling is whether to use 'correct' terms or those your audience understands. Sometimes these two things align with each other naturally. Often they don't.

This is something I've learned the hard way over time. When I started out, I thought I should make sure the labelling was the same as what the audience used. But the more I did this, the more I was unhappy with what I was coming up with. Your audience is often wrong, using terms that are out-of-date or just plain incorrect. Follow them and you risk not only losing credibility, but also making it harder for people who do know the content well.

The right answer is to use the most correct terminology you can use, in the context of what your audience knows. Correct terminology will describe the content well – helping people understand what a section of content is about. It may even help them use more correct terminology, which will help them learn and find more information.

If there is a big gap between correct terminology and the terms your audience uses, think about how you may deal with this on screen. For example, you may decide to include descriptions as well as labels, or provide different ways to get to the same content.

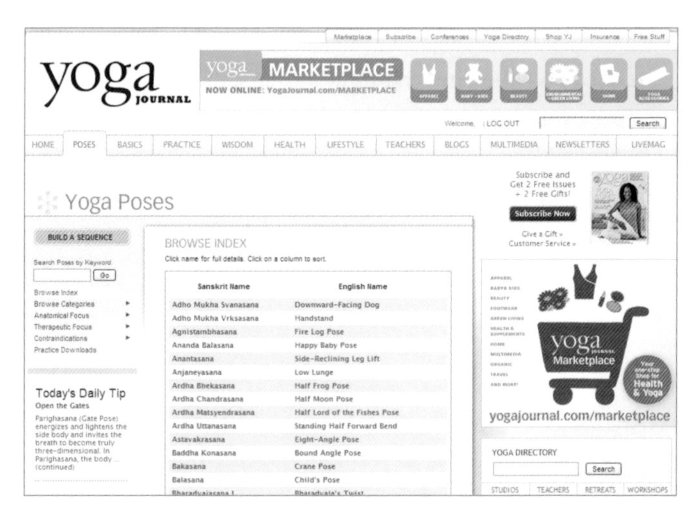

Figure 17 – 1. Yoga journal shows the Sanskrit and English name side by side (`yogajournal.com`)

Consistent

When it comes to terminology, consistency is very important. You need to be absolutely consistent within your own set of content – people naturally assume things that look the same are the same, and things that look different are different (who'd have thought it!). If you're going to use a particular label, stick with it throughout your site – don't say *Contact us* in one place and *Get in touch* in another. If two hyperlinks on a page go to the same content, label them the same way (or at least similarly enough that people know they're the same).

It can be handy, though not essential, to be consistent with content outside your own site. If there's a term everyone in your industry uses, and your audience is likely to know it, just use it. Let people use the knowledge they've learned outside your site to make life easier on your site. You can't go wrong with simple things like *Contact us, About us* and *Our services*. There's little point trying to be fancy here – it will only lose people.

People often ask me about consistency within a label set – for example, should they use all verbs, labels that all use the same part of speech or all one-word labels. I personally don't think it matters too much – I've never seen a usability test where someone anyone reacted to a bit of inconsistency. (Very occasionally someone will comment on it, but I've never seen it stop them from finding the right link.) But for the sake of neatness (which I do like) if you can make your label set consistent, go for it. It may make it slightly easier for your audience and will certainly stop people from nagging you about it! Never create a bad label just to make the set consistent though – that will certainly fail.

Use terms that your audience uses

While I said you should make sure your labels are accurate for the content they're describing, you'll often have plenty of room to work within this, and many ways to describe something. When making this decision, think about the terms your audience knows and understands, and use these (your user research will help you here).

Even within a single language, some words are more common in particular regions of the world, even down to quite small groups of people. Pay attention to these and use them where you can.

Be careful with jargon as well. I won't say you shouldn't use it at all. After all, I would never say 'Australian Broadcasting

Corporation' – everyone in Australia knows it as the ABC[1]. But only use jargon your audience knows, and make certain they do know it. (I once worked on a military intranet and had to resist the urge to remove the acronyms – staff did actually know them all.)

Figure 17 – 2. Imagine my surprise when I showed this image to an American audience in a workshop and asked what it was (we call it a stubbie holder, but the audience were yelling out coozie)

Clear as possible

Clear labels are obviously better than unclear labels. Here are a few easy ways to make sure your labels are clear.

Use as long a term as you need to describe the content or idea. Don't try to find a shorter term if it makes the label less clear or more abstract – go with the longer label. If you need many long labels for something like top level navigation, that's fine. Design navigation that lets you use longer labels and is suitable for the words you need to use – not the other way around.

Use words that are as concrete as possible. For example, don't use Small, Medium and Large if you can better describe what these labels actually mean.

[1] With acronyms, it's particularly important to know what terms your audience use. If I were using ABC on a site aimed at Americans, they would assume it meant 'American Broadcasting Company'

Make sure your labels clearly explain the content they represent. People should be able to guess what might be in a section by the label and get pretty close. My daughter's school's website has a section called Parents (not For Parents, just Parents). I thought it might contain news specific for parents, or ways for parents to be involved in the school (after all, it's a school website – most of the content is for parents). Imagine my surprise when I found out this is where the canteen and after-school care information was – something I'd previously looked for and thought wasn't around. The label just doesn't communicate what is included in the section.

Don't use cute, obscure labels. Well, I guess you can, but you risk people not clicking on them. If you absolutely know your audience is willing to explore your site, go ahead. But if yours isn't the type of site people will be willing to explore, make your labels plain and clear.

That doesn't mean you can't use slightly informal language, or be fun in your labelling – just be clear at the same time. Clear labels aren't necessarily formal. Be consistent with your brand and writing style – use friendly labels if that's your voice, or use more formal labels if your writing is more formal.

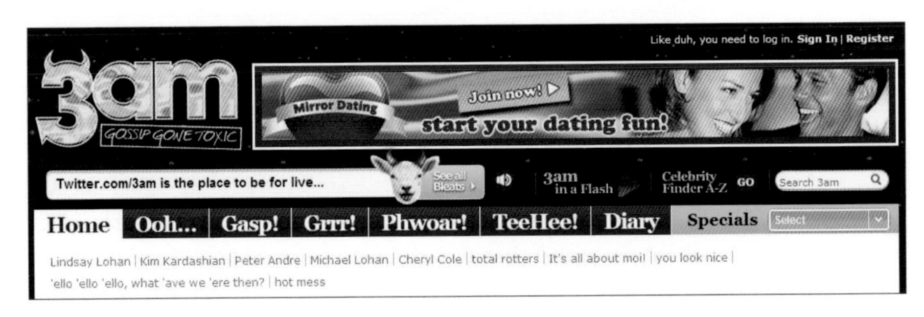

Figure 17 – 3. You can only get away with labelling like this if it really matches your brand (3am.co.uk)

Where to get ideas for labels

You can get ideas for your labels from a number of places:

- Content: look at the words used in your content and the labels they suggest.
- User research: your research will contain hundreds of words that describe how your audience phrase ideas and concepts. Make sure you look at your search logs – you'll see exactly what people are looking for.
- Card sorting: in a card sort, the last step is often for people to provide a label describing what the group of cards is about. I often find these labels a bit long or informal to use, but they can give you some ideas.
- What everyone else does: look around at competitors or other content like yours and see what other people do. If there's a consistent approach, you can do your users a favour and use that.

If you're tossing up between two terms, use google trends to see the popularity of particular terms.

Expect changes

Finally, expect labels to change over time. As you add more content to a site, or move things around, labels will need to change as well. Language is subtle and slight changes in words may be needed over time.

For intranet work, as organisations change the labels in common use also change. Older employees remember and use the old labels, but new employees will have no idea what to use. Keep on top of the terms being used and adapt over time.

Keep an eye on how people are using your site – in particular, watch search terms and see if there's any change in the terms people are using over time.

Chapter summary

No matter how well you group content and how easy it is to see on a page, success will come down to the words you use – the labels.

The best labels:

- Call things by their correct name
- Are consistent
- Use terminology that your audience uses
- Are as clear as possible

Further reading

For more information on labelling, see `http://delicious.com/practicalIA/labelling`

18

How to create an IA

Let's imagine you've done all the things we've talked about so far. You know what you're aiming to achieve for your client or business. You know about your users, what they need and how they'll approach your information. You understand what your content is about.

And you know lots of things about groups, classification schemes, IA patterns and labelling.

Guess what? You're ready to create the IA for your site. ("Finally!", you say.)

This is the scary part of the whole process. Now you have to go and create something.

How you actually go about doing this will depend on how you work and how you think. (It will be slightly different for everyone.)

If you like working stepwise through things – this leads to this leads to this – you may be wondering 'how' to step from the information you collected to come up with the perfect information architecture. Sorry, but this step isn't linear (and, as you may remember from chapter 10, there is no one perfect outcome). If you like linear processes that show how you got to an outcome, you may find this a bit hard.

If you're a more intuitive, creative type, this step may be easier for you. You may be more comfortable taking that creative leap and synthesising everything into a new IA. You'll probably find this fairly easy (as long as you've collected enough inputs).

Here's a step-by-step guide to help you work through it.

Step 1: Decide what do you need to create

First, think about what you're doing at this step.

If you're working with a hierarchical pattern (or even a combined hierarchy and database pattern) you're probably trying to come up with top level groups and sub-groups.

If you're working with mostly database content you're probably trying to come up with attributes for your content.

Step 2: Just do it

Now, draft your information architecture.

Did you expect more?

Look, you've done all the preparation you need. As long as you know what you're trying to create, and you've gathered enough information about your users and content, there's no point fiddling around.

At this point, the best thing is to let everything you know swish around in your head and just make something up. Yes, just have a go at it. Draft a set of top level groups or attributes.

Yes, right now.

Really.

Go do it – start scribbling on a piece of paper or a whiteboard, or just work through it a bit in your head. Once you get over the fear of the blank piece of paper or whiteboard and start, it will all begin to flow.

I wrote a blog post about this once and said 'just make it up'. Judging by the comments, some people thought I was saying you should make it up out of nothing. I'm not suggesting that at all. Make it up based on what you already know. You won't be pulling it out of nowhere – you'll be synthesising everything you already know.

But don't try to make it perfect. Just get something (or maybe a couple of things) down as a starting point. Don't agonise over trying to get the perfect answer straight away.

Step 3: Check it

This step is more important than the previous one. No matter how experienced you are, your first draft of an IA will not work perfectly. Mine never do either, and most experienced IAs tell me the same thing. But you won't know that until you check it.

Again, this step is different depending on whether you're working with a hierarchy or database content.

If you're working with hierarchical content:

- Look at your draft groups. Think about what you know about your audience. (Start by thinking about just your core audience or core tasks.) Does it look like these will make sense for what they need to do? Will they understand the groupings? Will the right things be grouped together? Will they understand the labels?
- Then look at your content. Slot it into your draft groups. Does it all fit in? Does it fit in easily, or could some things be in more than one place? Is there content that doesn't really fit anywhere?

If you're working with database content:

- Look at the attributes of each type of content. Look at what you know about your audience and what they need. Will those attributes give them good ways to filter, sort or otherwise narrow down your content? Will they understand what each attribute actually means?
- Get a sample of the content and assign the attributes to the sample content. Can you assign it all easily? Are there some objects that don't quite work as well as others? Are there some attributes that you realise need some more work?

Step 4: Revise it

For both types of content, go back to step 2 and revise what you've created.

Look at your draft, what you know about your audience, and your content. See if it looks like it will work.

Each time you do this, first check core tasks and core content. As you revise it, start looking at the more unusual tasks and content. Go deeper and play with more detail every time.

Step 5: Stop

You'll know when to stop revising. There's a point where you look at your draft IA, the audience needs and the content, and it just feels good. It feels simple and right and you can't tweak it much more.

I'm not sure if this happens to everyone (although talking to people in my workshops makes me think it's not uncommon), but when I do this step another strange thing happens. Not only does it feel good, I also feel totally stupid for spending so much time to get there. "Why did I think it would be so hard a couple of days ago? It's so obvious. I should have been able to do it faster."

That's one way I know it's going to work. I feel that way because I've managed to move from something messy to something simple and elegant. Hard thinking went into it, but it looks so obvious at the end.

Step 6: Discuss

In a project, this is a good time to start talking to other people about the draft IA. Talk to your client, your colleagues or your subject matter experts. However, don't do it until you've worked this right through – there's little point showing them a half-baked idea.

When you talk to them, be prepared to explain how you came up with what you did. Be prepared to explain the ideas that didn't work out and you threw away, and the rationale for the things you kept. But most of all, be prepared for nitty-gritty detailed questions about edge-case content and user needs. I'll tell you a secret – if people are talking to you about detailed edge cases, the core is good. Otherwise they'd be picking holes in the core idea.

If they are picking holes in the core idea, listen to them. Think about what's going on and why they don't understand the core idea. In all my experiences doing this, I've learned that if a lot of people have a objections to the draft IA, it's coming from somewhere. And in the long run it isn't going to work.

The last time I presented a draft IA that I thought was okay, some of the subject-matter people had reservations about it. They expressed it politely as, "I'm still not sure about this but we'll see what happens". I was halfway through writing the content when I finally realised they were right – it wasn't going to work out. My mistake in this case was I didn't understand the content as well as I thought I did (and it was based on some tricky legislation), so I didn't see that it wasn't quite going to work. I rewrote the content and re-jigged the IA at the same time. And I went back and said, "Remember when you said this may not work? Well, it didn't".

Tips for this process

As a series of steps, this process is fairly straightforward. Here are some extra tips for doing it.

How many content groups?

How many content groups are too few or too many? As you may predict, there's no right answer for this – it depends a lot on your site and content.

You want people to easily find whatever they need for their current task. That involves three steps:

1. looking through the list of groups
2. ignoring the things that aren't relevant
3. choosing between the things that might be relevant

You might think fewer groups would make this faster. And certainly the first step will be. But if you have fewer groups, the groups themselves can become more abstract and harder to interpret, making the second and third steps harder.

What if you had more groups and less abstraction? Well, the first step – looking through the list – would be slower. But the second and third steps should be faster as the content is less abstract.

As you can see, it's a balance. If you're not sure which way to go, create two versions using this process. Test both with your audience and see which one works better.

A comment from one of my blog posts illustrates this perfectly:

> *"I don't want to sound like a smartass (or whatever the Australian equivalent is), but the perfect number for items in a navbar is ZERO and each item added after that is a compromise.*
>
> *Zero items requires zero interpretation by the user and every item after that requires increasingly more complex interpretation. I know zero items isn't practical (or politically realistic), but I think it's worth thinking of the challenge as "what do I absolutely need to add to this list?" rather than "how can I whittle down this list?"*
>
> *Having said that, I agree with you that long lists can work just fine (and that users proving it in testing is a powerful way to sell it internally). The key to long lists is the speed with which a user can ignore everything else other than what they're looking for. If we can make it more about ignoring than interpreting, we have a better chance for success. For example, if you put an alphabetical list of a hundred names in front of me and my goal is to find my own name, it is an exercise in ignoring the 99 items that aren't my name."*
>
> Dan Willis, uxcrank.com

Navigation design

As you draft the IA, you will have ideas for navigation. Though you should work through the IA first (to get your groups and labelling right), you can't really separate the two. Sketch your navigation ideas so you don't forget them, but concentrate on getting the IA done at this point.

Which classification scheme to use

One thing people ask me all the time at workshops is whether they should organise their content according to an audience scheme, a topic-based scheme or something different. Apart from reminding them that audience schemes are hard (see page 175), I usually recommend they draft both. One of them will just work out better than the other. It really is the easiest way to resolve these types of questions.

If you have two approaches you think work well, another way to choose between them is to run a usability test (which you should do anyway – see chapter 19). This will usually give you a clear indication of which one will be more effective.

If you end up with both schemes working, or if one works well for one audience and one works well for another, think about how you could use both in your website. Maybe you'll mainly structure the content around topics but provide an audience-based entry point as well (see the section about focused entry points patterns in chapter 16).

If stakeholders hate it

If your client, stakeholders, authors or subject-matter experts are very negative about the IA, or have fixed ideas about how you should have done it, you may want to:

- See if you've actually missed something, or taken it too far. Go back to the beginning for the parts that people are particularly negative about and rework it. It's hard to throw away existing ideas and start again, but this may be just what you need to pick up what you've missed.
- Work their idea right through using the same process as above. See if it works. If it doesn't, take detailed notes about the parts that didn't work and why so you can explain it to them. As you'll learn with experience, something that looks sensible and straightforward on the surface often isn't.

Team or individual

You can do this by yourself, or with a team. I find it easier to think through the initial draft by myself. For anything complex I find it hard to think about the IA, audience needs and content all at once while discussing it with people at the same time. If you're the same and work in a team, you could all create first drafts independently (and do at least one round of checking content and user needs) and then get together to work through the best parts of each.

If you are doing this in a team, try not to fall into the trap of talking about whether you should approach it in a particular way. For example, don't have a long discussion about whether to use 'Products and services' as a single group or a combined one. Try both out with your content and user needs and see which will look better.

The mechanics of the process

Are you wondering just how you should do this? Should you create a site map (more on site maps in chapter 20) in a computer drawing program, a mind-mapping program, or even a spreadsheet?

It doesn't really matter how you go do it as long as it suits how you work. Sometimes I jot everything I know on sticky notes and shuffle them around my desk until I start to see some patterns that work. Sometimes I stick all my user research and content ideas around my whiteboard and scribble for a while. Sometimes (and this is more common for me) I sit in my comfy office chair with my feet on the desk and play around in my head (which really freaks project managers out as they think I'm doing nothing). Occasionally I sort it out during a run or a swim. Sometimes I'll do this with a client and a whiteboard and lots of markers. It really depends what works best for you.

The only way you shouldn't do is in front of a computer. Computer programs are great for writing down what you've come up with, but most people think more creatively when they're on their feet at a whiteboard or doing physical work like shuffling papers around a big desk. Even if you love to mind-map with a computer program, at least start by doing it on paper.

Figure 18 – 1. Content written on green sticky notes

Figure 18 – 2. User needs on white sticky notes

Figure 18 – 3. Shuffle around until they start working. Labels on pink sticky notes

Make notes of your rationale

As you work through the draft IA, make a note of the ideas you discarded and why you kept what you did. This will help when you are talking with your client or team and someone asks 'why didn't you do such-and-such'. You'll be able to remember what you thought about and explain clearly why it didn't work.

You don't have to create a big, formal document. Some scribbled notes will do, or even photographs of your whiteboards at various stages. I promise that as you work through ideas and discard some, you'll forget why you made particular decisions.

IA that changes over time

Some sites will have an IA that changes over time, as many types of content are based on a cycle. For example, the UX Australia conference site changes during the year as different milestones are reached.

If your site is likely to change over time, in a cyclical way, or just for extra content, make sure you include that in your IA

Sequencing in the IA

One other thing to think about is how you sequence the IA. In most cases, the order is fairly easy to figure out – there will be a natural order for things. Sometimes that order is by importance, sometimes groups in the IA will clump together and form natural subgroups that feel like they belong together.

The absolute worst thing you can do is to sequence alphabetically – alphabetical order is fine for A-Z lists (when people are doing a known-item information task), but not for navigation items. Alphabetical order is essentially random order. Spend time figuring out a sequence that makes some sense instead of defaulting to alphabetical.

Chapter summary

You're at the point when you're ready to create the IA. The best way to approach this is to just start – put pen to paper and get ideas down. Then:

- Check it works for both the content and the people
- Revise it
- Keep tweaking it until it's working
- Discuss it with your client, stakeholders, authors and subject-matter experts
- Test it (see chapter 19)

19

Testing IA

You're over the main hump of your IA design process. You're happy with the IA you've come up with, it fits your content, and should work well for the users.

Before you continue it's a great idea to test that assumption. Instead of just thinking and hoping it will work for the users, make sure it actually will.

This is called usability testing. It basically involves putting a draft of something in front of people, asking them to use it to do things they'd normally do, and checking it works for them. When you perform a usability test on something before you start to build it, you can find out what works, what doesn't work, and what you need to fix. It lets you see things that aren't going to work and make changes before it's too late.

Of course, usability testing can be done for anything. Although it's used a lot for software and websites, I've heard of retail outlets setting up test stores specifically to check changes to store layout.

For your project, you probably won't be doing usability testing on anything quite so large. You'll want to test your draft IA – your groupings and labelling. Eventually these will form the main way people find information or do tasks, so it's important to get them right, and to know they're right.

Usability testing at this point won't check everything you need to check for your final project. You'll want to do it again more thoroughly when you've designed the navigation, page layouts and content. However, the more things you try to test at once, the harder it is to figure out what aspect wasn't working – was the label obscure, or was the page so busy that people couldn't see the navigation bar at all? Usability testing just your IA lets you know that your groups and labels are working well. The other reason for testing your IA is that navigation and content have to work with it, so it's best to find any mistakes before you start working on these.

Usability testing isn't about checking whether the people can use your website. It is about checking that your website lets them do what they need to do. It's a subtle but important difference, and one to keep in mind when you're testing. You are testing your work, not people's abilities.

What you want to learn

Before you start testing your IA, think about what you want to get out of your test. This will help you decide how to run it and who to involve.

The main thing you'll be trying to learn is that your groups are sensible and your labels are good. You may want to check that your overall approach is okay (e.g. if you've used an audience-based classification scheme, that people expect to see your information in that way and understand the audience groups). Or you may not want to test the IA as a whole, but instead dive deep and just check a part of the IA that was hard to design or where stakeholders couldn't agree on the approach.

When to test

One of the biggest advantages of the approach I'm about to describe is that it's very easy to do. It doesn't take a lot of preparation and you get results quickly. Depending on your situation, you could set up a test one morning and have results that afternoon. It really is that easy to quickly test your IA. It's great to test quickly, make some changes and test again. So you really can test as soon as you have a draft IA you're happy with.

If you didn't get a chance to do good user research earlier in your project (and I know this happens for all sorts of reasons), you could take this opportunity to test your IA and gather some extra research at the same time. Even if you undertook some research early on, chances are some things came up in between that you wish you knew more about, or assumptions that you'd like to follow up. Combine an IA test with some simple research to help you make better decisions later in the project.

You could time your test with something else. (It takes so little time that it's easy to slot in with other activities.) If you're going to be communicating with your audience in some other way – perhaps a stakeholder or staff meeting to gather requirements for another part of the site – you could include a simple test of the IA alongside this.

How it works

This type of testing is quite simple. You're going to ask people how they would do a particular task or look for particular information using your new IA.

For example, if I wanted to test the IA of my conference website, I could ask people to find out some key things like how much it costs, what events are on particular days, and what they'll get out of the conference. I'm not really asking them to find the answers, as the content won't be available yet, but asking them where they would look for the information. I show them the IA step-by-step and ask them to indicate where they'd look – it's that easy.

This testing method works best for a hierarchy pattern (see chapter 16), simple database structures and combination hierarchy/databases (particularly for checking the top couple of levels). If you've used the subsites structure, you may want to test from the top levels, or test one or more of the subsites. It's also great for testing the focused entry points structure, as you can see which way different people approach information.

It's unlikely to work for most wiki structures – they don't really have an IA to test. You can test these later when you have some content ready (see chapter 24 for more about this).

It can work well for the top couple of levels of a catalog, but not so much for the deeper levels – especially ones that contain a lot of products.

Preparation

Before you start, you need three things:

1. A draft IA

The first thing you'll need is your draft IA.

It's okay if your IA is still in draft form. This is a perfect way to check what parts of the IA work and what parts don't. You don't have to test just one draft IA – you could try out different versions or different approaches.

It's also okay for your draft IA to list things in more than one place if you're unsure where you'll put them. This helps people feel like they've found the 'right answer', and gives you good information about the paths people will follow.

2. Scenarios

The second thing you'll need is a set of tasks or a list of things you know people may need to look for. In usability testing we call these scenarios, and they represent what people will do and look for during the test.

When you're writing these out, make sure they use the terminology people use and provide some sort of background or context to make sense of the task. In particular, you should avoid using the same terms as you have in your IA. If you do, it just becomes a treasure hunt for the exact word in your scenario.

For example:

- If you were designing a furniture website don't say "You need a new bookcase", because people will start looking explicitly for bookcases. Say "You've just moved house and have books in boxes everywhere" instead, which gets them thinking about what they'd do about that problem.
- If you have an intranet, don't say "Find the maternity leave policy". Instead, say something like "You've just found out you're going to have a new baby. What are you entitled to?".
- On your accounting software, don't say "Raise a receivable invoice". Try something like "You just delivered a report to your client and it's time to ask them for money".

Using these more realistic scenarios helps ensure people think about the task they may need to do, rather than just hunting for the exact word you're giving them.

There's no right number of scenarios to use. You want enough to cover a good proportion of your IA (or the part you are most interested in exploring) and a good proportion of the tasks people will do (so you can test that the main tasks are easy to complete).

As people go through the scenarios they'll see parts of the IA, and remember where they saw things. This is okay, as people do learn and remember in real life. But after a while people start to focus more on remembering where they saw something than thinking about where they would look for it.

I've found the best approach to balancing these two issues is to have enough scenarios to cover your content and normal tasks, and enough participants so they don't complete every scenario – they just do enough to keep the activity fresh.

It's also good to randomise your scenarios (if you write them out on index cards as I describe below, just shuffle them) so each person does them in a different order. This will make sure your test isn't biased by the order.

3. Participants

The third thing you'll need is a group of people who can give a small amount of time to be involved. As we discussed in chapter 6, the participants should be people who will be using your information.

The most important thing to note for this type of usability testing is that it only takes a small amount of time and commitment. Even a couple of minutes of input from people will give you some very valuable data. So the way you arrange your participants will depend a lot on your project situation. For example, when I do intranet work, I do face-to-face tests and basically arrange to see people at their desks. For website work, I'll set up an online test and invite people via email or via the website in question. If you can keep it low effort for people, it will be much easier to get them involved.

For more information about getting people involved, see the section on recruiting participants in chapter 6.

Method

The two main ways of running this type of usability test are face-to-face or online (yes, you can do both). The advantage of running face-to-face testing is you can talk to people. Just like other user research activities, you can ask people why they made particular decisions and what terms meant for them. This type of feedback help you understand why your IA is working (or not working) instead of just letting you know it is working.

Of course, it isn't always easy working face-to-face, which is where online testing can be particularly useful. The main advantage of online testing is you can involve people you wouldn't otherwise be able to meet face-to-face. And you can often involve more people than you would ever reach face-to-face, giving you a lot of useful information. Each method will involve different preparation.

On paper

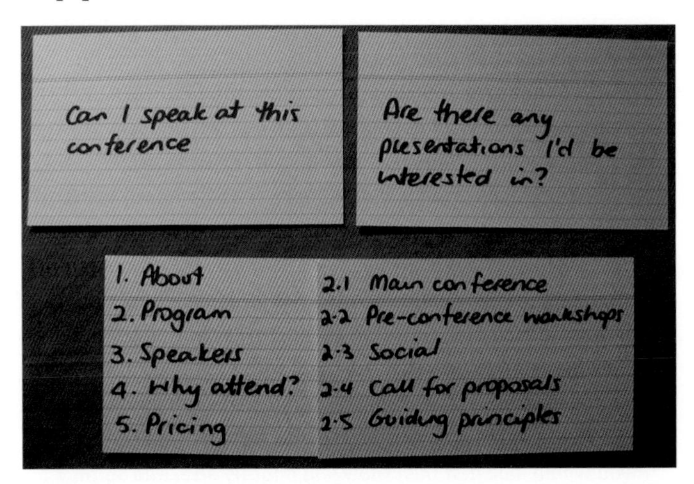

Figure 19 – 1. Scenario cards and hierarchy cards

If you decide on face-to-face testing, you'll need to prepare your IA and your scenarios. My favourite way of doing this is with a set of index cards.

For the IA:

- Write the top level categories on an index card. If you have more categories than will fit on one card, just continue on another. Write large enough that you can read it at arm's length. Number each category 1, 2, 3, 4, 5, etc.
- For each top level category, write down the second level categories in the same way. Again, if they don't fit on one card, just continue on another. It can be handy to use a different coloured card (so you can handle them more easily) but it's by no means essential. Again number these, this time using the number that represents the category above, followed by a number for the current level (e.g. 1.1, 1.2, 1.3).
- Continue for all categories and all levels.
- For the scenarios, write each scenario on one card (it can be handy to use a different coloured card for these too). I also usually label these as A-Z in the corner of the card. (The numbering and lettering system helps with record keeping and analysis.)

Come up with a way to explain the exercise. This helps you introduce the activity efficiently and helps people understand what you're about to ask. I usually say something like:

> *"Thanks for agreeing to help us out today. We've been working on improving [whatever your site is] and would like to check that what we've come up with is sensible for the people who will have to use it.*
> *I'm going to ask you to tell me where you would look for particular information. On this set of cards I have a list of things people do with this [site]. I'm going to show you one of these, and then show you a list of words that may end up being navigation on the [site]. I'll ask you to tell me where you would look first then show you another level and again*

ask you to tell me where you'd look. If it doesn't look right we'll go back, but we won't do more than two choices – after all, it's not a scavenger hunt. Don't worry if this sounds strange – once we've done one, you'll see what I mean. And if there are tasks on those cards (the scenarios) you wouldn't do, or that don't make sense, just skip them."

Bundle up your cards (plus some blanks and a marker) and you're ready to go.

Running the test

When you're with a participant, you pretty much run through the test the same way you described in your introduction. So first show them a scenario (or read it out if you like), then show them the top level card. Ask them to choose a group. For that group, show them the next level card, and so on until there is nowhere further to go.

If they choose a group and feel as if they've made the wrong choice (usually this will happen as they don't see anything that helps at the next level), go back one level and ask them to choose again. But just as you outlined in the introduction, only do this twice. After all, you want to know where they would look, not get them to hunt down the 'answer' to the scenario.

Run through the scenarios you have planned for this participant. If you feel like they are trying to remember where they saw answers instead of thinking about what they're looking for, that's a good time to wrap up.

If your participant needed to go backwards at any step, you may like to ask them what happened. Ask if they remember why they chose the particular group and what they thought would be in it. Be very careful not to make them think they've made a 'mistake' – remember, you're checking how good the IA is, not how good the participant is. But by asking you'll learn very useful information about what people think groups are about and how they expected to look for information.

When you're finished, thank the participant for their help and let them know what happens next.

When I'm using this method to test an IA, I sometimes notice a consistent problem in the IA – usually a label that just doesn't make sense. That's why I carry spare index cards and a marker. Rather than continue testing something I know isn't working, I'll change the label (by writing a new card) and continue testing to see if the new label works any better.

Recording results

As you work, record the participant's answers (this is why we put numbers and letters on the index cards). I like to have someone with me taking notes, as it can be tricky juggling cards and writing down selections (the test moves pretty quickly). All you need to do is write down the path for each scenario.

For example:

- A: 1, 1.2, 1.2.1 (no), 1.2, 1.2.6 (happy)
- B: 7, 7.6, 7.6.5

A helper can also write down the comments people make as they do the test, which are usually both interesting and useful.

After the test, I usually record the results in a big spreadsheet. I put the scenarios across the top, and the IA down the sides. Then I simply go back through all the results and tally where people looked for each scenario. Because I let people look in two places, I usually mark first choices with a big X and second choices with a small x.

It's a simple process, but it very quickly shows you patterns. For some scenarios, you may find there was a consistent approach. For some, there may be less consistency. Sometimes you'll find consistent answers that were quite different to what you thought would be the 'right' one.

Online

Preparation using an online tool will vary, depending on the tool. At the time of writing I know of three online tools that focus specifically on IA testing (all are quite new):

- TreeJack: From Optimal Workshop (`http://www.optimalworkshop.com/treejack.htm`)
- C-inspector (`http://www.c-inspector.com/`)
- PlainFrame (`http://plainframe.com/`)

The first two let you test the IA as a hierarchical tree. The third lets you test your IA in the form of navigation – i.e. the position of navigation bars on the screen. I usually create an IA before I know anything about navigation (something we discuss in chapter 23) so the tree approach works well for me, but it would be easy to mock-up a navigation approach and test with a bit more context.

All follow the same idea as the face-to-face test. You upload a hierarchy (your IA) and a set of scenarios. You write an introduction test and send it out via email or include a link to it on your website.

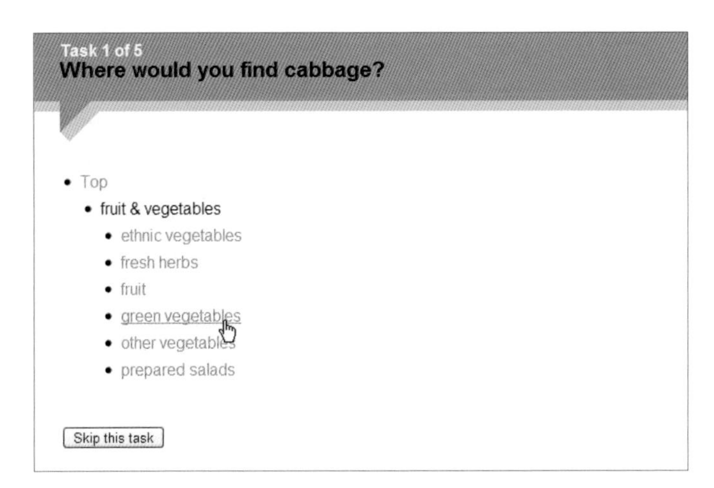

Figure 19 – 2. Treejack (`https://optimalworkshop.com/treejack.htm`)

	User	Clicks	Time	Notes	First click path
☑	1VQH5JLC	12	31		Contacts > My Connections
☑	1QKN3MH5	4	30		More...
☐	14QTDEYR	4	21		Contacts > My Connections
☑	1ONJIFSL	2	9		Inbox (11) > Compose Message
☑	1OAU4VH8	12	47		Home
☑	1XKSMY1V	2	16		Inbox (11) > Compose Message

Figure 19-2: The results from a PlainFrame test

Interpreting results

It's usually pretty easy to interpret the results of this activity. The spreadsheet I described above, or the outputs from the tools, show a fairly clear picture of what works and what didn't. When interpreting the results, think not only about what happened but why it happened.

First, think about whether the overall approach worked well. Did the test show you've chosen a good basic approach to your IA (particularly if you've chosen something like an audience or task-based classification scheme)?

Identify the scenarios where people looked in the same place you thought the content would be. You can probably be confident this will be a good location for that content.

For the parts that worked well, think about what made them work well and check that they worked well because the IA is suitable. You need to be a bit cynical here and make sure the scenarios didn't work well because you used leading language and people word matched, or because they always did that scenario 5th and had learned the IA.

When the results weren't what you expected, think about what happened:

- Did everyone think the information would be in a different place to where you thought you'd put it? If so, consider putting the information there. You may need to tweak the IA a little to fit it.
- Were some of your labels just not clear enough, or did people interpret them in a way different to how you intended? You may need to revisit the labels, the placement of content within them, or the categories themselves.

When you've finished analysing what worked and what didn't, go back to the process we discussed in the last chapter. Tweak the IA (or toss it out entirely and take a new approach) and test it again. Keep doing this until you're happy you have something that's going to work.

Tree testing with Windows Explorer

Brian Hoffman, Web Experience Specialist, EnergyCAP, Inc.

> *"I had done an open card sort, came up with top level categories, which things might go in them, and identified some terminology issues. But I wanted to test the results of the hierarchy I'd come up with and didn't think a closed card sort would achieve what I wanted it to – I wanted to test the whole hierarchy and not just the top categories.*
>
> *So somehow I came up with the idea of a tree test. I wanted a very natural interface for participants to use, so I ended up creating the hierarchy in a series of nested folders in Windows. The participants were then given tasks and asked to find things in the hierarchy by navigating through the folders and using a think aloud protocol.*
>
> *It worked really well and using an iterative testing process I believe I came up with a very solid start to the IA for the site."*

IA testing – 3 ways

Melinda Anderson, Freelance user experience consultant

"A couple of years ago a local (Australian) government client came to me for help. They were redesigning their very large, information-based website. They had devised a new site structure, but had not as yet involved users. They wanted to understand whether or not the proposed structure was likely to work before progressing into design and development. Usability testing was not possible because, being a largely static content website, there were a limited number of wireframe templates to be developed. This meant that they would not produce enough wireframes to make a prototype, and waiting until the website was nearly complete would pose a huge risk should the structure turn out to be flawed.

I had read about a method for testing on index cards[1]*. The client provided me with a copy of their proposed structure, which I converted to index cards. Armed with these cards and a list of information-seeking tasks, I went to the local library and (with the library's permission) canvassed participants. I found that participants quickly learned the structure and so later tasks didn't have as realistic results as earlier tasks. In addition, I found that juggling cards, trying to note down the paths the users took, and asking questions to understand their motivations was challenging. However, at the end of the exercise, I was able to go back to the client and make some strong recommendations on the key problem areas and the client went away happy.*

It was around 6 months before a similar project crossed my desk. A colleague of mine had discovered a tool to create a prototype site just with navigation. We decided to conduct information architecture testing following the standard

[1] http://www.boxesandarrows.com/view/card_based_classification_evaluation

usability testing approach. The client provided a site map and we developed a prototype. We used 6 participants from their primary audience. Again, participants learned the structure fairly quickly, so again after about 15 tasks, the results were slightly compromised. This time however, it was easier to capture the participants' journeys because I didn't have the manual task of flicking through cards. The testing gave us strong results and because an interview style approach was followed, we were able to collect feedback on labels, much like we had done with the card-based classification validation scheme. We fed back to the client in an informal wash-up and they went on to implement our recommendations.

Fast forward 2 years and I'm now working for an agency in London. A client requested usability testing on their new site; however, being predominantly static content, they faced the same problem as my first client – they didn't have a significant amount of interaction to test, and in order to get the most out of an hour long test session, they needed to produce a fairly comprehensive prototype. This was just not financially viable, nor was there enough time to develop a prototype.

While researching IA testing tools, I came across a new web-based software program (Treejack)[2] where users completed the study remotely online without a facilitator. As the client was not comfortable conducting the entire testing remotely using Treejack (they were unfamiliar with the concept of IA testing and were concerned that they would not get the results they were looking for), a small sample of the respondents were invited to our labs, and we observed them using Treejack to complete the tasks in a manner similar to the white site testing and usability testing. Treejack conveniently tracked the paths that users took and presented that information in a digestible format that made it easy and

[2] Treejack: `http://optimalworkshop.com/treejack.htm`

fast to identify key problem areas. In addition, by observing participants, we were able to collect comments and feedback regarding the proposed structure, that was not possible with the remote studies.

Whilst we got some great results, which we fed back to the client, we did find some issues with Treejack that we hadn't counted on. I found that the results could be compromised. Some participants liked to browse through the structure first to see what was in each section before back tracking and making a selection. Whilst this is consistent with the web browsing behaviour of some types of users, it did not suit the purposes of the study, which relied on users making first-instinct decisions. I also found that not all participants understood how to use Treejack, even though comprehensive instructions were provided (remembering that users don't tend to read instructions).

Since that first time using Treejack, I have completed further studies using this tool, these being predominantly remote studies with no facilitation. I have found that whilst it is cheaper to conduct the remote studies because the cost of a lab and facilitator is removed, the lack of direct interaction with participants means that only path information available, and it is up to the consultant to interpret this correctly. I also have to take into consideration that users may not interact with the application the way that we expect them to, which can compromise the results. That said, I still feel that the data capture feature makes it preferable to the manual approach of the card-based classification verification scheme.

Having used a number of different methods to test IA, I can safely say that I prefer to use an electronic prototype to index cards. I find that allowing the user to drive frees me up to observe, take notes, and ask more detailed questions. I think that it is better to do one-on-one interviews rather than remote facilitation because I can explore concepts and rationale with the participants, which helps me to better understand the results, and therefore provide more accurate recommendations."

Chapter summary

A usability test of your IA will let you check that it's working well before you design navigation and page layouts. A test involves:

- Deciding what you want to learn, and which parts you'll test
- Preparing the draft IA
- Preparing scenarios
- Arranging participants to be involved
- Running the test
- Seeing what happened and making changes to the IA

This type of testing can be done face to face, or via an online tool.

Further reading

For more information on testing an information architecture, see `http://delicious.com/practicalIA/ia-testing`

20 Communicating Information Architecture

In previous chapters I've talked about how you should design your communication around the needs of the people you'll be communicating with. This is just as important for the IA as it is for all other communication.

However, at this point I'm going to suggest you don't communicate the IA to anyone outside your immediate team. Of course you'll want to explain the groups, labelling and pattern you're going to use. And you'll want to describe how you came up with the groups, what will be in them, and why you know they're going to work well. But even so, you may want to hold off for a little while.

No, not because I think you should keep it under your hat or secret. I'm suggesting it just because people may not need to know about the IA.

In the past I've presented IAs to clients, stakeholders and my audience. Full of good intentions and transparency, I've shown people diagrams and spreadsheets showing the IA. I've explained the rationale behind the groups and all the issues we came across when deciding the labels. But the results were never particularly good. Why? At this point it's all too abstract – my diagrams and spreadsheets didn't connect to anything concrete and practical. Everyone walked away with different ideas about how the site would work.

So I suggest you communicate the IA after you've designed the navigation and page layouts. Show people the two things together and they can visualise how the site is going to work. It's much safer and less likely to cause confusion.

Of course, that doesn't mean you shouldn't write anything down after coming up with the IA. Just consider who to talk to about it at this point in your project.

Writing it down – Sitemaps

An IA is usually documented as a sitemap (an IA sitemap is different to the sitemaps you see on websites, but shows the same sort of thing). Sitemaps can be diagrammatic or some type of list.

I use two different types of sitemap, depending on the complexity of the project.

1. Conceptual sitemap

The first type of sitemap I use is a conceptual sitemap. Similar to the diagrams in chapter 16 (IA patterns), it shows a high-level representation of the site and its basic pattern.

A conceptual sitemap will usually show top-level headings, key pages or sections, and key relationships between pages or sections. It definitely won't show all the pages that will eventually be in the site.

This sitemap will almost always be a diagram. I'll use it in situations where I have a chance to explain it – its abstractness can be hard to communicate in writing.

There's no one way to draw this diagram. The shapes and connectors should be simple, and the diagram should not contain too much information. The idea behind it is to show the overall shape of a site at a glance, so don't make it too fussy.

I don't always use this type of sitemap, especially with small sites or larger sites that are straightforward hierarchies or databases. In these cases, a conceptual diagram just isn't necessary.

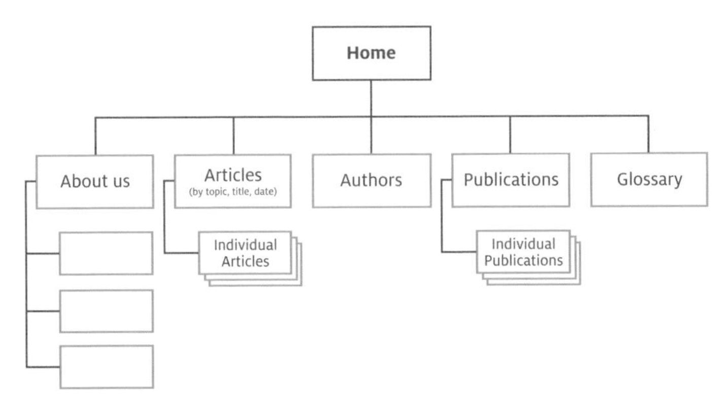

Figure 20 – 1. A conceptual sitemap

2. Detailed sitemap

The second type of sitemap is a more detailed one. Rather than trying to communicate concepts, this one's all about the nitty-gritty detail.

This type of sitemap can be done either as a diagram or some type of list. (I use a spreadsheet, but plenty of people use the outline view of something like Microsoft Word.) If you have to choose between the two, consider how hard it will be to update – for large sites, a diagram may be easy to see at a glance but inefficient to change.

Even detailed sitemaps that represent a lot of content don't need much in the way of drawing shapes. I use simple boxes and simple connectors, with each box representing a 'page' in the site. Where I have structured content like articles, news items or publications and there are too many to list, I show these as a stack of boxes. For special things like interactive tools, areas available only to logged in users or something else you can use colour or different shapes. Tailor the diagram to suit your own site and what detail you need to include.

For large sites, spreadsheets can be both very useful and much easier to maintain than diagrams. You can also use them for other things, including project tracking activities such as recording who owns what, who has provided content, which pages have been prepared, which have been checked, and much more. You can include columns for extra information and notes – which are all harder to do on a diagram. If you have a database-structure site, you can include the metadata in the columns as well.

Figure 20 – 2. Basic shapes for drawing an IA

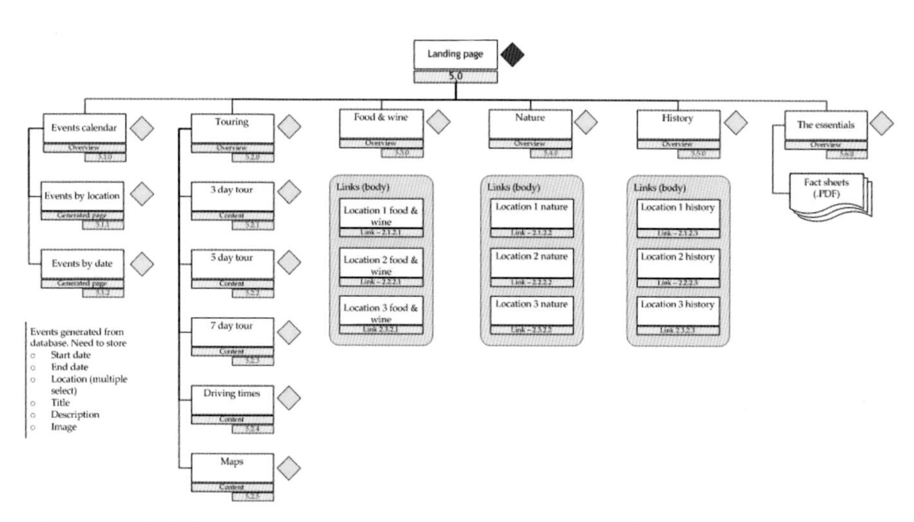

Figure 20 – 3. A detailed site map for a tourism website - the icons indicate which template to use, the pages are numbered to match the copy book

	A	C	D	E	F	G
1	www.environment.gov.au - Combined structure					
2	**No.**	**Title**	**Nav OK**	**Page titl**	**Sidebar**	**Fix**
3		**Home**				Remove heritage trails ad. Update nev
4	1.0	**ABOUT HERITAGE**	y	OK		
26	2.0	**HERITAGE PLACES**	y	OK		
27	2.1.0	**World heritage places**	x	y		Change nav to 'World heritage places'
28	2.1.1	Gondwana Rainforests of Australia - Barrington Tops Area				Sidebar link to NSW national parks is b
29	2.1.2	Gondwana Rainforests of Australia - Focal Peak Group				
30	2.1.3	Gondwana Rainforests of Australia - Hastings-Macleay Group				
31	2.1.4	Gondwana Rainforests of Australia - Iluka Nature F	Move dinosaur site here.			
32	2.1.5	Gondwana Rainforests of Australia - Main Range Group				
33	2.1.6	Gondwana Rainforests of Australia - New England Group				
34	2.1.7	Gondwana Rainforests of Australia - Shield Volcano Group				
35	2.1.8	Gondwana Rainforests of Australia - Washpool and Gibraltar Range				
36	2.1.9	Lord Howe Island Group				
37	2.1.10	Sydney Opera House				
38	2.1.11	The Greater Blue Mountains Area				
39	2.1.12	Willandra Lakes Region				
40	2.1.13	Royal Exhibition Building and Carlton Gardens				
41	2.1.14	Australian Fossil Mammal Sites (Riversleigh)				
42	2.1.15	Fraser Island				
43	2.1.16	Great Barrier Reef				
44	2.1.17	Wet Tropics of Queensland				
45	2.1.18	Australian Fossil Mammal Sites (Naracoorte)				
46	2.1.19	Purnululu National Park				
47	2.1.20	Shark Bay, Western Australia				
48	2.1.21	Macquarie Island				
49	2.1.22	Tasmanian Wilderness				
50	2.1.23	Kakadu National Park				
51	2.1.24	Uluru - Kata Tjuta National Park				
52	2.1.25	Heard and McDonald Islands				
53	2.2.0	**National heritage places**				
54	2.2.1	Kurnell Peninsula (S)				
55	2.2.2	Brewarrina Aboriginal Fish Traps (Baiames Ngunnhu)				
56	2.2.3	Sydney Opera House				
57	2.2.4	First Government House Site				
58	2.2.5	North Head, Sydney				

Figure 20 – 4. A detailed sitemap in Excel. This was being used to record migration testing as well

Cross links

People often ask me how to show cross-links on a sitemap. After all, the final site will include links between key pages. I don't try to show these on the sitemap – on a diagram it is just too much information. You can include it in a spreadsheet if it's important to record key links. But the best place to identify cross links is within whatever you are using for content (I usually use a big document that contains all the copy and all the links).

Depending on where you live, it might even be faster to walk or ride and avoid traffic congestion.

Walking kids to school or riding with them has lots of benefits. Your local school might be interested in starting a walking school bus [http http://www.travelsmart.gov.au/schools/schools2.html].

Use public transport

Depending on where you live, public transport [Take action>Travel smarter>Use public transport] can be cheaper and less stressful than driving. You'll also help reduce air pollution and traffic congestion.

Avoid peak hour traffic

Peak hour can be the most stressful time to drive. Stopping and starting in heavy traffic increases wear and tear on your car and uses more fuel than normal driving.

Work from home

If you're in a situation where you can do all or some of your work from home, you can save on fuel, maintenance and parking costs. You might also have more free time.

Car pool or car share

Car pooling and car sharing [Take action>Travel smarter>Car pool and car share] can cut your transport costs and help remove the need for your own car or the second car.

Figure 20 – 5. Part of a copy book, showing crosslinks and external links

Maintaining the sitemap

Another question people often ask me is how to maintain the sitemap after the site has gone live.

I rarely bother doing this. A sitemap is necessary during a design or redesign phase to keep track of the new IA, and maybe to manage the production of the site. But I think that the sitemap of a built site is the site itself.

The only reason you would want to keep a separate document is if you were managing the site manually (without a content management system of any type) and needed to keep track of things like owners, date last updated, date pages were added. But I know few people who don't use some type of content management system these days, so you probably won't need to maintain a sitemap. If you want to for some other reason, a spreadsheet will be easier to maintain than a diagram.

What else to include

So far we've discussed what to include in the actual sitemap. But two things are much more important to document – the rationale behind the IA, and how to maintain it into the future.

The rationale describes the reasoning behind the IA as a whole, and is incredibly useful when other people have to figure out where to add content or make changes to the IA without you around. Include information about:

- why you chose the overall approach
- what each section is about – the underlying idea
- what each section should include

If you tested the IA, make sure you include details of what you learned during the testing.

Just as important is information about what you decided not to do. Make sure you describe the ideas you threw away and why you did so. For example, if you started off thinking you'd use an audience scheme and found it didn't suit the content or didn't work in testing, that's really handy for someone to know. If you tried alternate labels for categories, describe why you decided against using them. This is very, very important. If you don't document these, guess what's going to happen? Some manager is going to toss out your work and use one of the crappy ideas you threw away.

Also document how to maintain the IA into the future. This is similar to the rationale as it describes the IA as a whole and what should be in each section, but it should also provide guidelines on what to do in the future. Think about the types of content that should be added, and how to choose where to locate them. Think about what would happen if the site doubled in size – how should someone manage the IA as that happens? This process also helps you check the IA is scalable and that you've considered future requirements.

Communicating IA effectively

Gary Barber, radharc, radharc.com.au

> *"I have seen this happen too many times, you design a sexy IA, and six months later all the good work and benefits of the IA work have been lost.*
>
> *To overcome this issue you need to either train the client in the dark arts of an IA, how you make categorisation decisions (nice but not practical), or provide some reference documentation.*
>
> *I have found that over the years the best type of documentation is the one that is very concise, in bullet points and focuses on the elements of the IA or the interactive design. All you want to provide is information to help them make that categorisation decision. Often this just comes down to comparing like with like information.*
>
> *The critical thing with this "Where do I put this manual" question is the method of presentation of the information.*
>
> *I have worked with government agencies that have requested a PDF of the "Where manual". I knew instantly where this would end up on the shelf and eight months later it was evident the manual had not been reference.*
>
> *Similarly in a large company, I delivered this type of documentation via their online help system. The problem here was that no one used the Intranet – so same end result.*
>
> *Documentation is great, but it's a waste of time if it's not used. So how do you overcome this?*
>
> *Simple, you have to match the type of documentation with the client's real internal processes. Just like all users*

aren't the same, so all clients aren't the same. It's a good idea to observe and research the people that are responsible for the day-to-day maintenance of the site. Even if it's just a few minutes, you'll get an idea of the type of documentation they respond well to.

I have found that depending on the personality of the maintainer the following methods have worked well for my clients:

- *A decision tree of the category system using flow diagrams: Designers and developers respond well to this. Usually a few large poster size printouts. However, there can be issues maintaining the decision tree.*
- *A wiki of the decision tree process: This uses the auto linking of the wiki to link up the decision touchpoints to flow through to the final category, with a description of the category and examples.*
- *Powerpoint/keynote presentation: This is basically the same as the wiki above, however the slides are manually linked together. This can be subject to version control issues.*
- *Word document / PDF: This tends to work well for editors and copywriters. I include a simple list of the categories based around the site IA, again with detailed descriptions and examples. The issue is there is no decision support system with this document. The document is also subject to version control issues.*
- *Spreadsheet: This is usually the basic documentation, it's a simple spreadsheet with the categories listed in a tree like structure, a brief description and a few examples. It's often extended from the site map. Now I have never seen this type of documentation work well, except with fellow IAs – maybe that says it all.*

Whatever is used it has to be simple, easy to get to, use and maintain. If it takes more than a few seconds to access and start the decision process, I have found people will just not use it."

Chapter summary

Document your IA, but consider whether you want to show it to the client or anyone outside your immediate team – it may be better to leave it until you have designed the navigation and page layouts.

For internal use, the IA is usually documented as a sitemap. I use two types:

- A conceptual sitemap shows the overall approach to the site.
- A detailed sitemap shows all pages and a lot of detail. It may be a diagram, but works well as a spreadsheet.

More important than the sitemap is your document explaining the rationale for the IA so people can maintain it over time.

Further reading

For more information on how to communicate IA, see `http://delicious.com/practicalIA/communicate-ia`

Part 5

Designing navigation

We've figured out our groups, tested them and talked to other people about them. And we're pretty confident that we're on the right track.

It's now time to take the last step in our IA journey and design ways to help people get around your site and between pieces of your information – navigation. This section describes different approaches to navigation, how to design it, test it and communicate it.

Navigation core

Navigation extras

Designing navigation

Testing navigation

Communicating navigation

21

Navigation core

Navigation is a fairly all-purpose word that refers to the methods we design that let people move around information. It includes navigation bars, hyperlinks, buttons and other clickable things.

Navigation is more than just a way of getting people around a site. It can also:

- let people browse to the content or functionality they need
- show the context of the information
- show what is related and relevant
- help people find information they didn't know about

Navigation is more than just a single bar at the top of the page. It's an entire system that combines different pieces for different needs.

Types of navigation

Here are some common elements of an overall navigation system.

Navigation bars

The simplest approach to navigation is a navigation bar – a horizontal or vertical bar that shows the categories of the site. Navigation bars can be used for both simple and more complex sites.

A **horizontal navigation** bar stretches across the page, usually right at the top, or beneath some sort of banner or logo. It may contain the same information on every page, or change depending on the section of the site you're in.

A horizontal navigation bar is suitable when:

- you have a small number of top-level items that can fit across the screen
- you aren't likely to be adding new top-level items
- your labels are short enough to fit into the horizontal space
- you aren't likely to translate the site into a language that uses long, compound words (which take up more space)
- you want to maximise the amount of page width available for content

Simple horizontal navigation bars can usually display 1-2 levels of a site.

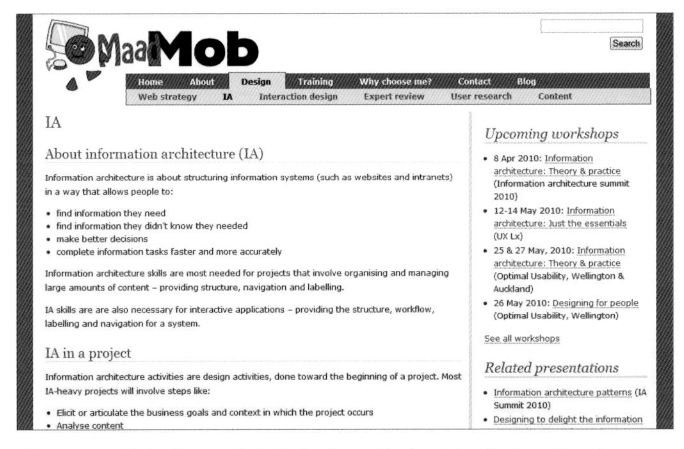

Figure 21 – 1. My business website is simple, and horizontal navigation allowed me to use the full page width for content

Figure 21 – 2. Horizontal navigation doesn't have to be at the top of the page – but it's important that people see it and recognise it as navigation (`alfaromeo.com/`)

A **vertical navigation** bar sits at the left or the right of the screen and is most useful when:

- you have more top level groups than would easily fit across a screen
- you may add or change groups over time
- some groups may have long labels
- you may want to translate the website

Vertical navigation is also good for hierarchical sites with a few levels. One of the most common navigation patterns is to display the pages for the section you are displaying, indenting the sub-categories to show their relationship.

Figure 21 – 3. This website uses simple left-hand navigation (`blackestate.co.nz`)

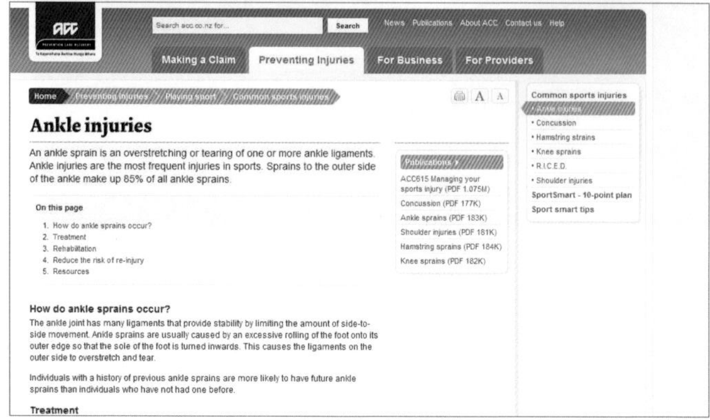

Figure 21 – 4. ACC uses right-hand navigation. In usability testing, this performed just as well as left-hand navigation (`acc.co.nz`)

If you want to use this approach, make sure each level is visually distinct and the indentation is big enough for people to see the relationship between items. This helps them understand where they are in the site and the context of the current information.

Although it's more common to find navigation bars at the left of the screen, there's no reason they have to be there (though some people say they should be there for languages that read right to left). Right navigation bars let the content area be the focus of the page. And as long as they're easy to identify as a navigation bar, they're just as easy to use as left-hand navigation.

Inverted L

By combining horizontal and vertical navigation bars we get inverted-L navigation. This pattern usually has a horizontal navigation bar that's consistent right across the site, and a vertical navigation bar for each section of the site.

This approach is good for large sites, particularly those with the subsites pattern I described in chapter 16.

Case Study: UX Australia

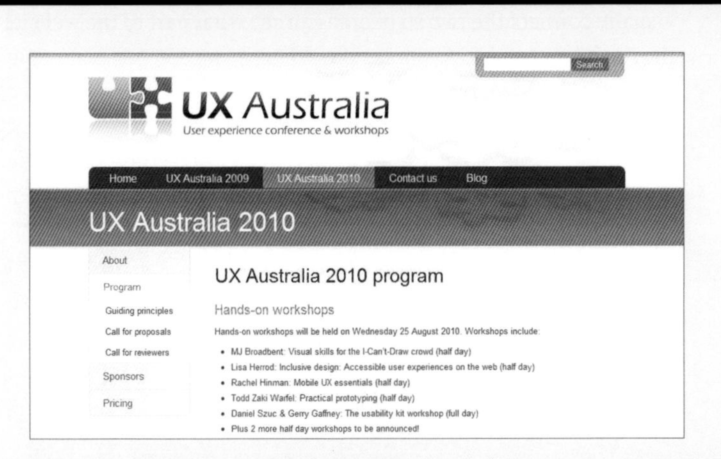

Figure 21 – 5. UX Australia has horizontal navigation for the major sections, and rarely changes. The left navigation bar is a 2-level hierarchy for the current conference, and changes throughout the year as planning progresses.

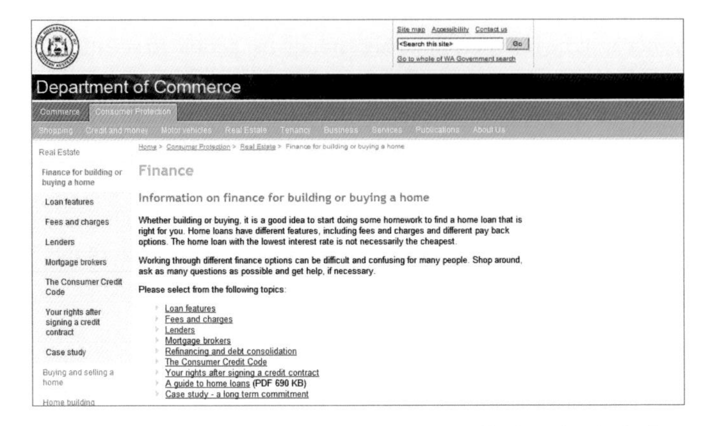

Figure 21 – 6. The Department of Commerce WA has a 2-level horizontal navigation bar plus a 3-level vertical navigation bar - a good model for a large hierarchical site (`http://www.commerce.wa.gov.au/`)

Tabs

Tabbed navigation is just a variation of the horizontal navigation bar, and is suited to the same types of websites. However it will always have a second level of categories, and it's important to visually connect the two so people can see what part of the website they're in.

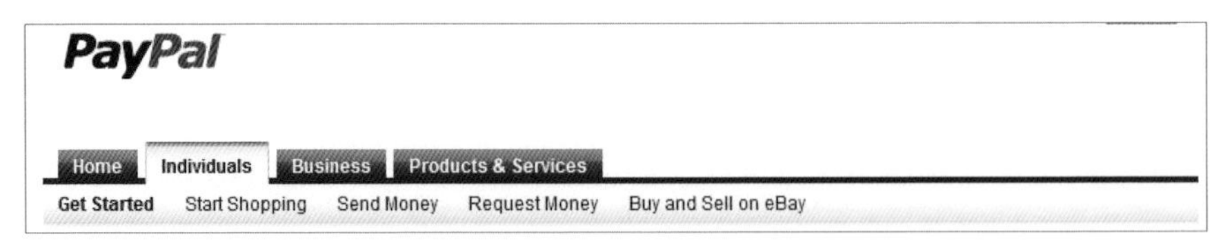

Figure 21 – 7. Paypal has 2 levels - the top is tabs, the second is a horizontal navigation bar (`paypal.com.au`)

Drop-down

Drop-down navigation uses a horizontal navigation bar, and when someone hovers over a top level category the second level categories are shown.

The main advantage of drop-down navigation (and flyout navigation, which I'll explain next) is people can see what's included in the next level category without having to click into it. This not only helps them navigate more efficiently (it's one less page to load) but also helps them understand what the site covers and what each category is about. By looking at what is in the next level, they get a better idea of the category.

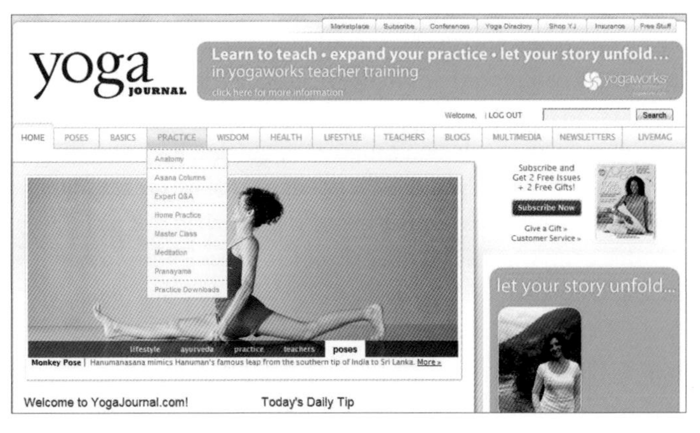

Figure 21 – 8. Drop-down navigation on Yoga journal lets me see the next level of the site without clicking into it (`yogajournal.com`)

Flyout

Flyout navigation is similar to drop-down navigation (showing the next level in a hierarchy without people having to click into it) except it's used for vertical navigation bars.

The main disadvantage of flyout navigation is it can be hard to use, as people need to carefully move their mouse across then down. If you know your audience will struggle to select the navigation items (e.g. if they won't have the fine motor skills needed) consider a different approach instead.

Flyout navigation can show a third level of hierarchy.

For both flyout and drop-down navigation, consider these issues:

- Long menus may go off the bottom of the screen, making it impossible to get to the bottom items. Test on a variety of screen resolutions to make sure this doesn't happen.
- If they appear too slowly or disappear too quickly, they may be frustrating to use. Test people's reaction to them before releasing.
- Many implementations require javascript, which is still not supported everywhere. Make sure people can navigate without javascript available.

Figure 21 – 9. The flyout navigation on Amazon is easier to use than most. It stays out longer, and you don't have to be quite as precise with your mouse (`amazon.com`)

Figure 21 – 10. Tabs and dropdowns and flyouts, oh my! (`frys.com`)

Giant drop-downs

A fairly recent navigation type that's becoming more common is very large drop-down boxes containing many links. Just like normal drop-downs, the advantage is they let people jump deeper into the site without clicking through every level. And if they're grouped and laid out well they can show a few levels of the site – not just the next level.

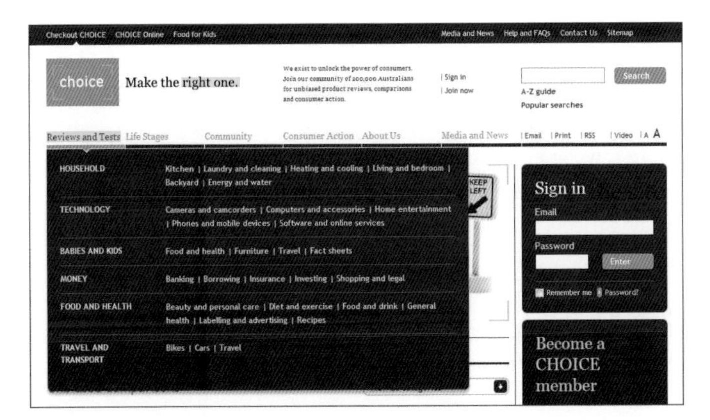

Figure 21 – 11. This giant drop-down provides access to deep content, and is laid out well so you can still find what you need (`choice.com.au`)

Whole page

Some sites contain a home page that uses the whole area for navigation, usually integrating the navigation into the graphic design. In these types of sites, other pages will usually have another navigation type for the rest of the site – the home page approach doesn't carry through.

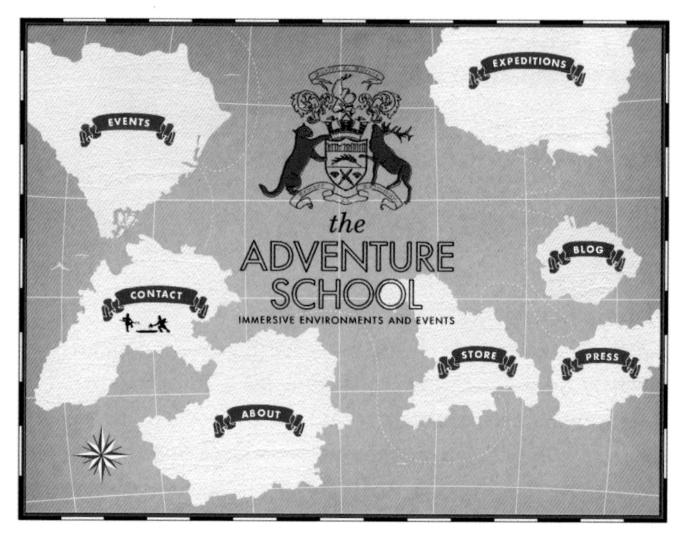

Figure 21 – 12. This home page is only navigation (`theadventureschool.com`)

Page body navigation

Although we spend a lot of time designing navigation bars, people spend most of their time looking at the body of the page, using the navigation bars when the page body doesn't help or they already know which category to choose. But in a lot of situations, navigation happens mainly in the body of the page.
Within-page navigation includes lists, indexes and summary content that leads to more detail.

This style of navigation offers a lot of flexibility and variation. Within-page navigation is also particularly common for database-structure sites with a lot of content – it's much easier to use the page body than to include a long list of items in navigation bars.

Figure 21 – 13. BBC TV has most of the navigation in the page body (`bbc.co.uk/tv/`)

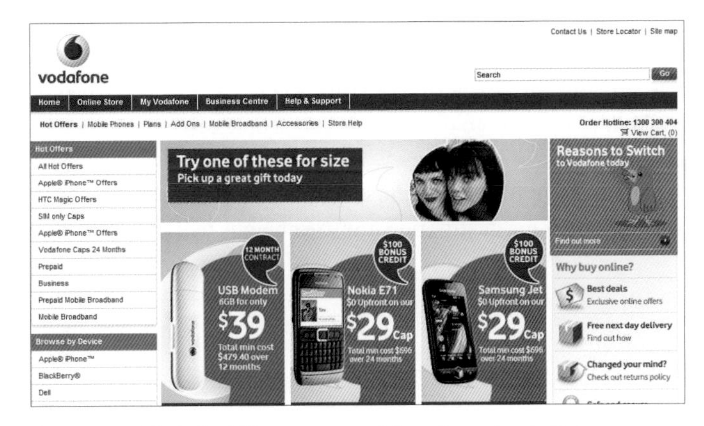

Figure 21 – 14. The body of this page serves as information and navigation (`vodafone.com.au/personal/`)

Contextual links

Another way to achieve in-page navigation is via contextual links. This is common in many websites, though wikis are undoubtedly the prime example.

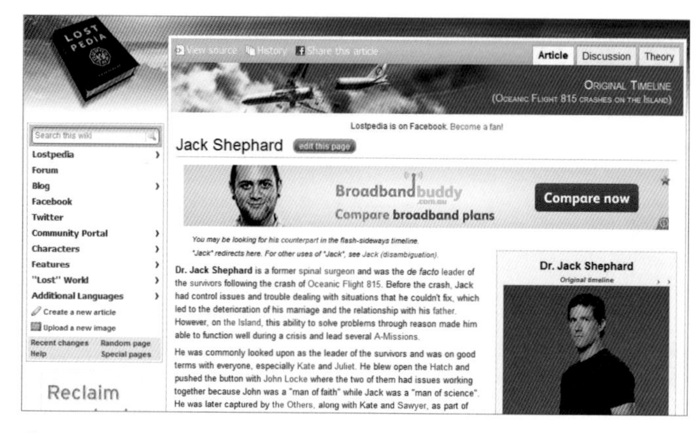

Figure 21 – 15. In the Lostipedia, most of the navigation is via contextual links (`lostpedia.wikia.com`)

For contextual links, here are two issues to keep in mind:

- Make sure they're clearly visible. Use a colour that fits within your brand but is different to the body text so people can tell where the links are.
- Use the tips from the chapter on labelling to make sure the links clearly describe the destination and are obvious to their readers.

Related links

Related links are a very common type of navigation item. As the name suggests, they allow access to content that's related to the current page. They allow you to highlight content you'd like to expose to people, and help users to find things they may be looking for.

Related links can be manually identified by content authors as they prepare their content, or automatically by the system. This is another good use of metadata – if your system lets you do it, you can automatically generate related links based on metadata from the current page.

When choosing related links, or rules to generate them, make sure they really are related and useful. Don't include things you want to promote that aren't related to the current content – it will just annoy the people who really want to find information.

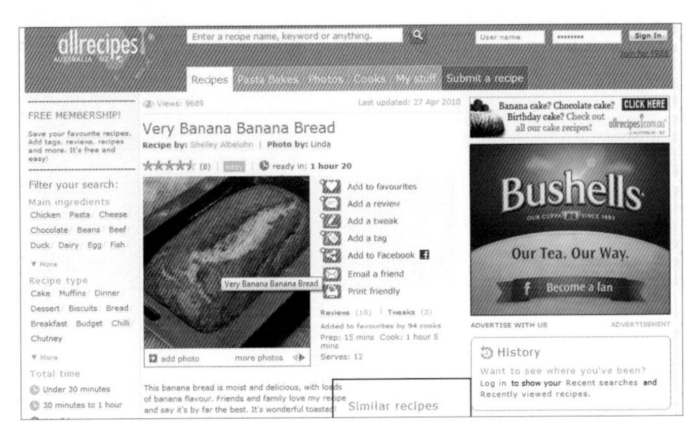

Figure 21 – 16. Allrecipes has a section for similar recipes (`allrecipes.com.au`)

Figure 21 – 17. Amazon has many related links - this one is created by looking at what other people bought (`amazon.com`)

Chapter summary

Navigation refers to the methods we design that let people move around information. It includes navigation bars, hyperlinks, buttons and other clickable things.

Common types of navigation, and what they're good for, include:

- Horizontal navigation bars are great when you have few groups with short labels that aren't going to change a lot
- Vertical navigation bars are good for more groups, longer labels and more change
- Inverted-L navigation lets you combine horizontal and vertical navigation bars for large sites
- Tabs are just 2-level horizontal navigation bars
- Dropdown and flyout menus let people see what's at the next level making it easier for them to jump to content and see what's in each group
- Full pages devoted to navigation are okay for some home pages
- Links in the body of the page, either as navigation, in context or as related links let people get to content as they are reading

Further reading

For more information on navigation design, see `http://delicious.com/practicalIA/navigation`

22

Navigation extras

In the last chapter we looked at the main types of navigation bars and approaches. This chapter is all about other ways to help people get around your content.

Breadcrumbs

Breadcrumb trails are used on many websites – mainly hierarchical ones. The breadcrumb trail is the strip you see near the top of the website that shows the position of the current page in the hierarchy. They can help people understand the current page by showing the section it belongs to, which often provides context and a better understanding of the content. Breadcrumb trails can also give people an easy way to move to a broader level of the website - handy when they land in the middle of the site as the result of a search.

Occasionally someone will tell me breadcrumbs should show where you've been, not where you are (after all, that's what the metaphor is about). But it doesn't make sense. If people land in the middle of a website and follow a bunch of contextual links they really don't care where they've been, and they can use the back button if they need to go to pages they've seen.

Breadcrumb trails are definitely an addition to your main navigation scheme. During usability testing I've seen people who don't see them at all, or don't understand what they mean (along with plenty who do). So don't rely on them as your only navigation mechanism.

When designing a breadcrumb trail:

- Include all levels of the website.
- Place the breadcrumb trail beneath the banner and navigation, but above the page content.
- Hyperlink everything except the current page.
- If you want to show the relationship between the items, use the » (`Alt+0187`) character instead of the >> (greater than) to avoid screen-reading software saying 'greater than, greater than'.

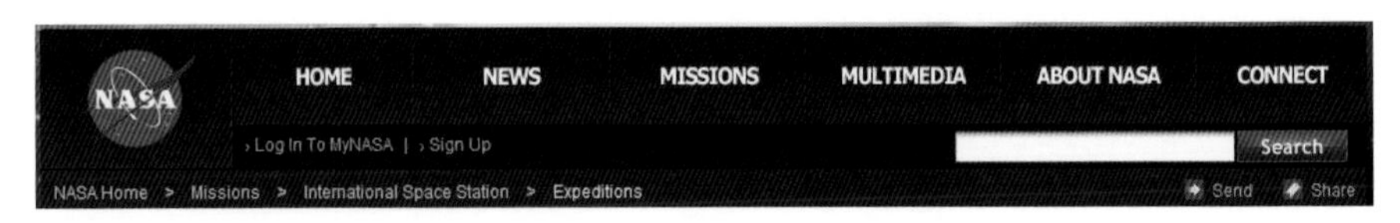

Figure 22 – 1. NASA's breadcrumb navigation (`nasa.gov`)

Tag clouds

Tag clouds are used in websites that use tagging to describe content. A tag cloud shows a visual representation of the tags. In most implementations, the size of each item in the cloud relates to how commonly the tag has been used (with larger sizes showing they have been used more often).

Although tag clouds have become more common in the past few years, they still are not well understood. People regularly misinterpret what the different sizes mean, and many find the visual approach quite confusing. This is one area where you really should do usability testing and make sure your users know what's going on.

Case Study: UX Australia

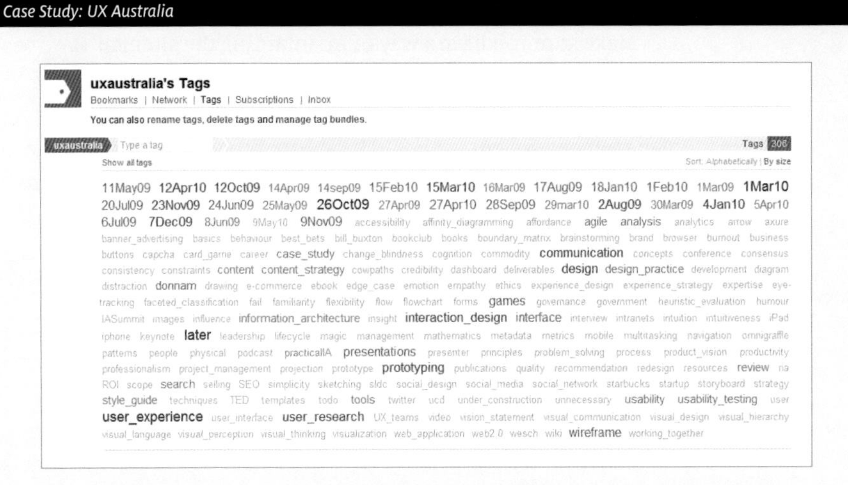

Figure 22 – 2. The social bookmarking service delicious was one of the first sites to use a tag cloud. This one shows the tags for articles included in the UX Australia newsletter (`delcious.com`)

Site maps

In the early days of the web every site had a site map – a single page that listed all pages. They disappeared for a while (or at least became less popular) but have been re-appearing in the past couple of years.

Site maps serve two different audiences:

- Humans (yes, people) who want to see everything at a glance and avoid going step-by-step through the site. This is a fairly common behaviour when people know what is available but aren't sure which section it's in.
- Search engines (not people) that can more easily see what content is in a site and get to all the pages.

For both situations you'll want to list as many pages as possible – both humans and search engines want to get deep into a site without much effort. For small sites this is fairly easy.

For large sites you'll have to make a decision about how much to include. While you may not be able to list every page, you may be able to list all the major sections of the site. This may be enough to get people and search engines deep enough into the site.

Make sure you have a way of maintaining the sitemap. (I think this is one of the reasons they fell out of popularity for a while – they can be hard to maintain.) If you're using a content management system, it should be able to produce and update the site map automatically. If you'll need to do it manually, make sure you have procedures so it can be kept up-to-date.

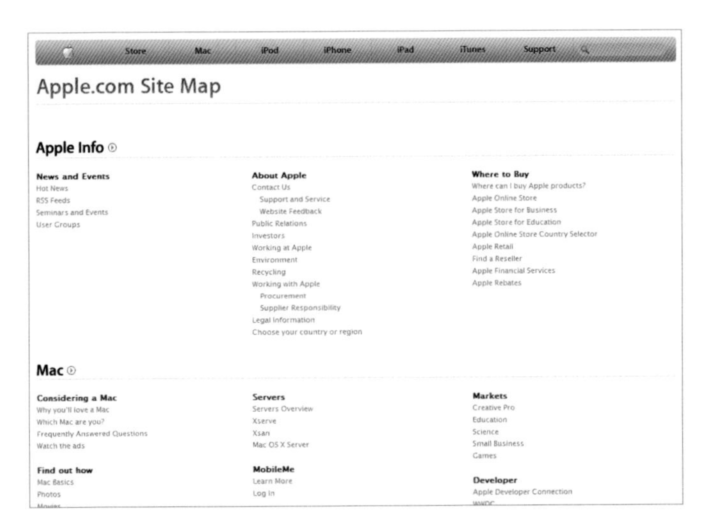

Figure 22 – 3. The Apple sitemap includes a lot in a small space, and is still easy to read and understand (`apple.com`)

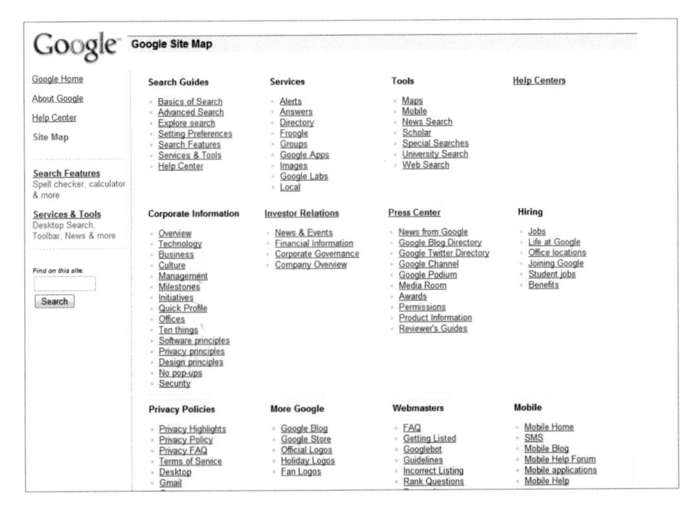

Figure 22 – 4. The Google site map is a good way to find products and Google content (`google.com`)

Big footers

A fairly new trend, and one that often eliminates the need for a site map, is to use a large footer at the bottom of every page. This section, like a site map, helps people to jump between content pages and search engines to find content. And because they are at the bottom of the page, they are out of the way for people's everyday tasks.

If you want to list everything, they are suitable only for small sites. But they can be used on large sites to list the main areas of the site.

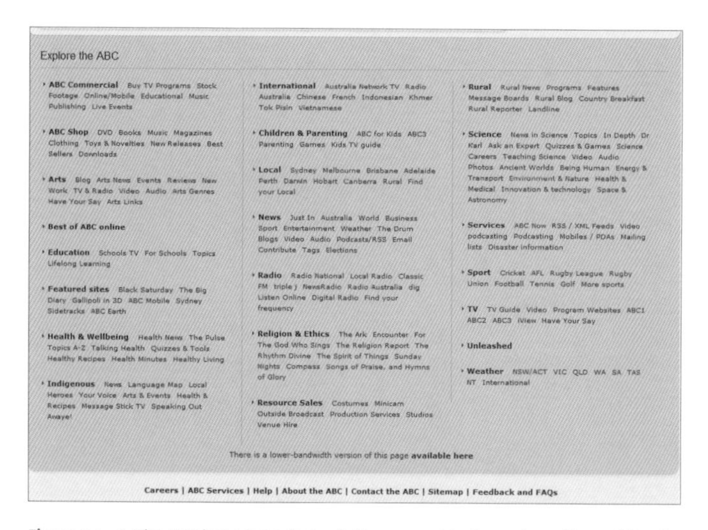

Figure 22 – 5. The ABC has a large footer, letting you get to the main sections of the site (`abc.net.au`)

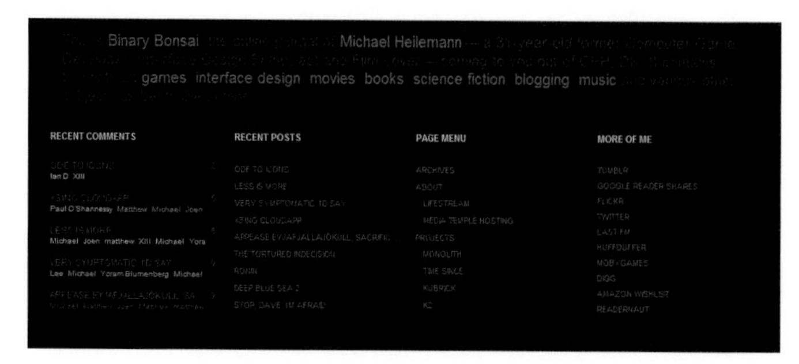

Figure 22 – 6. This portfolio site has little main navigation in the page, but a lot in the footer (`binarybonsai.com`)

A-Z indexes

An A-Z index lists out key content in an alphabetised list. A-Z lists are very useful for the known-item information tasks we talked about in chapter 10 – when people know exactly what they're looking for and what it's likely to be called. They're also a good way to help people understand the difference between their terminology and technical terms (by displaying the two together) and adapt to new terms over time.

In a good index:

- The term used in the index matches whatever term the person has in mind when they approach the index (e.g. an index that uses 'Refrigerator' when the user is thinking 'Fridge' won't be much help).
- The index has a good coverage of the content. It may not include every page, but will include every topic or major area covered by the site.

Of course, this isn't unique to the web – the same issue exists in printed back-of-book indexes.

As with site maps, A-Z indexes also help search engines to locate content.

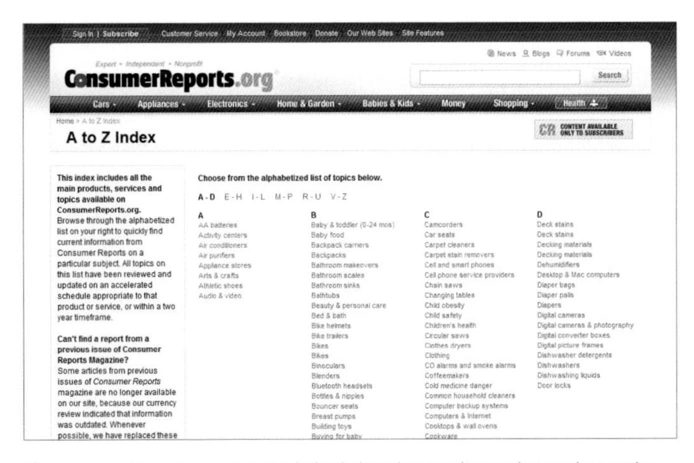

Figure 22 – 7. Consumer reports A-Z index helps when you know what product you're interested in (`consumerreports.org`)

Link-rich home pages

For some large websites the main goal of the home page is to help people get to the content they're interested in. (Some home pages are designed to reinforce a brand, send people in a particular direction – anything but help people get to content.)
A good approach can be to include lots of links on the page. This is called a link-rich page and is a great way to let people jump straight into content. More links provide more opportunity for readers to spot the content they are interested in and follow a link.

The main challenge with link-rich pages is that they need to be well-organised visually. The links need to be grouped well, labelled well and easy to read.

Figure 22 – 8. The New York Times home page is packed with links (this shows about 20% of the page) (`nytimes.com`)

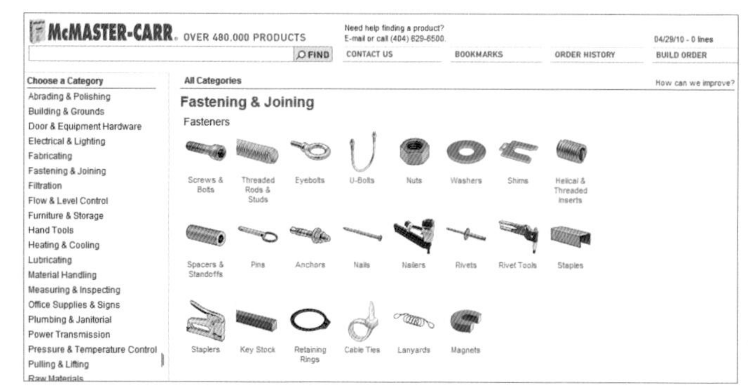

Figure 22 – 9. As is the McMaster-Carr home page (this shows about 5% of the home page) (`mcmaster.com`)

Filters

Filters allow people to narrow down a large set of content. They are great for content sets, where the content has a range of attributes and people may want to approach the site with different starting points.

As we discussed in chapter 9, people often approach large sets of content with particular criteria in mind. For example, when buying a car you may be interested in a particular body type, fuel efficiency, safety and other features. A good filter will let you choose the criteria that matter to you and see results that match just those criteria.

To design a good filter, you really need to know a lot about your audience and what matters most to them. As with other aspects of IA, labelling is also very important.

Figure 22 – 10. Real estate websites need good filters to let you focus on the criteria that matter (realestate.com.au)

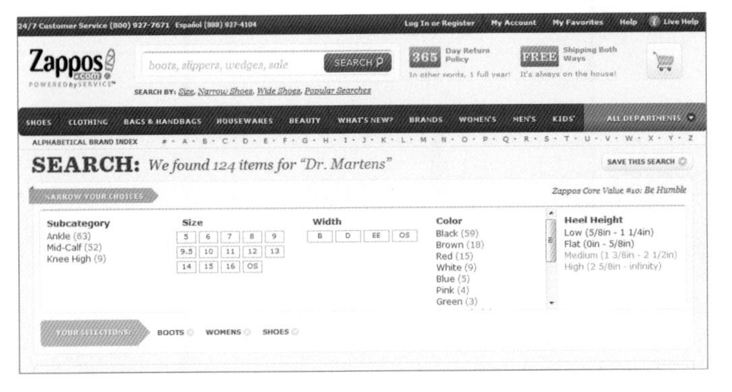

Figure 22 – 11. Zappos lets you filter by a number of criteria to narrow down the results list (zappos.com)

Faceted browse

Faceted browsing is a particular type of filter. Instead of choosing a set of attributes like a filter, you browse step-by-step, narrowing down the result set with each step. You don't have to enter a search term, can start narrowing down with any attribute and can never get a zero result (something that can happen with other filters).

My favourite example is epicurious – a recipe site. Their iPad app (which, by the way, is great) uses faceted browse to help narrow down to a recipe:

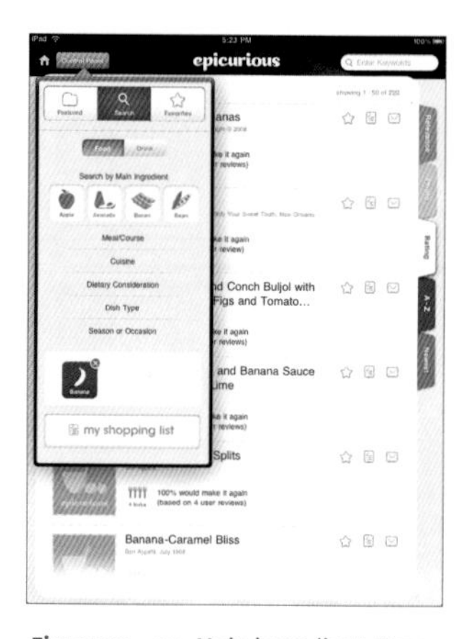

Figure 22 – 12. Main ingredient=Banana

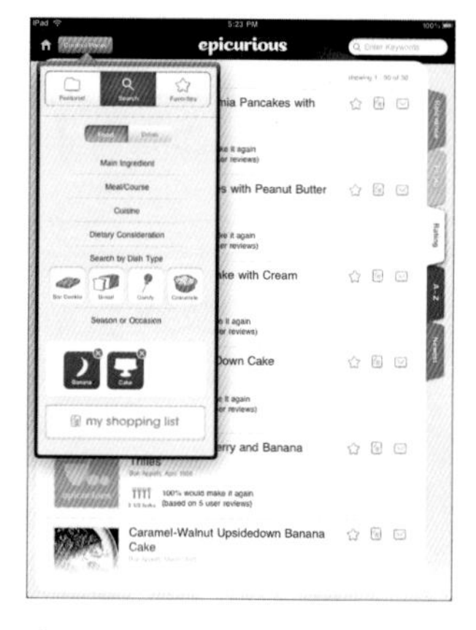

Figure 22 – 13. Dish type=Bread

Figure 22 – 14. Meal/course=Breakfast

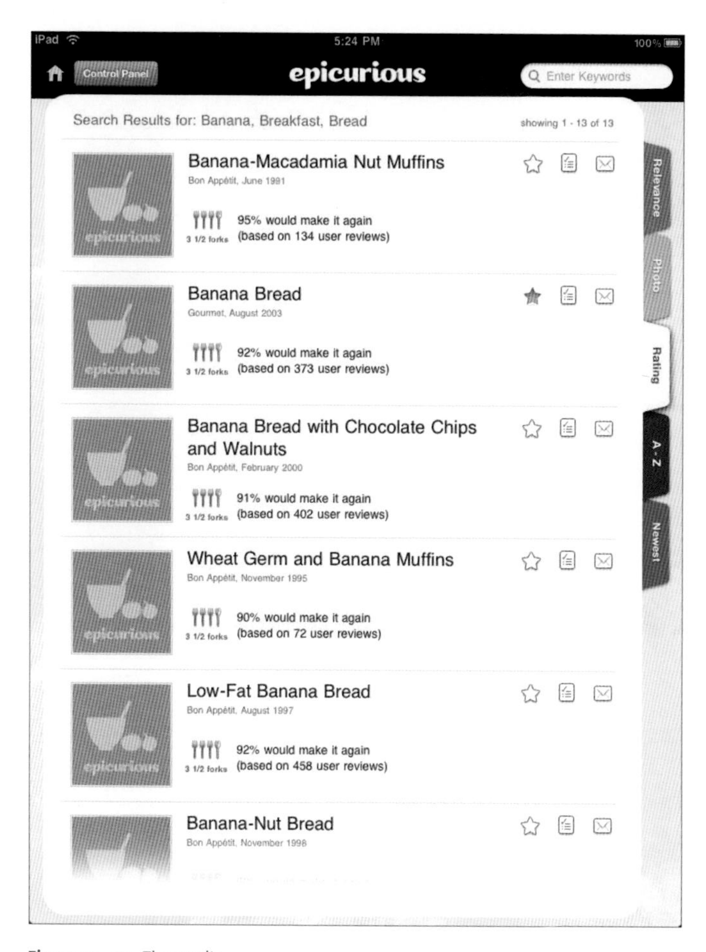

Figure 22 – 15. The results

In the situation I just showed, I would have come to the same point no matter what path I took. I could have chosen Breakfast, Bread, Banana and still ended up with the same list. The key point is that I never hit a dead end and followed my own path, not the designers'.

Faceted browse is available on an increasing number of sites, but may still be unfamiliar to many people. Make sure you thoroughly usability test it – people may be fine when moving toward content, but may not be sure how to modify their path or get rid of an attribute.

Chapter summary

Special navigation approaches include:

- Breadcrumb trails, which let you see where you are in a hierarchy
- Tag clouds, which provide a way to navigate via tags (but should be tested carefully)
- Site maps and A-Z indexes, which let people jump straight to content when they know exactly what they are looking for
- Link-rich home pages, which are great for content-heavy sites where people need to get to products quickly
- Filters and faceted browsing, which lets people narrow down a large set of content to just the criteria they want

Further reading

For more information on navigation design, see `http://delicious.com/practicalIA/navigation`

23

Designing navigation

It's time to get out your paper and pencils, or whiteboard and markers, and design the navigation for your site.

I'm quite serious about you doing this with paper and pencils or on a whiteboard. The last place you should be designing navigation is in front of a computer. While they're great for documenting what you've decided, they can really limit your creativity when it comes to design.

Start with the content page

Believe it or not, the home page is not the most important page on your site. The humble content page holds that honour. So when you start designing your navigation system, this is the best place to start. There are two reasons for this:

- The content page is where people will spend most of their time. It's where they'll have success or failure, and most likely where they'll be when they want to move to another page in your site.
- It will probably be the first page people see. It depends on the type of site you're working on, but in a lot of cases people come from a search engine. Where do they land? More often than not on a content page. And when this happens the content page is effectively the home page to your site.

Start working with the main content type for your site (or types if you have more than one). But before you start to draw anything, go back to everything you learned (from your goals user research and content analysis) so you know:

- What needs to be on this page
- Where people will want to go next – will they want more detailed information or other information on the same topic
- If people need to move between different sections of the site, or whether they're more likely to explore everything in the current section

- Where you would like them to go next – to related products, more expensive versions of the same product, etc.
- Whether it matters if they don't go anywhere and just jump in and leave

For example, on an intranet content page people will often want to know who to contact. On a recipe site they'll want similar recipes. On movie sites they may want to go to movies with the same actor or director.

One way is to start with the most important goal or information need, the product that creates the most revenue, or the function that's most frequently used or requested by people. Get this working, and then see if it needs to be varied for different content or different goals. Once you have a set of pages roughly assembled, revisit the goals and needs.

For small sites, you may be able to work through this for most of your content pages. For large sites you may need to sample a set of content pages and think this through to look for patterns.

Once you've thought about it, start sketching. Draw what needs to be on the page, and sketch out navigation approaches that will help people do what they need to for this page. Don't try to get it 'right' – try lots of different approaches and ideas.

Next, work on the pages that link to content pages

When you've got some scribbles for the content page, start with ideas for the pages that would link into the content pages. You may have several types of these pages:

- For simple hierarchies, the page may just need to list out the content in the section.
- For database structured sites, you may have more than one way to get to the content.
- You may design gallery pages (see chapter 16 – the Catalog pattern) or comparison pages.
- Don't forget to think about A-Z indexes, site maps and other helper pages.

These are crucial pages in your site – they are the places where people will make a decision to click on a content page. Get these wrong and people won't click through.

As with the content page, sketch. Draw different approaches to these pages and how people would experience them. Think of the different types of tasks people will be doing, and the decisions they will be making at that level and design for that.

Depending on the structure of your site, you may have another level of index pages, linking to the pages that link to the content. Tackle these in the same way.

Then do the home page

When you've finished sketching your content pages and index pages (pages that lead into content pages) then do the home page. Honestly, if you start on your home page you'll spend so much time on it you won't allow enough time for the other page types. Not only that, you risk designing navigation that only works if people work from the home page inward.

Home pages generally need to:

- Communicate who the organisation is
- Highlight particular content or features
- Allow people to navigate to where they want to be

When you design navigation for the home page, you will be designing more than just navigation bars. For many home pages, everything is ultimately navigation to content deeper in the site.

When designing home page navigation, think about:

- How much of the navigation you've designed for other pages is relevant to the home page? For example if you use top and left navigation within the site, you may only need the top navigation on the home page.
- Is there anything on the home page that isn't for navigation? (And should there be?)

- What needs to be on the home page, and what does it navigate to? For example, you may want to include news, links to individual articles, campaign advertisements that link to campaign pages, quick links to key pages, etc.
- What do you know that may be difficult for people to find, and so deserves some home page space to help them?

Home pages are difficult and frustrating to design. Not because they're inherently hard to lay out, but because everyone has an opinion about how to do them. More than any other type of page, sketch lots of versions and be prepared to make changes. But also be prepared to use what you know about the project goals and people's needs to push back on some suggestions and explain your decisions.

Revise

Just as you did when you designed your IA, after you've sketched your content pages, index pages, special pages and home page, revise them:

- Think about the business goals, people's needs and the content, and make sure the navigation will support it
- Check that the navigation will support the IA well
- Sketch and tweak and check it until you're comfortable it will work for your site

If you're wondering whether to take one approach or another (top navigation or side, no navigation bars, large footers) try them all – work through the whole site, see what would happen, and see what works best.

Chapter summary

When you're ready to design navigation for your site, don't start with the home page. Start with the content page – identify what people need to do on that page and design navigation that suits it. Then design the pages that lead to content pages, and then finally design the home page.

Sketch lots of versions and expect to change it as you go.

Further reading
For more information on navigation design processes, see `http://delicious.com/practicalIA/navigation-process`

24

Testing navigation design

In chapter 19 I described how to test the draft IA before you designed the navigation. This chapter is all about testing the navigation.

When I described how to test your draft IA, I suggested you do it in isolation – without the navigation or content – and just focus on the IA. To test the navigation, I'm going to suggest the exact opposite – that you test it with real content, and as much of it as possible.

The main reason is that although we design things like navigation bars, most navigation happens within the body of a page, much of it via contextual links. To properly test the navigation, you need to test these links and the content around them. Of course, you'll also want to check that your navigation bars, tag clouds, breadcrumbs and other navigation elements work as well.

Usability testing for navigation and page layouts is similar to usability testing for a draft IA. But you'll be trying to test more – the labelling, navigation design, page layout and content. It's more detailed, and a much bigger test than just a quick test against a hierarchy.

Get help

All through this book I've been trying to give you enough information so you can do it all yourself without having to buy another book. But for testing your navigation and content, I think it's better if you do get some help or learn some more. On the surface, usability testing looks easy – put people in front of the site and watch them work. But it's also easy to make mistakes and not know you've made them. Poorly-written scenarios can lead to answers that don't reflect real-world use. You may struggle to not tell someone what to do when they get stuck. You may have trouble figuring out why people are having problems. And it can be very easy to misinterpret what happens.

I strongly recommend you do usability testing – it's the only way to make sure you've actually done a good job for the people who will use your site. You will have made mistakes (I still do) and it is the best way to pick them up. But if you've never done usability testing before I suggest you get help from someone who has, or buy one of these two awesome books that will help you avoid common mistakes (both focus on a simple approach to usability testing):

- *Rocket Surgery Made Easy,* by Steve Krug
- *Handbook of Usability Testing,* by Jeffrey Rubin and Dana Chisnell

Both books provide general information on how to test, so here are some specific things you'll need to do to plan for your test.

What you want to learn

For a usability test of your navigation and page layouts, you can be testing practically everything in the site. I suggest you focus on checking:

- Does the IA still work now it has been made into navigation?
- Can people see the main navigation bars and know how to use them?
- Do people notice and use other navigation elements such as related links?
- When do people use navigation elements other than contextual links?
- Where it's relevant, can people use within-page navigation elements such as comparison features?
- If you've used something less common, such as faceted browse, how well do people understand what to do with it?
- What content works well (and what doesn't work quite so well)?

You may want to focus on areas you found hard to design, or where there were a lot of comments and changes as you worked through the navigation design.

When to test

The best time to test will be after you have content prepared. You may not need all the content you'll eventually have in the site, but the more content you have, the more you'll get out of the test.

If you know some of your content will take a while to get ready, don't think it's necessarily to delay your testing. Run an initial test on whatever you have so you can get feedback earlier rather than later. You can always test again when more content is ready.

If you haven't finished the graphic design, you can test without it – use a fairly plain visual approach, or even test a black and white version. You'll need to test again with the graphic design finished to make sure people can still see and use key features. But as with the content, don't delay your testing until the graphic design is finished – it's better to get some feedback rather than wait.

You don't necessarily have to build the whole site to test it. A rough working prototype can be good enough, again to get some initial feedback and make sure you're on the right track.

Some people recommend testing a paper prototype (a paper version of the site). To be honest, I'm not particularly fond of paper prototype testing for IA projects. It's great for some situations – early versions of web applications to test the basic workflow, or to test different versions of single pages. But most IA projects have a fair amount of content, and making a paper prototype means you have to create a paper page for each content page, and then manage them during the test. And for anything other than small sites, it can be quite hard to handle.

I recommend you create a basic computer-based prototype – it doesn't need advanced features like search, login areas or within-page updates. Just keep it simple and static so you can get some feedback easily. (There's more info about prototypes, including prototyping tools, in chapter 25.)

If you're using a content management system, it may be easy to create a draft site to test. Otherwise a basic HTML prototype may be good enough.

Preparation

Preparation is similar to the IA testing. You'll need:

- a draft site (real or prototype)
- scenarios
- participants

The only real difference is that testing the navigation and pages will take longer than IA testing. People will be actually working through the scenarios instead of just telling you where they would look and reading the content. Plan for the test to take longer – anything up to an hour is normal and gives you a lot of good feedback.

You can do the testing face-to-face or remotely[1]. Face-to-face testing is always best as you can see how the participant is reacting during the test. However, remote testing is great if you can't meet people face-to-face. Remote testing uses screen-sharing software and a voice connection (phone or internet-based) so you can see what the participant is doing. The available tools are getting better and better, and it's a good option that makes usability testing a lot more accessible.

[1] See this website for information about remote testing and tools to help: `http://remoteusability.com/`

Other tips

Other tips for testing navigation and pages:

- Don't start all your testing from the home page. Start from somewhere inside the site occasionally to mimic what would happen if someone landed in the middle from a search engine (or followed a link from another site).
- Ask participants to think of things they'd want or expect to find on the site and try to locate them. You can learn some interesting things about users' expectations for site content and relationships.
- As participants work, occasionally ask them what they expect to find behind different links. This can give you great clues about how people interpret terminology when they first see it.
- If people consistently use search during the usability test, think about rewording your scenarios. They may be just trying to put in a scenario keyword instead of thinking about what they want to find.
- If people don't click on something you expected them to, wait until the test has finished and then ask them if they noticed it and what they thought it was. You may learn that it didn't look like navigation, that people didn't look at that part of the screen, or that the terminology was poor.
- If half of your participants look in one place and half look in another, ask them what they thought would be in the section they didn't look in. You may learn something important about the group or labelling.

Chapter summary

It's vital to test your navigation and page layouts before you release, with real content and real links.

But usability testing this detail can be tricky. Get someone involved who can help you or read up about testing before you have a go.

Otherwise the testing process is similar to testing the IA, just more detailed.

Further reading
For more information on navigation design, see `http://delicious.com/practicalIA/testing-navigation`

25 COMMUNICATING NAVIGATION

Navigation and page layouts are commonly drawn and documented as wireframes.

Wireframes are design drawings without any visual treatment. They're usually done in simple lines, with few colours. Their purpose is to show what will be on a page, without final graphic design or interaction.

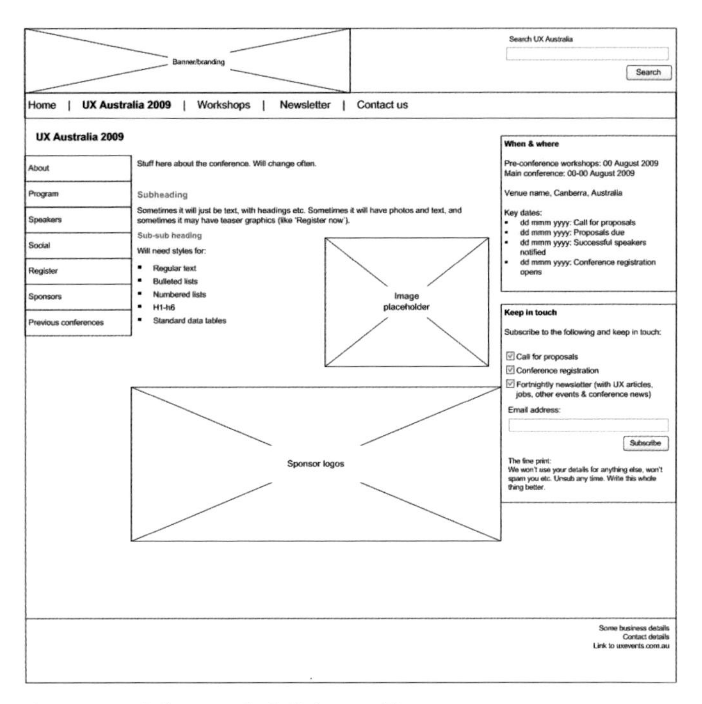

Figure 25 – 1. Wireframes are basically boxes and lines

Wireframes themselves aren't particularly hard to draw – they're just lots of straight lines and text. And you can do them in any drawing package – Visio, Illustrator, InDesign or one of the many online prototyping tools[1].

[1] See `http://delicious.com/practicalIA/prototyping/` for a list of tools

What makes wireframes hard is deciding:

- How much detail to include
- How much of the site to draw

How much detail to include

I've mentioned this in other chapters on documentation, but it's very important when talking about wireframes – the amount to draw, and the amount of detail to include depends on the purpose and reader of the wireframe. Wireframes that give a management-level stakeholder a broad idea for the shape of the site should contain a lot less detail than ones showing a developer how to build the site.

Wireframes will be used by a wide range of people on a project. The main readers, and their main concerns include:

- Project team: To discuss different ideas and approaches.
- Subject matter/content authors: How will their content fit into the site and be represented in it? What parts of a page do they have available?
- Managers: Have you met business needs? (And "where's my stuff on the home page?")
- Developers: Exactly how should this work, and how will I implement it?

Types of wireframes

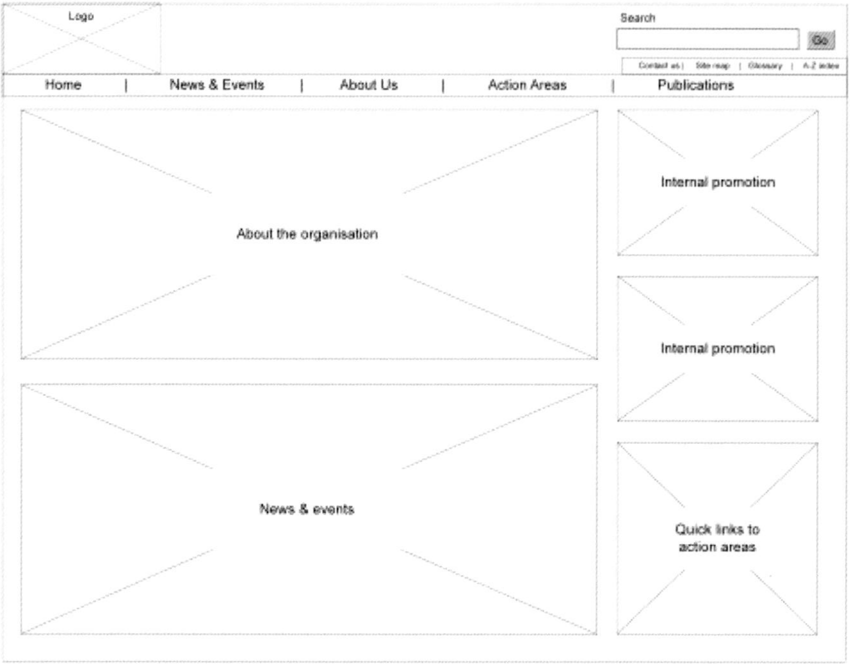

Figure 25 – 2. A reference zone wireframe

Reference zones

The wireframe above shows very broad content zones only. This type of wireframe is good for:

- discussing big ideas without worrying about detail
- showing the high-level approach across a whole site – highlighting consistent and different placement of elements
- exploring different layouts with a team
- discussing high-level flows and ideas without getting into detail

When you use this type of wireframe, make sure people understand it's only meant to communicate broad ideas and positioning, or they may wonder why you haven't 'finished' the work. Also keep an eye out for whether people understand you – many people find these types of wireframes hard to understand as there isn't enough detail for them to work with.

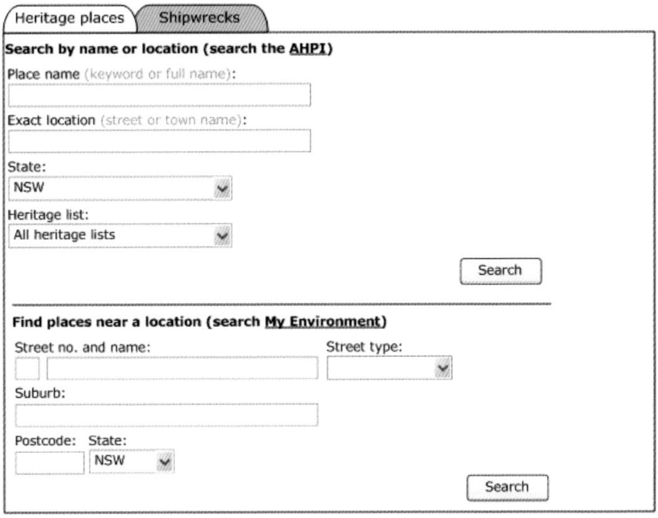

Heritage places
Shipwrecks
Search by name or location (search the AHPI)
Place name (keyword or full name):
Exact location (street or town name):
State:
NSW
Heritage list:
All heritage lists
Search
Find places near a location (search My Environment)
Street no. and name:
Street type:
Suburb:
Postcode: State:
NSW
Search

Figure 25 – 3. Detailed wireframe

Detailed

This type of wireframe shows as much detail as will appear in the final site. It will include final wording of all navigation items and all content.

As you can imagine, you probably won't use this type of wireframe for every page in your site – creating the content for every page is just too much work. But it's great for special pages where the full details need to be spelt out (particularly any interactive pages), and as an example of particular page types.

When you use this type of wireframe, you'll probably want to introduce ideas with something broader before showing this type of detail. It's easy (and common) for people to get distracted by irrelevant details (like wording of content) and forget to focus on the more important aspects of the design.

Combination

Wireframes don't have to be only broad, or only detailed. The next example shows a combination of both. It doesn't show the content, but it does show all the headings and the layout. This wireframe helps people focus on what you want to discuss or show – the less important parts aren't shown in as much detail. I use this type of wireframe more than any other.

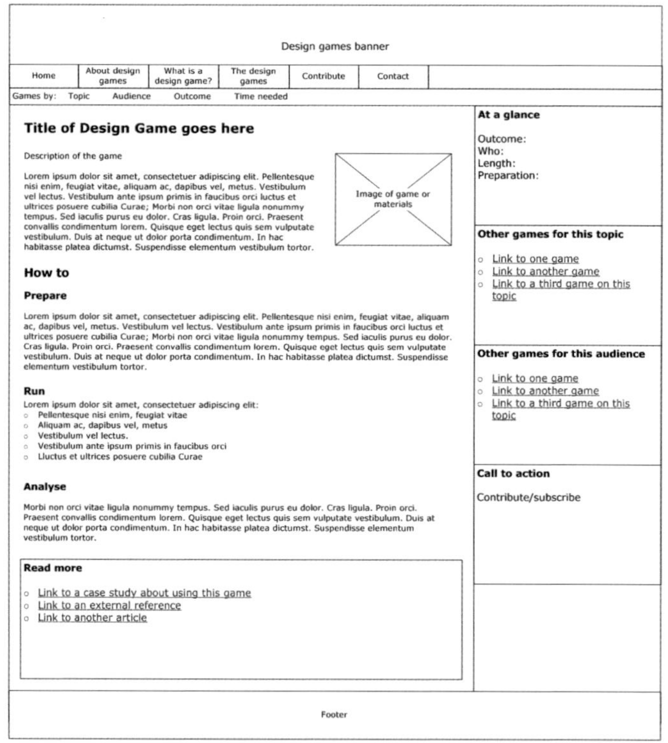

Figure 25 – 4. This wireframe shows detail in specific areas, but not everywhere

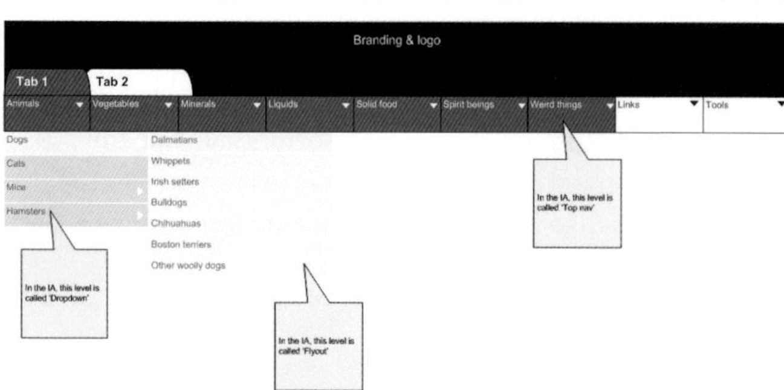

Figure 25 – 5. This is another quite detailed example. In this case the content isn't important, but the way the navigation should work is detailed

Specification wireframe

The final type of wireframe is even more detailed. Not only does it have all the interface details, it also has enough annotations for a developer to build it without having to ask you anything.

This type of wireframe is necessary when you're ready to have a system built. Developers need to know exactly what text should appear on the screen, where the data comes from and goes to, and what action occurs for every link and button. They also need to know about any variations that might occur if the data is longer than it looks, and how the individual screen will work.

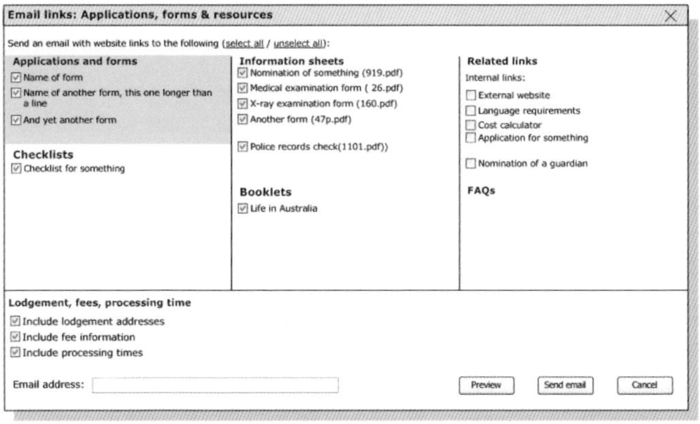

Email links: Applications, forms & resources

Send an email with website links to the following (select all / unselect all):

Applications and forms
Name of form
Name of another form, this one longer than a line
And yet another form

Checklists
Checklist for something

Information sheets
Nomination of something (919.pdf)
Medical examination form (26.pdf)
X-ray examination form (160.pdf)
Another form (47p.pdf)
Police records check(1101.pdf))

Booklets
Life in Australia

Related links
Internal links:
External website
Language requirements
Cost calculator
Application for something
Nomination of a guardian

FAQs

Lodgement, fees, processing time
Include lodgement addresses
Include fee information
Include processing times

Email address:

Preview | Send email | Cancel

Triggers

- User selects 'Send to client>Send links via email' from AFR1

Content

- Same as AFR1
- Instead of tabs, display as three columns
- All content able to be selected

Actions

- Cancel : closes pop-up window with no action
- Select 'select all': select all checkboxes
- Select 'unselect all': unselect all checkboxes
- Preview: change view to a preview of the email that will be send to client (still to be drafted)
- Send email: send an email to the client that includes all links the user has selected (email layout and content to be defined)
  - Need to determine: what is displayed in the email - short names or full form names
  - Need to define what is included for the lodge, fee, processing times

Figure 25 – 6. A detailed specification wireframe

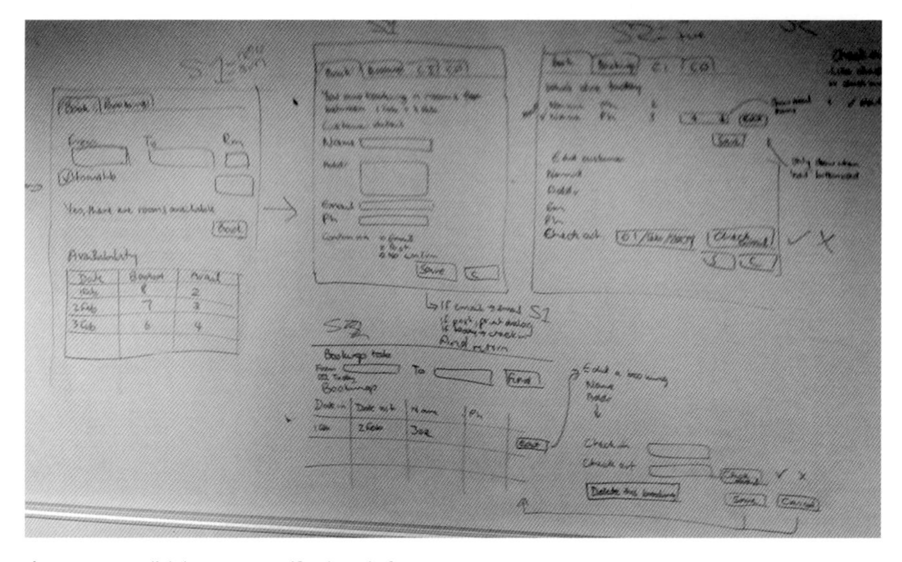

Figure 25 – 7. A slightly strange specification wireframe

Believe it or not, the wireframe above contained enough detail for the developers to build. It was never written down in any more detail than this. What made it work is that we all worked through the design process together, and so had a common understanding of what needed to happen. It was built within a few days of sketching, and because it was so recent, everyone remembered exactly what all the strange squiggles were about. The only changes made after the build was to change some of the on-screen text that wasn't properly defined in this version.

Page description diagrams

A quite different way to communicate page layout design, and one that works particularly well when you're working with graphic designers, is a page description diagram. This is an 'anti-wireframe' in that it doesn't include any drawings at all. Instead it describes the elements of a page in words. It lists what needs to go on a page, and describes which parts are the most important and need the most emphasis.

What to include in a wireframe

Drawing your wireframes is one of those tasks that's never quite finished. You can keep refining them, adding more details and annotations, until the cows come home.

To avoid this, think of your wireframes as being made up of three levels:

1. Absolute essentials: Those things the wireframe will be useless without. When you're pressed for time, or already working closely with the people who need to use the wireframe, this is where you can stop.
2. Explanations: Things that aren't essential, but will help people understand what the wireframe is about – annotations, background information, important things to pay attention to.
3. Information design: Better visual approaches, so people can more easily understand what you're communicating.

Prototypes

I was talking at South by Southwest Interactive[2] last year about wireframing with my friends Nick Finck and Michael Angeles (our talk was called *Wireframes for the Wicked*[3]). During the presentation someone tweeted that we were 'Old skool IAs', and should be talking about prototyping.

The only reason we didn't talk about prototyping is that we'd decided to talk only about wireframing, and to allow more time for questions than talking. Otherwise they were right – prototyping is a very important way of communicating navigation and page layout design.

A prototype is a more interactive version of a wireframe. It can be done on paper or on a computer – the key is that people can do something other than look at it.

---

[2] http://sxsw.com/interactive

[3] Our talk is here: http://www.slideshare.net/nickf/wireframes-for-the-wicked

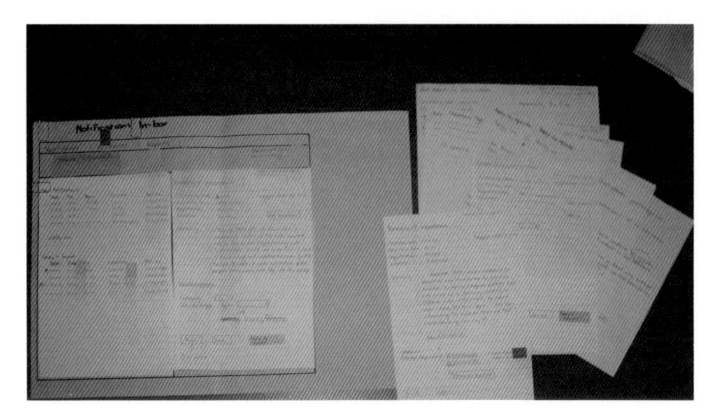

Figure 25 – 8. A paper prototype of a web application

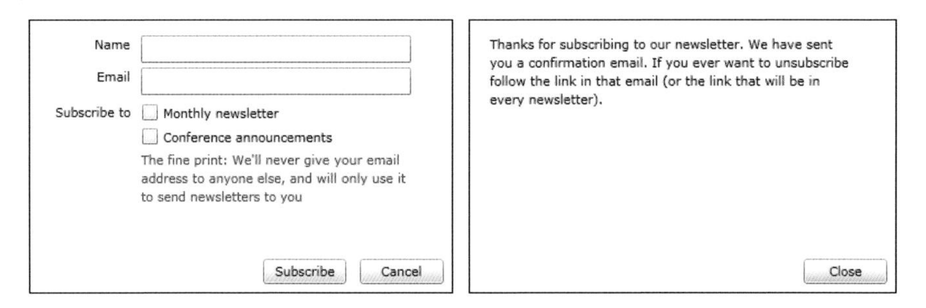

Figure 25 – 9. A prototype subscription form using Microsoft Expression Blend – it took me about 5 minutes to create a basic working prototype

As with wireframes, the amount of detail you'll include in a prototype depends on what you need to communicate and who you're communicating with. Paper prototypes are great for showing initial ideas and how someone would move through a site (but are tedious to make if you want to include all page detail). Detailed computer prototypes can mimic the final site well enough that you can really demonstrate how the site will work.

Communication tips

Introducing wireframes

When I'm working with a new client, stakeholders or people who'll be using a site, I take some time just to explain what I'm about to show them. A lot of people will never have seen a wireframe, and will wonder why you haven't 'finished it'. Clients accustomed to being presented with pixel-perfect visual designs may be expecting something different.

I usually explain that it's a draft, and as the idea is to get feedback we've done only enough work to communicate the ideas to them (i.e. we didn't want to waste time and money making it perfect when it's only a draft). I also explain that it's black and white, shows the ideas but not the final visual approach, and only contains example content.

It can help to show people a before and after from another project – showing how the line drawing changes to something finished and how the two relate to each other.

Using sketchy wireframes

A trend, and one that's quite effective, is to create computer-drawn wireframes that have sketchy lines and handwritten typefaces. The advantage of this approach is it's much more obvious that the wireframe is not real and not finished. It's a subtle difference, but people are much more comfortable providing feedback and ideas on things that look unfinished than look finished and perfect.

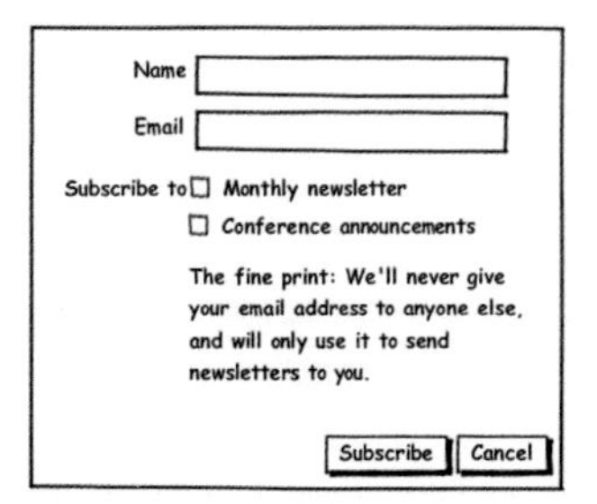

Figure 25 – 10. A sketchy wireframe (from Balsamiq mockups - `balsamiq.com`)

Tools and templates

Almost every month I get an email with an invitation to preview a new prototyping or wireframing tool – they're popping up all over the place. You don't have to invest in these tools though - standard drawing tools like Visio and OmniGraffle can create very basic prototypes and quite good drawings.

I'll keep a list of tools on the book website, but here are some to start with:

- Eightshapes Unify: This is an InDesign-based documentation system. It contains templates, common page layouts and symbol libraries to get you started. `http://unify.eightshapes.com/about-the-system/`
- Konigi wireframe stencils: For OmniGraffle, this contains a broad set of components to use in wireframes. `http://konigi.com/tools/omnigraffle-wireframe-stencils`
- Nick Finck's stencils: This is similar to the Konigi stencil set, but for Microsoft Visio: `http://www.nickfinck.com/blog/entry/visio_stencils_for_information_architects/`
- Balsamiq: This prototyping tool is currently the most popular, allowing you to create simple sketchy prototypes online.
- Axure: Very established software for creating clickable prototypes: `http://www.axure.com/`
- Microsoft Sketchflow: At the far end of the prototyping spectrum is Sketchflow, which lets you create everything from quick sketch-style prototypes through to quite complex interactive prototypes with re-usable code.

For more: `http://articles.sitepoint.com/article/tools-prototyping-wireframing`

Chapter summary

Navigation and page layouts are usually communicated via wireframes (simple line drawings) or prototypes (simple working versions).

As with all communicating, figure out what your readers need to know and provide that level of detail. Wireframes and prototypes can be done at various levels of detail:

- Reference zones show broad zones on a page only
- Detailed wireframes show all detail, but usually for specific pages only
- A combination lets you focus more on those aspects you need to communicate
- Page description diagrams don't include drawings, just descriptions of what's important

Further reading

For more information on communicating navigation design, see `http://delicious.com/practicalIA/communicating-navigation`

Conclusion

So we're done. You now have a brand-spanking IA that works really well for your organisation, audience and content. And the navigation design lets people get around your content, find what they need and discover what they didn't know about. The project is finally over!

No, of course it isn't.

IA projects are never over. There's always a new need to meet, new content to add, and the shifting sands of everyday life dealing with content.

Even if you're working through this book for a project you still aren't done. You've worked on the IA and navigation, but there's still work to do on the content, as well as the graphic design. The branding hasn't been discussed at all (you really don't want me talking about that), and the site still has to be built or rebuilt. There may be tons of work still to go.

The good thing is, carefully designing the IA based on a good understanding of what you need to achieve, what people need, and your content means any additional work should go fairly smoothly. The IA work really does create the foundation and blueprints for the rest of the work to come.

What next

I've covered a lot in this book, but you may still be wondering what to do for a particular issue on your project. You may have to make loads of decisions I haven't covered at all, or covered in only a single sentence that doesn't give you much to go on.

How do you make these decisions?

For every question I've been asked in a workshop, there's one answer. I don't even have to say, "Well, it depends".

Information.

The more you know, the easier it is to make good design decisions. And to get that information you can:

1. Research for your particular problem
2. Research about what other people did
3. Just do it

In the first three parts of the book I talked a lot about the first type of research – learning enough about your goals, your audience and your content that a lot of your decisions are straightforward and obvious.

I can help you with the second type of research as well. At the end of most chapters is a URL for further reading, and I'll be maintaining a list of the best articles on each topic.

And the third – well that's my favourite approach of all. You can answer most questions by just having a go at solving them. You might even try tackling your question with a couple of approaches. But as I said when I talked about coming up with the IA, just do it. Make it up and see how it works. Work it right through and put it in front of your audience to see how they react. Tweak it and try again. Stop thinking and fussing and just have a go.

You're ready – go do it!

Attributions

In order of appearence

1 About information architecture

Xero ~ http://www.xero.com || Adobe ~ http://www.adobe.com/ || Australian Transport Safety Bureau ~ http://www.atsb.gov.au/ || Foursquare ~ http://foursquare.com/ || Yoink ~ http://www.yoink.com/ || Australian Government ~ http://webpublishing.agimo.gov.au

2 Understanding people

YouTube ~ http://www.youtube.com || alanstairs~ http://www.flickr.com/photos/alanstairs/4073602871/ || nForm ~ http://nform.ca/ || IMBD ~ http://imdb.com || BBC ~ http://www.bbc.co.uk || Top Gear ~ http://www.topgear.com || Wine.com ~ http://wine.com/ || Wikipedia ~ http://en.wikipedia.org || eMusic ~ http://emusic.com/ || Google ~ http://google.com || Yoga Journal ~ http://www.yogajournal.com/ || Amazon ~ http://amazon.com/

3 Understanding content

UX Australia ~ http://www.uxaustralia.com.au/ || ABC~ http://www.abc.net.au || Upcoming ~ http://upcoming.org/ || Lonely Planet ~ http://lonelyplanet.com || Last.fm ~ http://www.last.fm/ || Etsy ~ http://www.etsy.com || Bunnings warehouse ~ http://www.bunnings.com.au || Paypal ~ http://www.paypal.com || Monash ~ http://www.monash.edu.au || Dell ~ http://www.dell.com.au || CHI ~ http://www.chi2010.org/ || choice ~ http://www.choice.com.au || A List apart ~ http://www.alistapart.com ||

4 Designing an information architecture

Chrisig ~ http://www.chisig.org || White house ~ http://whitehouse.gov || Freelance switch ~ http://www.freelanceswitch.com || Toys r us ~ http://www.toysrus.com || Wordpress ~ http://wordpress.org/ || Gap ~ http://www.gap.com/ || Linkedin ~ http://www.linkedin.com/ || ANU ~ http://www.studyat.anu.edu.au || Flickr ~ http://www.flickr.com || 3am

~ http://www.3am.co.uk/ || Adobe ~ http://www.adobe.com/ || Optimal workshop ~ https://optimalworkshop.com/ ||

5 Designing navigation

Maad Mob ~ http://maadmob.com.au/ || Alfa romeo ~ https://alfaromeo.com/ || Black estate ~ https://blackestate.co.nz || AAC ~ https://acc.co.nz || Department of commerce ~ http://www.commerce.wa.gov.au/ || Frys ~ https://frys.com || The adventure school ~ https://theadventureschool.com || Vodaphone ~ https://vodafone.com.au/personal/ || Lostpedia ~ https://lostpedia.wikia.com || All recipes ~ https://allrecipes.com.au || NASA ~ https://nasa.gov || Apple ~ https://www.apple.com || Binary bonsai ~ https://binarybonsai.com || Consumer reports ~ https://consumerreports.org || New york times ~ https://www.nytimes.com || McMaster-Carr ~ https://www.mcmaster.com || Realestate ~ https://www.realestate.com.au || Zappos ~ https://www.zappos.com || Epicurious ~ http://www.epicurious.com/ ||